An Encore for Reform

Otis L. Graham, Jr. is Assistant Professor of History at the University of California, Santa Barbara. A native of Arkansas, he received his B.A. at Yale University and his M.A. and Ph.D. at Columbia University. He previously taught at Mount Vernon Junior College, Washington, D.C., and California State College, Hayward.

An Encore for Reform

THE OLD PROGRESSIVES
AND THE NEW DEAL

OTIS L. GRAHAM, Jr.

New York   OXFORD UNIVERSITY PRESS   1967

To my parents and my Anns

Acknowledgments

The brevity of the following remarks leaves me very unsatisfied, but no written acknowledgment, however lengthy, could adequately express my debt to those who have helped me understand these reformers.

I benefited from conversation and correspondence with Helene M. Brewer, Lawrence G. Brooks, Richard S. Childs, Irving Norton Fisher, Philip Dunne, Raymond B. Fosdick, Lois Teal Hartley, Denison B. Hull, Don Irwin, William H. Irwin, Charles Louis Marburg, Scott Nearing, Madeline Pardee, Anson Sheldon, Miss Ruth Shepard, Helen Taussig, Rexford Tugwell, Joseph Tumulty, Jr., and Henry A. Wallace, among others. Librarians beyond count have been gracious and knowledgeable. I am grateful to Clarke Chambers, Robert A. Harper, Joel Tarr, and Rod Nash for informed criticism. Tad Kuroda provided able research assistance, and my friend and colleague Samuel F. Wells lent invaluable support during our joint researches and discussions in Boston. To President Peter D. Pelham and the Trustees of Mount Vernon Junior College I am indebted for a research grant for the summer of 1964, and I owe an additional debt to Dean Flora Harper and to my colleagues on that faculty for constant encouragement. Richard Rice, of California State College at Hayward, facilitated my work at an important point.

I am indebted to Perkins Bass for granting me access to the Robert Perkins Bass papers at Dartmouth College, and to John Crane for access to the Charles R. Crane papers at the Institute for Current World Affairs, New York. The following libraries and individuals kindly gave me permission to quote from their collections: Bancroft Library, University of California at Berkeley, from the Wallace Irwin and Hiram Johnson papers; Columbia University Oral History Collection, from the Frederick Morgan Davenport and Burton J. Hendrick interviews; Franklin D. Roosevelt Library, from the Roosevelt papers; Mr. Ralph Hayes, from the Newton D. Baker papers; Harvard University, from the Oswald Garrison Villard papers; Huntington Library, from the Marshall Stimson papers; Mrs. Amos Pinchot, from the Amos Pinchot papers; Social Welfare Archives Center, Minneapolis, from the Survey Associates papers; State Historical Society of Wisconsin, from the Richard T. Ely and Raymond Robins papers; Mark Sullivan, Jr., from the Mark Sullivan papers; Joseph Tumulty, Jr., from the Joseph Tumulty papers; William L. White, from the William Allen White papers; Yale University and Irving Norton Fisher, from the Irving Fisher papers. I have been given permission by Holt, Rinehart and Winston, Inc., to quote from Edgar Lee Masters, *Across Spoon River,* and by G. P. Putnam's Sons to quote from George Creel, *Rebel at Large.*

The manuscript was read by many, but I am particularly grateful for the advice of Barton J. Bernstein, Sigmund Diamond, James Shenton, and my brother, Hugh D. Graham.

Two men especially guided and corrected me. William Leuchtenburg, whose enthusiasm and erudition were offered so unstintingly, has added me to that crowd of historians who would not think of proceeding without his counsel. Finally, I would like to thank Richard Hofstadter, who lent his incomparable historical judgment and stylistic precision to the improvement of my efforts, while never letting me forget the importance of intellectual independence.

As for my wife, I would put her name ahead of mine on the title page, but for the errors that neither she nor any of the foregoing could induce me to remove.

OTIS L. GRAHAM, JR.

Santa Barbara, California
February 1967

Contents

An Encore for Reform

I

From Progressivism to the New Deal:
Tradition and Innovation in the Liberal Past

> So, at this opening of a new age, in this its day of unrest and
> discontent, it is our part to clear the air, to bring about
> common counsel; to set up the parliament of the people
> . . . to make classes understand one another. Our part is to
> lift so high the incomparable standards of the common in-
> terest and the common justice that . . . a new day of
> achievement may come for the liberty we love.
>
> WOODROW WILSON

American history and biography for half a century or more have
told the story of reform and reformers—the story of liberalism.
And although one hears today with increasing frequency the jus-
tifiable complaint that conservative figures, business organizations, and entire periods of complacency and political calm need
more attention, the instinct of historians and the public is sound.
Not only is liberalism in its broadest sense the sole American tradition, as Louis Hartz has shown, but in its more familiar sense,
meaning that current reformist-humanitarian-pragmatic political
creed which has caused us all to forget that the label ever meant
anything else, liberalism has been the most conspicuous force
shaping our politics. And, using political power as a lever, it has
helped transform American society in the twentieth century.

We know the essentials of the story of liberalism. Although
what is now called liberalism is a set of political assumptions and
tactics that matured in the heyday of Alfred E. Smith and became
dominant during Franklin D. Roosevelt's New Deal, twentieth-
century liberalism has its obvious antecedents. The moral and
ethical values of the liberal tradition, political democracy, the
maximization of individual freedom, humanitarianism, equality,
have been actively and conspicuously at work in this country

from the colonial beginnings. As all our written accounts tell us, in the periods of the American Revolution, Jefferson, Jackson, and the antislavery effort, these values have appeared to be the primary causes of successful punitive uprisings against oligarchies political and economic.

Early liberalism presented largely a negative aspect, and sought to realize its goals for the most part by dismantling or limiting political power. When, under the impact of industrialism, liberalism began to adjust its definition of freedom to include popular employment of a regulatory state, its eighteenth-century and nineteenth-century antecedents, while still inspirational, lost some of their practical relevance. But men were not lacking to provide a new sense of direction. The re-definition of freedom, the critique of laissez-faire, the intellectual preparation of a creed for a popular interventionist state—these were provided by turn-of-the-century thinkers such as Dewey, Ward, Beard, and Croly. Dynamic political leadership taught the forces of liberal reform to employ the new tactics, and in a series of uprisings over half a century, liberalism performed a transvaluation of means in the pursuit of the ancient ends. It is a triumphant historical record, culminating in the 1930's with the creation of that long-desired welfare state of liberal predisposition.

These are the main outlines, and they are not in dispute. Beyond this, there is controversy—not only the predictable disagreement about the general adequacy and wisdom of what liberalism has built, but also about the extent and nature of its borrowings, especially in the 1930's, from the American past. Were the New Dealers continuing in the reform tradition, capping the efforts of earlier reformers, making "the reparation," in Burke's phrase, "as nearly as possible in the style of the building"? Or was there a gap in ideals and methods sufficiently separating the New Deal from what had gone before so that we distort all phases of the liberal record by linking them seamlessly together? In the worn language of historical problems, we are not yet agreed on the origins of the New Deal and on the degree of continuity between it and the American political past.

I I

With a sort of irresistible logic, the attention of students of the New Deal has returned to the progressive era, where reform got its twentieth-century start.[1] Clearly it was the progressive who first struggled with the full range of modern social problems: how to limit and control private economic power as the Founders had limited political power; how to surmount industrial warfare without damage either to the capitalistic order or to the American insistence upon justice; how to keep careers open to talent, and talent attracted to innovation; how to preserve individualism in an organizing world; how to make the cities livable; how to preserve self-government from enervation.

To reconstruct that reform effort is to describe the intricate legislative struggle, the operation of a new Federal or state regulatory agency, the details of a new form of municipal government, or the rise to political power of a reforming politician. It is to relate a now-familiar panoply of accomplishment: electoral reforms, the regulatory and welfare legislation of the pre–World War I period, the settlement houses, the organizations dedicated to social betterment.

But progressives themselves explained their efforts primarily by reference to ideals, and were proudest of the structure of ideas they produced, both by analysis and by prescription. Political action was dependent upon a determination of values and a rational plan of correction and control. Therefore their movement, while almost entirely political in its tangible expression, left behind what was to them an equally important legacy—a body of ideas for the guidance of like-minded men, ideas which took the form of values and the techniques to realize them.

This being true, the large question of the relation of progressivism to the New Deal has led generally to an effort to identify and weigh the intellectual debt of the New Dealers; to a lesser extent, attention has centered in institutions, laws, and personnel. Was progressivism, in temper, in method, in social base, in ultimate intention, an early and formative version of Franklin Roosevelt's welfare state? Or did the New Deal improvise out of new social and intellectual materials a governmental framework for American life which owed little to, in places even affronted, the progressive vision? Was the New Deal, which unquestionably fashioned the contemporary political world, the culmination of a continuous reform movement that lasted, with brief interruption,

1. For an example of the search for political re-orientation through re-study of the progressive era, see Karl E. Meyer, "Progressivism Reconsidered," *The Progressive*, XXVII (September 1963), 23-6.

from the Civil War to Pearl Harbor, or did it break with that tradition in vital ways? Whatever the focus, on ideas or men or institutions, the question of progressive–New Deal continuity has become one of the important interpretational problems in our historiography, sharing with the other areas of controversy a certain boredom of terms, a lack of clarity in concepts and definitions and methodology, but constituting nevertheless a problem whose resolution is vital to the understanding of the recent past.

III

Continuities between progressive and New Deal records are most conspicuous in the form of shared "ideas"—that is, in normative judgments and goals, as well as in substantive analysis of contemporary ills and in proposals for remedy. The two movements belabored a common enemy, the menace of private economic power unrestrained either by adequate laws or sense of responsibility; both knew the anger of "conservatives" of all types who had reasons to fear an aroused democracy. As George Baer fled before one Roosevelt, so Irénée Du Pont was to flee before another.

In both periods, the dominant rhetorical note was the pre-eminence of the People's Business, of the need to restore the balance between the public good and private gain. Both set in motion a new cycle of concern for society's underprivileged, and employed freely the concept of "social justice" in coming to their defense. The progressives formulated those two famous answers to the problem of corporate size, the New Freedom and the New Nationalism, and the New Dealers borrowed liberally—even indiscriminately—from both. The imprint of Wilson's New Freedom, with its eager antimonopoly sentiment and its confidence that public action in the familiar areas of taxation, tariffs, and money would cure industrial America's ills, may be seen upon the Banking and Exchange regulation of the early New Deal, the assault on the sprawling holding companies, and the occasional aid to small business and small agricultural enterprise. The bold stamp of T.R.'s New Nationalism, willing to see business and industrial combination so long as government held supervisory and co-ordinating power and the weak were ungrudgingly aided, adorns not only the relief measures but the NRA and AAA attemps at planning a way out of wasteful competition. Reformers of both periods developed a hostility to the courts, and turned against the abstract constitutional defenses of conservatives a corrosive judicial realism. More important and more generally, both sought most of their ends through an enlargement of the state, abandoning to the conservatives the ancient liberal devotion to laissez-faire.

There were other and more tangible continuities. New Dealers altered the Federal Reserve System to their own uses, and extended the idea of Federal regulatory commissions to the stock market, radio frequencies, and air routes. They used the nation's intellectual talent as eagerly, if not as systematically, as Robert La Follette and Francis McGovern had used the University of Wisconsin. And the most imposing connection of all was surely that remnant of progressive survivors so visible in the service of Roosevelts' New Deal. There was the Wilsonian element, beginning with Franklin Roosevelt himself and including Josephus Daniels, Cordell Hull, William McAdoo, Joe Robinson, and others, who were bonded over to the New Deal when the party of Wilson came to power again. And observers have also seen in the services rendered by Bull Moosers like Harold Ickes, Senator Edward P. Costigan, and later by Henry Stimson and William Allen White, the signs of that strong carry-over from the Bull Moose group which a reading of the 1912 Progressive platform led observers to expect.[2]

These affinities, then, in ideas, institutions, and personnel are impressive evidence of an extensive kinship between these two reform movements, giving modern liberalism claim to roots which turn the corner of the century. In this perspective the progressive generation, fortunately for Franklin Roosevelt, had thought hard and fruitfully about the means to a more liberal America, and he had only to apply their theories, and some of their veterans, to the task of social reconstruction.

If the men and ideas linking the two periods are obvious, so are the discontinuities. Some of the ills and enemies of the progressive generation, such as Boss Rule, prostitution, or alcohol, were ignored by the New Dealers. Conversely, the New Deal took up an acute economic problem which progressives had never faced, as Richard Hofstadter has said. The New Deal was distinguished by a different political and moral style, by that freewheeling pragmatism and tough-mindedness which set men like Harry

2. Here, and in the discussion that follows, those with a close interest in the literature should refer to the Bibliographical Essay at the end of this book.

Hopkins, Maury Maverick, and Tommy Corcoran apart from men like the Pinchots or Burton Wheeler or George Record.

The new type of politician and the new type of adviser that converged with Rooosevelt on Washington reflected the changed social base of the Democratic party. The newly militant labor element, the urban immigrant voters, the Negro, these had entered American politics since progressivism and were largely responsible for the changed moral and social attitudes within this unlikely reform instrument, the Democratic party. Add to these considerations of style and personnel the fact that so much New Deal legislation—the Wagner Act, AAA, TVA, Social Security, Public Housing—had only the faintest roots in the pre-Depression period, and the case for discontinuity may be seen as a strong one.

In the case of an historical problem of such complexity, with the evidence so various and often so contradictory, the best accounts produced so far are qualified and tentative. Progressivism, of course, was neither wholly kin nor entirely alien to the New Deal, its survivors neither solidly for nor against. Rather, the many elements of progressivism strayed into a confused and largely uncharted diaspora amid the general realignment of American political and social forces after World War I.

Both cases are in some degree persuasive. There is much evidence of a direct reform bloodline: the physical survival and continuing usefulness of reformers of the Ickes-Norris variety; the obvious debt of NRA to the ideas of the "Concentration School" going back to Van Hise and Croly; the whole unchanged rhetoric of "the people" arising in wrath to chastise "malefactors of great wealth"; the continued use of the label "progressive" among friends of the New Deal and among left-of-center reformers in Wisconsin and California.[3] Yet to anyone conversant with much

---

3. In Wisconsin, the Wisconsin Progressive party of 1934 and the National Progressive party of 1938; in California, Raymond Haight's Commonwealth-Progressive party of 1934. Aside from these parties, the label "progressive" appeared many times in the discourse of the day or in the titles of political organizations of all types. Its use generally signaled sympathy for the New Deal, but the word migrated leftward as the decade wore on and became an important word in the communist lexicon. The history of the word is therefore as complicated as the history of the body of ideas the movement generated.

progressive thought at the more popular levels—a good example would be Winston Churchill's novels *Coniston* (1906) and *Mister Crewe's Career* (1908), which faithfully represent the progressive ethos—or to anyone unable to dismiss the progressive credentials of F.D.R.-haters like James R. Garfield, Bainbridge Colby, or James A. Reed, or the slightly less angry William Allen White or the two Pinchots, the case for pregressive–New Deal similarity bogs down in crippling qualifications.

I V

The principal barrier to the creation of an assessment of twentieth-century reform politics that will win general acceptance is the vexatious variety of progressivism. The New Deal had its labyrinthine confusions, to be sure, but it *was* focused at one political level and confined to one party—and to a brief five- or six-year period. Progressivism spread its work over at least a twenty-year period,[4] operated at municipal, state, and national levels, infil-

---

4. Or longer. Municipal reform groups were forming in several American cities in the 1890's, and the settlement house movement began in the 1880's. At the other end, the state of Louisiana, for example, did not even begin its progressive rejuvenation (a somewhat limited one, under Governor John M. Parker) until 1920.

---

trated two parties and founded another, and spread many of its energies into non-political fields such as social work, settlements, and education. It was neither chronologically nor geographically compact, and there was no undisputed leader to give it coherence.

For many years, historians, lacking an appreciation of the complexity of the progressive movement, and without the monographic studies which are only now bringing that complexity into full view, generalized about progressivism on the basis of what was known of the ideas, and to a lesser extent the actual achievement, of a few prominent politicans and theorists. The fondness of the historian for intellectuals and politicians combined with a professional carelessness about the representativeness of its evidence, and this produced summaries of the progressive contribution which perched upon the flimsiest evidential structure.[5]

5. Daniel Aaron's *Men of Good Hope* (New York: Oxford University Press, 1951), for example, is a useful study of Emerson, Parker, George, Bellamy,

But this is by now a widely appreciated hazard, and there has consequently been a general appeal for more caution in generalizing, at least until better specialized studies of the movement appear. Important work has been done on conservation, social work, temperance, contests over regulatory legislation, and other areas of progressive effort. Every year sees more regional, state, and local studies, as well as an extension of competent biographies. Class analysis has been accomplished for California progressives, for Progressive party leaders, for all the reformers listed in W. D. P. Bliss's *Encyclopedia of Social Reforms,* for Iowa progressives, for Taft Republicans, for Massachusetts political leaders, and for Pittsburgh municipal reformers. There seems to be a growing awareness that five or six progressives don't make—perhaps must always distort—the movement, and this is all to the good. Ideally, distinctions will not make generalization impossible, nor generalizations make important distinctions invisible.

One of the most useful distinctions has referred to a doctrinal difference, and is quite old. This is the New Freedom–New Nationalism dichotomy, the classic formulation coming in the election of 1912. It is an attractive and risky pair of categories, and part of the intent of the present study is to look into the validity of the ideological divisions implied in these terms—terms which up to now have been too valuable to release, but too crude to use without a host of encumbering qualifications.

Arthur Link has separated "advanced" progressives from the others in a further attempt to manage the heterogeneous whole by subdividing it. He identified them as a coalition made up of social justice groups, labor, and farm elements, which emerged toward the end of 1914 as Wilson's early reforms passed into law, leaving certain needs untouched.[6] This division, rough as it is, seems to me a rather valuable beginning, and shows a fine understanding of the original Wilsonian impulse. In a recent article, John Braeman tried to establish a "traditionalist" and "modern-

---

Lloyd, Howells, Veblen, Brooks Adams, and Theodore Roosevelt—but Aaron talks throughout as if he were discussing some entity, progressivism. Reflecting a more glaring error, Andrew Scott's labored rebuttal of Hofstadter's *The Age of Reform* (New York: Alfred Knopf, 1955), which appeared as "The Progressive Era in Retrospect," *Journal of Politics,* XXI (November 1959), 684-701, is narrowly based on the Bull Moose element and especially on the platform of that party, although one would never guess it from the tone.
6. *Woodrow Wilson and the Progressive Era, 1910-17* (New York: Harper and Brothers, 1954), p. 54.

ist" distinction, using recent biographical studies of seven progressives.[7] Anyone working with progressivism feels the urgent

7. Braeman, *Business History Review*, XXXV, 581-92. Given
the complexity of the movement, we must work for some set of
defensible categories so that we may talk about it intelligibly at
all, and attempts to fashion typologies of this sort are to be
encouraged. But we must expect a good many false starts. The
hazards of even an informed effort to generalize and yet avoid
the sampling errors of others are amply demonstrated by Daniel Levine's book, *Varieties of Reform Thought* (Madison:
State Historical Society, 1964). Critical of studies based on too
few progressives, Levine settled for Jane Addams, La Follette,
Edgar Gardner Murphy, Beveridge, Gompers, and the Civic
Federation of Chicago. The best that can be said is that he was
working in the right direction, especially in the chapter on the
Civic Federation.

need of such clarification, and while Braeman's categories carry us
little beyond Link's, both represent an important effort to release
the many minority elements which made up progressivism from a
convenient subordination to some general view.

An understanding of the mesh between the two reform periods
has also been hampered by disagreement concerning the role of
ideas. Although progressives were proud of the tangible monu-
ments to their hopes, the electoral reforms and regulatory agencies and the militant citizen's organizations of many types, it remains true that *ideas* were their chief product. They wrote books
with high hopes of their effect, read each other's books and were
moved by them, had unbounded faith in exhortation and revelation. A basic progressive belief was in the possibility of a conscious re-ordering and subsequent control of society and its direction, a re-ordering accomplished by a public awakened by ideas, a
control guided by trained intelligence and backed by right values. When James Harvey Robinson spoke in 1909 of the importance of the study of ideas as preliminary to "the career of
conscious social readjustment upon which mankind is now em-
barked," he spoke as a progressive and for progressives.[8]

It is true that they thought themselves hardheaded, and that
there was a strain of realism in their thought which effectively
demolished the abstract formulations of the social thinkers of the

8. James Harvey Robinson, *The New History* (New York: Macmillan, 1909),
p. 130.

1870s and 1880s. They had a passion for facts, most often economic facts; witness the Brandeis brief in the *Muller* case, Charles Beard's book on the Constitution, or the Pittsburgh survey of 1907-08.[9] But these efforts reflect no narrow economic determinism, but rather a confidence that men could be persuaded, that truth mattered and was a match for any economic force or corporate complexity.

So, fundamentally, their faith was in the word, written and spoken, and it was in that coin that they dealt most comfortably. They were willing to work, and did work, through appropriate political or social action, and were not oblivious to the need to revive old institutions or create entirely new ones as instruments of their purpose. But their deepest belief was in popular education. Rush Welter's recent book treats the entire progressive effort, with great perception, as essentially a massive attempt to educate the American public.[10] Ray Stannard Baker, in a letter to Louis Filler commenting on Filler's *Crusaders for American Liberalism*, wrote, "I am glad you emphasize the educative rather than the reforming impulse. We had, at least I think I had, no dogma at all, but we were concerned about what we considered the evil conditions developing in our life and we wanted first of all to understand them. . . . I had a kind of faith, perhaps naïve faith, that if I could make people see the situation as clearly as I did they would immediately put an end to abuses." [11] And Fred Howe was to repeat that revelation in his invaluable autobiography, *Confessions of a Reformer:* "It was mind that would save the world, the mind of my class aroused from indifference, from money-making, from party loyalty and coming out into the clear light of reason." [12]

Always preferring exhortation to analysis, they might well be thought of as a kind of secular clergy, absorbed with right values, with self-evident, established ideals. The action component, as

9. Robert Bremner's *From The Depths: The Discovery of Poverty in the United States* (New York: New York University Press, 1956), presents this progressive emphasis upon the concrete as the distinguishing characteristic of their thought. I am especially indebted to this excellent study.
10. *Popular Education and Democratic Thought* (New York: Columbia University Press, 1962). See also the suggestive remarks of Lawrence Cremin in his *The Transformation of the School* (New York: Alfred A. Knopf, 1961), chap. 3.
11. Baker to Filler, June 7, 1938, Box 106, Baker MSS, Library of Congress.
12. New York: Charles Scribner's Sons, 1925, p. 322.

important as it was, was secondary to the theoretical and the pro-phetic. Their greatest achievement was to mobilize facts and neg-lected social values, and while they were avid for reform now, they did not need to rest their case before history on what they accomplished on the law books of today. The truth was out, social evil was unmasked, and the appropriate remedies had been for-mulated for the next generation that would finish the work. Therefore a large part of their legacy took the rather abstract form of social analysis and prescription. Such laws as they passed, such institutions as they erected might be perverted or altered by others, but the rhetorical deposit is fixed. Unhappily, while pro-gressivism is rich in ideas, there is considerable dispute as to how, or whether, to use them. The literature on progressivism mirrors this disagreement. Conflicting accounts of progressivism, and by inference, of the New Deal–progressivism connection, have come from intellectual historians who take ideas more or less at face value, as against those who feel that what progressives verbalized about their intentions must be subordinated to other evidence or ignored entirely.[13] If we find, as many have, that there is a close

13. Intellectual historians who have approached progressivism through its leading thinkers are, for example, Daniel Aaron, Louis Filler, Sidney Fine, Eric Goldman, and Henry May. An interest in ideas of a more popular and less coherent sort, com-bined with attention to the economic or social situation of the speaker, characterizes the work of men like George Mowry, Richard Hofstadter, or Joseph Gusfield. Then there is a group of historians such as Samuel P. Hays, Gabriel Kolko, or Robert Wiebe, whose focus is the political infighting of interest groups, and who reduce political rhetoric to the vanishing point in determining what progressives wanted. They prefer other evi-dence concerning progressive goals (concrete legislation or other action), concerning what bothered them (their class situ-ation and especially how it might be changing), and concern-ing their program (not what they called for, but what they were satisfied with).

resemblance between the verbalized assumptions, indignations, and remedies of progressives and New Dealers, the goal being "social justice," "democracy," or "reform," the enemy being "self-ishness" or "special interests," the remedy being "the positive use of government," could we then accept this joint use of verbal symbols as confirmation of a deep identity? To what extent may we trust the rhetoric of reformers to inform us of the complexities and qualifications which, unspoken, attend the bluntly stated means and ends of progressivism? Is it possible to take an interest in progressive ideas as they stated them, without being misled by the notorious propensity of mere political talk to mask a less elegant reality?

These are some of the formidable difficulties confronting those who would try to weigh the evidence for the incorporation of the progressive impulse and heritage into the aggressive liberalism of the 1930's. Progressivism was sufficiently fragmented so that it remains inaccessible to those easy generalizations with which we long to make it manageable. The truth about it comes in small assertions, in the limited, the qualified, the discrete statement. No paragraph will suffice to trace out its effects on recent history.

In addition, we may have reasonable doubts as to whether those progressive ideas, when they are located and measured inside the New Deal, accurately reflected progressive aspirations. Can we ever be sure that New Deal action, even when based in the most obvious ways upon ideas and expressions borrowed from the progressive lexicon, represented an accurate translation of progressive language?

V

History gave the conservatives just over a decade of peace, and visited them again with reforming Democrats. We know that progressives had been young, and we know that many survived. This study was conceived to exploit that circumstance, by systematically recruiting a broad sample of those reformers and recovering their own perceptions of the reforms of Franklin Roosevelt. The New Deal made physical contact with the progressive impulse through this surviving remnant, and their intellectual and emotional responses to the New Deal constitute a vital form of evidence about the progressive inheritance.

I have therefore tried to reconstruct the thinking of surviving progressives, working from published accounts by their own hands—autobiographies, articles, letters to editors, essays—supplemented wherever possible by unpublished manuscripts, and finally from biographies and other secondary accounts. Did they greet the New Deal with sustained enthusiasm, with abhorrence, or with some degree of feeling in between? What did they think about the relation of New Deal reforms to their earlier efforts? What were their judgments as to mistakes and missed opportunities? A number of difficulties present themselves at once. "Progressive," as we have seen, is a most unsatisfactory designation. What will assist us is a determination to recognize the divisions inherent in progressive reform, to generalize only upon a broad sample that includes most of the various subdivisions within the movement. I have recruited an eclectic sample (see Appendix I) of reformers who took part in the protest and alterations of the period from about the turn of the century to the election of 1916. All have at some time been called—by themselves, contemporaries, or historians—progressives.[14] They differed in reform activ-

---

14. It is possible to question the progressivism of many in this sample, as its eclecticism allowed many a lukewarm reformer to be selected. Even the most cautious of them, however, such as James C. McReynolds or Carter Glass, could lay some claim to a connection with progressive reform.

---

ity, class origins, education, geographic origins—differed in more ways than it is necessary to recapitulate here. Taken together, the sample reflects, I hope, the diversity of progressive styles and interests, while at the same time maintaining a reasonably accurate proportionality between the various elements of that spontaneous uprising of Americans bent on corrective action in the days of Roosevelt, Taft, and Wilson.

The sample was obtained from organizational lists and from secondary accounts, and represents reformers from seven general areas: national politics, state politics, municipal politics and reform, voluntary associations formed to advance social justice, intellectuals (writers, professors, "muckrakers"), social gospel representatives, and consumer's groups. To insure balance and to secure as many of the influential reformers as possible, I culled the name of every progressive from three major historical studies of large phases of the movement. The sample reached the figure 400; of those, 168 survived to observe the New Deal through a completed term.

But even if the sample broadly reflects the important characteristics of the original movement, and is sufficiently large to provide reliable data on at least the progressive leadership, if not the rank and file, further problems are inherent in the technique. For one thing, what assurance is there that the old men of the 1930's were essentially the same in political outlook or social attitude as they had been when they battled the trusts or a corrupt city council in the day of Theodore Roosevelt? Old men change their minds, goes the popular notion, and almost invariably become more conservative. If this bit of folklore be true, a study of a surviving remnant can shed little light upon what history has made, through the passage of time, inaccessible.

For several reasons, I believe that the men examined here were guided in their political judgments during the 1930's by the same goals and values that had brought them into progressivism twenty years before. There are a few cases of deep philosophical apostasy, when one appears to be dealing with virtually a different human being: the post–World War II Oswald Garrison Villard, for example, or George Creel or Reginald Wright Kauffman in the same period. Almost all of them had seen their confidence in the intelligence, sometimes even the motives, of "the people" damaged by the events of World War I and the disappointing years that followed. The years after 1917 were years of deep attrition against their energy, their assumptions, their leadership, and, of course, their prospects.

But it is surprising how often the study of the social and political ideas of the same individual in both periods reveals the original ideals and preferences intact. Certainly the charge of apostasy was rejected by many of the old progressives themselves. Those who opposed the New Deal were especially sensitive to suggestions that they had retreated to a comfortable conservatism because of age or success, and reformer after reformer insisted that his position had not changed, only the circumstances. While age may have worked its subtle alterations upon political mood, subjectively the old progressives had no sense of having turned their backs on old principles. Indeed, they were often aggressively convinced of the tenacity of the old ideals.[15]

---

15. The analogy with abolitionism suggests that old reformers tend to retain rather than to lose their original commitments, even if they retire physically from the struggle. See James M. McPherson, *The Struggle for Equality: Abolitionists and the Negro in Civil War and Reconstruction* (Princeton: Princeton University Press, 1964).

If the progressives' response was not warped to the right by the passage of time, it might be objected, it certainly must have been by the moorings of Republican loyalty, by resentment at being shouldered from leadership by a new and unusually young reform element, by increasing wealth, or by the natural—and very progressive—tendency to oppose those in power. As for progressives who were Democrats in the 1930's, the pressures must have run the other way, toward a tolerance of the new liberalism.

These are serious concerns, and in the pages that follow I shall try not to underrate the effect of the changes progressives had felt by the time of Roosevelt's accession to power. Nonetheless, I am convinced that they carried into the 1930's, with few exceptions, those political and social attitudes which animated them in the days of their revolt.

While presenting certain problems, the approach through the testimony of survivors reduces one hazard which is perennial in the study of ideas. Parted by time and death from their human sources and the circumstances of their birth, verbalized ideas may be bent to novel uses by successive generations. The original intent is easily lost as a phrase or an argument or a line of thought is stripped of its surroundings. It was not possible for progressives even in their most formal expressions of political philosophy— such as Croly's *The Promise of American Life,* or E. A. Ross's *Sin and Society*—to eliminate ambiguity entirely. And of course verbalized ideas are even less precise copies of what is intended in the more general level where most progressives operated—the political speech, the political platform, essays, articles, novels, letters. But if sufficient attention is paid to the speaker's situation, the site and the circumstances, and what the speaker did after he had spoken, it is possible to realize much of the meaning of political expression.[16] The difficulty lies always in recovering the surroundings. The more we know about the setting in which ideas emerge, the longer we are able to observe the idea and its owner in practical situations, the better we understand those phrases which seem often so deceptively self-evident.

Because one reform movement pressed so close upon another in the first half of this century, a living remnant repeated progres-

16. Rush Welter argues this point persuasively in his article, "The History of Ideas in America: An Essay In Re-definition," *Journal of American History,* LI (March 1965), 599-614.

sive thinking under new conditions, a repeat performance granting the historian an invaluable second exposure to the progressive ethos. One has a priceless second look at progressivism, the
authentic progressivism of survivors operating under new conditions, and that double-exposure does serious damage to any easy
assumption that an "idea" has about it a quickly discernible
meaning and a sturdy timelessness. The idea of using government
as an instrument of conscious social betterment, to cite a central
example, was certainly at the heart of the progressive experience,
and remains the basis of much of the argument for continuity
between progressivism and the New Deal. The importance of the
setting in which the idea was expressed, a setting too complicated
to be stated along with the central idea, and at any rate assumed
by contemporaries, may be seen in the instance of progressive
Henry L. Stimson.[17]

---

17. Stimson was a T.R. progressive, but as Taft's Secretary of
War he remained loyal to the administration in 1912. He,
along with the entire Roosevelt school, advocated a "strong
central government and a liberal interpretation of the Constitution." (Quoted in Elting Morison, *Turmoil and Tradition:
A Life of Henry L. Stimson* (New York: Houghton Mifflin,
1960), p. 127.)

Stimson, a man Theodore Roosevelt once referred to as "the
only man who is anywhere near as radical as I am," said in 1912
that government was not "a mere organized police force, a sort of
necessary evil, but rather an affirmative agency of national progress and social betterment." [18] This sort of statement was typical
of Stimson and a great many other progressives, both in and out
of the New Nationalism group. Nothing could be more plainly a
foreshadowing of how the New Deal was to use Federal power.
Yet Stimson was to oppose Franklin Roosevelt's domestic reforms
as unbearably coercive, and in so doing clarified his earlier plea
for active government. When he voted for Landon in 1936,
when he agreed with Joseph P. Kennedy that the only way to
teach F.D.R.'s forces the folly of the New Deal was through "suf-

---

18. The Roosevelt quotation is repeated in R. N. Current, *Secretary Stimson*
(New Brunswick: Rutgers University Press, 1954), p. 22; the Stimson quota-
tion is from Arthur M. Schlesinger, Jr., *Crisis of the Old Order* (Boston:
Houghton-Mifflin, 1959), p. 18.

fering," he was not repudiating his earlier faith in Federal activism, but further defining it.[19] He wanted a bolder government

19. Kennedy's remark, and Stimson's agreement, are recorded in Stimson's Diary, entry for July 27, 1938; Henry Stimson MSS, Yale University Library, New Haven, Conn. Kennedy told Stimson that he "lay awake nights" worrying that Roosevelt's inflation would take away all the money he had saved for his children. I suppose this is one case where liberals can be glad that, as with most of the fears of the well-to-do in the 1930's, Kennedy needn't have bothered.

in 1910, but he assumed that its aims would be principally to encourage and stimulate business. If this was not sufficiently explicit, if the emphasis in T.R.'s day seemed to be on benevolence, it was only because that setting required an appropriate stress.

In the 1930's, the situation had changed—meaning Stimson's career situation, the prospects of the parties, the nature of the available leadership, and especially the mood of the nation. He then, without ever retreating to a laissez-faire position, began to enunciate the boundaries of the reformist philosophy as he unhappily watched F.D.R.'s government transgress them. To New Dealers, Stimson's early preference for strong executive leadership in the pursuit of a national interest may have sounded like an early appeal for just what they were doing. But we would never have known just what Stimson meant when he called, in ringing campaign phrases, for an enlargement of government, had he not lived through the New Deal. He did like to see government take on new powers, however, and although his objections did not arrest the process, he was able at least to clarify the meaning of his resort to government by adding the limits and providing the qualifications that in earlier days had not seemed necessary. Once they had been added, they gave the remarks of 1910 rather a different thrust.

As the center of our concern is men rather than ideas, we work within chronological limits which are often breached. When ideas set off across the historical landscape, moving by word of mouth or transmitted from page to mind to page, with all the distortion involved in that process, they assume a life of their own, and that life is the proper study of one form of the history of ideas. But we should be very clear, more so than we have been, that when these ideas leave the individuals professing them, their continuing study tells us something valid about the ideas but nothing reliable at all about the individuals. If we are to understand the progressives, there can be no history of progressive thought beyond their deaths.

At this point it should be clear that the subject of this book is a double one, since I deal both with the question of continuity and discontinuity within the American liberal tradition and with what might be called the after-history of the progressive mind. In concentrating on the latter, I have attempted to shed light on the former, but it is of central significance that it is the progressive mind that I have been concerned with, not the New Deal mind. This has much bearing on the matter of continuity and discontinuity, since I am quite aware that there is another quite different way of getting at it. To examine the progressive mind in the post-progressive period is to discover what many students might consider an arresting measure of discontinuity: there were so many progressives who did not approve of the New Deal at all. But I have no quarrel with the common-sense judgment that there were indeed very important points of continuity between the two movements. Suppose one were to approach the whole subject from a different angle of vision and ask instead whether the New Dealers approved of progressivism, whether they believed they had inherited something from its experience, whether they took any inspiration from its example. It is easy to believe that one would then be disposed to emphasize the points of continuity more strongly, and that one's sense of the relationship would be different from that portrayed here. Every political movement tries to legitimate itself by reference to more or less accepted movements that have preceded it, and the New Deal is no exception. New Dealers could look back to the reforms of Theodore Roosevelt and Wilson and their contemporaries as precedent for what they were doing, could draw upon the increasing resort of progressives to state intervention, their enlarged concern with the general welfare, and their spirited attack against "special privilege." If a majority of surviving progressives cherished a rather unfavorable image of F.D.R. and his works, it does not by any means follow that F.D.R.'s supporters had to look back upon progressivism in a similarly unfavorable light. A few, no doubt, followed Thurman Arnold in being somewhat condescending to progressive moralism, but it is my impression that most of them saw much more to praise than to condemn in the progressive movement as a whole. To take full account of this would be important to any attempt to take stock of the continuities in the American liberal past.

For their part, the progressives could testify only to what they had originally meant, not to the potentialities inherent in their own intellectual formulations in the hands of a less restrained generation, nor to the sincerity or validity of all claims to apostolic succession. As the result of a speeding history and the longevity of a generation of reformers, progressives and progressive ideas had a second encounter in the 1930's with some of the unfriendly forces working to rob them of what it had been their *raison d'être* and destiny to try to preserve. We shall be interested to see who they identified as friend, and who as foe.

V I

Despite its effort to deal with a reasonably large number of persons, this essay stands largely in the tradition of impressionistic historiography. But it is impressionism with a difference. Precisely because it does deal with numbers, some effort has been made to use quantitative techniques, even though I am well aware that the results expressed may offer a greater show of definiteness than the actual substance of events may warrant. While data such as age, residence, and formal education are firm enough, such things as being a "reformer" or "against the New Deal," while I have often dealt with them statistically, are not of a comparable definiteness. We deal here with political opinion— or rather expressions of political opinion—among men who cannot be systematically polled; and even if they could be, such matters include so much that is unique that we are not often justified in reducing them to cold figures.

But while I do not wish to fall into a false sense of definiteness, it seems to me that the urge to quantify in the study of politics is a healthy one. If we must venture finally upon impressionistic judgments, they will be the more accurate if we sample widely, classify as carefully as human units permit, and count before we weigh. And if the effect of ideas eludes precise and final quantification, there need be no antagonism between a continuing interest in political thought and a disposition, in the words of Lewis

Namier, to "find out who the guys were" in sociological and political situation.

I am aware of one final, familiar problem. It seems obvious that the emergence in the last ten years of a vigorous radical Left, accentuating the difference between real radicalism and "mere" liberalism, must have the effect for most of us of further pushing the old progressive movement—now more than fifty years in the past—deeper into the dusty attic of the American experience, where we entomb those social movements and ideas which seem to have less and less relevance to present dilemmas. The Saul Alinsky campaigns in the slums, the Students for a Democratic Society, the militant sector of the Negro movement, the Viet Nam protest groups—these angry reformers of the 1960's demonstrate a disdain of paternalism, a distrust of improvements which come as gifts from the powerful to the powerless, which is in dramatic contrast with the spirit of that generation which believed in Uplift.

And it cannot help the progressive reputation that the Left is now struggling so desperately to solve problems which the progressives either ignored (the situation of the Negro) or tinkered with so ineffectively that the problem is still with us (war and peace, poverty). The sudden boil on the political Left cannot but heighten our sense of the conservatism of the progressive movement, causing us to stress not so much the useful part of their record—the organizations they founded, the laws they passed, the stimulus they gave to American self-criticism—but the negative side, where progressivism appears as a defensive movement generated amidst a moralistic middle class wishing to strengthen the grip of its cultural style and get power, insofar as it could, back into its own hands. This new perspective should be welcome, for the standard memories of the progressive movement which are too congratulatory fail to detect, even to try to detect, the shortcomings of that cautious uprising of the better classes. Finley Peter Dunne's Mr. Dooley, viewing the world from his bar on Chicago's South Side, brushed off progressivism as simply the American people beating a carpet, and we are better able now to see why he thought so.

But there is danger in this shift of perspective, even though I would agree that it is helpful and probably permanent. Much will be lost if we forget how hard it was for the progressives to awaken themselves, and then some part of the influential public, to undeniable national ills, how much of their lives they poured into astonishingly difficult campaigns to forge an inch ahead, how much they set in motion so that later assaults on injustice and the waste of human and natural resources would not have to start at rock bottom. I hope the account which follows preserves the right balance between their frailties and their courage, and places the blame for such archaism and irrelevance into which they and their doctrines may have fallen upon the pace of a century which divides one generation from another with such relentless thoroughness.

The roots of the New Deal went deep and tapped more than ideas; it rooted itself in social classes, pressure groups, and ancient grievances, all juxtaposed against a recent and baffling economic disaster. The New Deal owed debts to institutions, such as the National Conference of Social Work, the Regional Planning Association, the Reconstruction Finance Corporation, or the War Industries Board. Insofar as these debts were intellectual, however, it was always official New Deal doctrine to credit the progressives with a large degree of spiritual and intellectual paternity. But even if progressive platforms had been their primers, there is room for considerable speculation as to whether the New Deal liberal had really resumed the old progressive tasks. Such is our good fortune that we may allow the progressive himself to define the place of the progressive impulse in a world suddenly gone modern.

II

The Culmination of Progressivism:
I The Fight Against the New Deal

> Nothing could be a greater departure from original American-
> icanism, from faith in the ability of a confident, resourceful,
> and independent people, than the discouraging doctrine
> that somebody has got to provide prosperity for the rest of
> us. And yet that is exactly the doctrine on which the govern-
> ment of the United States has been conducted lately.
>
> . . .
>
> I don't want a smug lot of experts to sit down behind closed
> doors in Washington and play Providence to me.
>
> WOODROW WILSON

Franklin D. Roosevelt was elected four times, writes Henry Steele
Commager, "but no student can fail to be impressed with the
consideration that on each occasion the majority of the wise, the
rich, and the well-born voted the other way." [1] To the wise, rich,
and well-born should be added the majority of the old progressives, and for them "voting the other way" meant opposing the
reform movement which most of them had been hoping for since
the disappointments of Wilson's second term.[2] Accounting for

---

2. Of 168 surviving progressives, reliable information regarding
political attitude in the 1930's exists for 105. Of these, 60 opposed the New Deal, 40 supported it, and 5 were aligned consistently to the left of it. See Appendix I.

---

that defection cannot be easy, but that accounting provides a
major insight into the jumbled origins of liberalism. Had defect-
ing progressives abandoned reform, or were they speaking in the
name of reform principles when they scored the New Deal? If
the New Deal was not reform after their liking, what had reform meant in the days of progressive effort, and wherein did it

1. *The American Mind* (New Haven: Yale University Press, 1950), p. 354.

differ from the hopes and achievements of the second Roosevelt? No political discussion is more sterile than the "conservative" criticism of the New Deal. Any student of the New Deal is familiar with the parade of imaginary horribles that gripped the minds and dominated the speech of the opponents of the New Deal. The rhetoric of political conflict in the 1930's had a quality of hyperbole that seems unusual even in a country for which political talk has always been a major form of release and therapy. Americans have never been held accountable for what they utter in the heat of a political campaign, but the silly season of many political figures in the 1930's provided a performance which is unequaled in exaggeration and sheer unwarranted fright. The only possible use to which their talk of dictatorship, the end of the Republic, class revolution, etc., may be put is as a clue to the depth and nature of the deprivation being worked against certain men and classes in America.

Progressives who opposed the New Deal joined in some of this language, as must be expected in a decade of general fright and intellectual confusion. It would seem that there would be little profit in making any extended reference to what they had to say about the New Deal, for we have a book on the American Liberty League and a close study of the anti–New Deal argument generally, and it is rather arid stuff.[3] But a progressive was a peculiar sort of conservative when he was conservative at all, and when he came to condemn the great reform effort of the 1930's he was generally aware that his behavior was paradoxical. His criticisms, therefore, tended to be a bit less indiscriminate, a bit more carefully rendered, a bit more frequently preceded by hard thinking than most anti–New Deal utterances. Taken together, the 60 anti–New Deal progressives produced a running conservative commentary which, although not without its bleak stretches of unrestrained hysteria, makes it clear that the New Deal affronted the progressive spirit and that it bit more deeply in some places than in others. There is much in this body of criticism that is valuable, revealing the moral and intellectual quick

3. See George Wolfskill, *Revolt of the Conservatives: The American Liberty League, 1933-40* (Cambridge: Harvard University Press, 1962), and Thomas P. Jenkin, "Reactions of Major Groups to Positive Government in the United States, 1930-40: A Study in Contemporary Political Thought," *University of California Publications in Political Science*, I (1945), 243-408.

of a certain type of progressivism, and, no less, the areas where the novelty of the New Deal was most destructive of ancient reform methods and ideals.

For most of the surviving progressives, 1932 was the year to vote for the Democratic Roosevelt and the promise of change. It is true that the years had deeply sapped the reform commitment of almost all of them—driving some to the abandonment of all interest in reform, forcing more to a sort of physical truce, and bringing disappointment to all. But the economic breakdown at the end of a complacent decade reawakened many to the unfinished business of progressivism, and behind men like the Pinchots, Richard T. Ely, or Marshall Stimson, who had never given up hope of making further changes in America, gathered most of the old progressives, eager by 1932 to vote for and perhaps even to participate in a revival of reform.[4]

---

4. A few, of course, were not eager at all. Men like James C. McReynolds and Charles Evans Hughes had long since decided that the world was about as good as men could make it, and that it had better be let alone. Of the 60, I should say that only the following were apparently so complacent that not even the Depression could generate some mild form of reformism: William S. Bennet, Jonathan Bourne, Charles Evans Hughes, James C. McReynolds, Atlee Pomerene, James A. Reed, and perhaps Henry Stimson. The rest, although they may not have been actively involved with reform (and some were, such as Amos Pinchot), either maintained at least formal contact with a reform group (Newton Baker, for example, remained a supporting member of the National Consumer's League during the 1920's), took an occasional interest in a progressive cause (John Mandt Nelson, for example, acting as treasurer for the La Follette campaign of 1924), or at the very least allowed the Depression to revive within them social criticisms long dormant. That is to say, they thought the country needed another progressive era in 1932. Their subsequent rejection of the New Deal must then be seen, not as a dislike for reform, but as a dislike for reforms that were not progressive in spirit. It should be emphasized that "giving up" in the 1920's did not mean that a man was no longer a reformer. The reform impulse showed a surprising resiliency. Fred Howe "retired" to the Nantucket moors in 1925, disillusioned with "the State" and reform in general; eight years later he was working for the New Deal. See

Howe, *Confessions of a Reformer* (New York: Charles Scribner's Sons, 1925), pp. 340-43.

Franklin Roosevelt was known to only a few of them—to A. Mitchell Palmer, who helped write the Democratic platform of 1932, to Burleson and Newton Baker and Carter Glass from joint service under Wilson, to Justice Hughes from the early days in New York politics. But Roosevelt promised a vigorous if undefined reform administration, and had the support of most of those in either party who identified themselves as men of progressive spirit. The symbol of that progressive endorsement was the National Progressive League, organized to support Roosevelt in September of 1932, and headed by George Norris and Frederic C. Howe.

The "hundred days" were a whirlwind, an impossibly brief period in which to enact, let alone understand, the mass of legislation that was made law. These were days of intellectual confusion for both administration and onlookers, but the confusion was harder to bear from the outside. It was hard to tell which advisers were guiding the President, but it was virtually certain that most were new and unknown men. It was hard to discover what the New Deal intended simply by following, in the papers, the switchbacks from economy to relief spending, from a rather conservative banking act to the Federal adventures in industrial and agricultural planning. The result of this confusion was that Roosevelt for a while held the support of that substantial number of progressives who had been with him in November, and it was not until the summer of 1933 that the defections really began.

By June it began to be clear that Roosevelt had not taken the plain, high road of clean government and antimonopoly, but had gone a new and disturbing way. The first sign had been his choice of advisers. Among Democrats of progressive lineage, Hull was in the cabinet, Glass, McAdoo and Robinson in the Senate, but none of them were intimates. Roosevelt, when he could have consulted experienced Democrats, seemed too often closeted with professors from Columbia or Harvard or Cornell.[5] At the other

5. Roosevelt never established with the old Wilsonians the sort of ties they hoped for, and the distress many of them felt may be read most conveniently in the anxious letters that Albert Sidney Burleson sent to Dan Roper—who was as close as he could get to Roosevelt—urging tariff reduction and a balanced

budget. But, since it can be argued that Burleson was never much of a progressive, I would suggest that the response of Joe Tumulty was representative of a common sense of some kind of betrayal which seems to have struck almost all the old Wilsonians. The New Deal deeply distressed Tumulty, who had been Wilson's private secretary and a New Jersey progressive before his connection with Wilson. Because he finally voted for Roosevelt in 1936, and never openly broke with his party, he could not be set down as an opponent of the New Deal. But his dislike of it was instinctive and hard to conceal, and only party ties—and perhaps the memory of Wilson—kept him from a break. I have categorized him among those variously ambivalent, even though he clearly thought progressivism and the New Deal worlds apart. He spoke with special poignancy of the old men who, for him, symbolized the true spirit in American politics, and suffered at their neglect by Roosevelt. "Personally, being an individualist," he said in 1936, "I do not like regimentation or planned economy any more than you do." Admitting that he was "not intimately acquainted with" the Brain Trust, Tumulty went on: "There is, however, a group of prominent Democrats, that I have wintered and summered with since 1913 —Vice-President Garner, Cordell Hull, Pat Harrison, Joe Robinson, Jesse Jones and Senators Lonergan and Maloney of Connecticut, Congressmen Rayburn of Texas, O'Connor of New York, Vinson of Kentucky, McCormack and Walsh of Massachusetts, Ashurst of Arizona, Barkley, Bailey and Byrnes. . . . When you are asked to leave the Democratic Party, take a walk, desert—you part company with these fine men. . . . Will you Democrats find yourselves in any pleasanter company in the Republican Party? . . . No, somehow, I must remain true to the old traditions, to the old friends." (From "Address of Joseph P. Tumulty, New Haven, October 26, 1936," pamphlet in possession of Joseph Tumulty, Jr.)

---

extreme, he appeared to encourage close relations with Farley, Hague, Curley, Guffey, men whose connections to machine politics would hardly bear scrutiny. The result of his choice of advisers (and of those who were *not* asked to advise him) was that there seemed to have been erected a strange new government, out of tune with the Congress and the nation, whose first principle was coercion and whose ancestry and ultimate direction were dubious. The drift of the old reformers to the Right began that summer.

It is clear that NRA was the chief persuader. It was NRA, with its encouragement to monopoly and its Federal supervision of wages, hours, and standards, which not only convinced that small group of old progressives who had thought that nothing good could come of a Democratic President that they had been right all along, but which added men like Bainbridge Colby, Carter Glass, and A. Mitchell Palmer, Democrats all, to the list of those now opposing reform.[6] "Arbitrary, senseless, and brutal," Glass called

6. Of course, the political import of NRA was largely in the eye of the beholder, so contradictory were its purposes. There were progressives to the left of the New Deal, like Oswald Garrison Villard (at least in 1933-34), who feared that NRA was the first step to Fascism.

NRA before voting against it in the Senate, and he followed his disapproval with a refusal to allow the law to operate at his two Lynchburg (Virginia) newspapers.[7] Few progressives who saw in NRA an unnecessary and dangerous coercion could match Glass's unique brand of stubborn resistance, but his general sentiments could be matched almost endlessly from diaries, letters, and published opinions of many an old reformer.

After NRA, the New Deal seemed to drive progressives out by attrition rather than through any one dramatic measure. Those who defected almost invariably grounded their resentments in the areas of New Deal spending, labor policy, bureaucracy, and the supposed drive for dictatorial power by the executive. Disturbed by deficit spending, for example, James R. Garfield wrote in his diary as early as July 2, 1933: "Fifty-two years ago today father was shot! What would he think of present day public finance and the proposed fantastic economic experiments?"[8] And later in that year, on November 19: "Father's birthday. I wish men would remember his splendid work for sound finance and act upon his proposals which were successful in those days." And on the last day of 1933, in a reflective mood: "Our national affairs chaotic with grave danger of disaster unless the road to inflation is blocked and we return to sound money."[9]

That same concern over the reliability of money appeared early

7. Glass MSS, Box 312, University of Virginia Library, Charlottesville.
8. Diary entry of July 2, 1933, Box 16, Garfield MSS, Library of Congress.
9. Diary entries of November 19 and December 31, 1933, Garfield MSS.

and often in the letters of many old progressives. In 1936, S. S. McClure, then almost eighty, wrote to William Allen White: "I write to you in a kind of despair. I accidentally was led to make a study of the national budgets of all the nations of the world. I was surprised to find that the nations that prospered and got out of the depression did so by following the economic principles established during the nineteenth century. . . . It seems to me that these facts . . . back up Landon. . . . I put in months of work getting my stuff together, but I can't get it out. . . . For old times' sake, I would like to have you weigh this problem I have put up to you, on why the stuff won't go." [10]

10. McClure to White, October 5, 1936, White MSS, Box 182. McClure had fallen on very hard times by the 1930's, but did not repudiate the system that had given him, by turns, wealth and poverty, fame and obscurity. He eked out an existence in New York, living at the Murray Hill Hotel, writing occasionally for E. A. Rumely's National Committee to Uphold Constitutional Government. His voice rose, Ida Tarbell reported, only when he spoke of F.D.R. Louis Filler saw him in 1939, surrounded with old copies of *McClure's Magazine,* trying to mine them for material on a book about America in 1939. He was never able to get beyond the wisdom of 1912, when, in his autobiography, he said that all our ills could be cured by the commission form of city government. See S. S. McClure, *My Autobiography* (New York: F. Ungar, 1963), and Peter Lyon, *Success Story: the Life and Times of S. S. McClure* (New York: Charles Scribner's Sons, 1963).

The election of 1936 found most of their grievances crystallized, and most of those who were to oppose the New Deal already in opposition, sure now of their objections, and glad of the chance to air them in the public talk of a campaign. Republicans who had been friendly in 1932—Hiram Johnson, White, Gifford and Amos Pinchot, Chase Osborn—were, on the New Deal record, disappointed and inclined to prefer Landon. A number of Democrats had bolted, men like James A. Reed, Carl Vrooman, William Randolph Hearst, Bainbridge Colby. Others like Glass and Burleson and Newton Baker said nothing in support of the President and were known to be unhappy with much that had been done. By October 1936, probably more old progressives were set to vote against the New Deal than to endorse it, and the October 19 letter of eighteen Bull Moosers opposing Teddy Roosevelt's cousin was symbolic of that shift.[11]

Roosevelt was openly supported by the Progressive National Committee headed by La Follette and Norris, it is true, and the letterhead of the Committee showed the names of Costigan, Paul Kellogg, and Peter Witt, all of whom dated back to the period before World War I. But the progressives who met at Chicago in September of 1936 to form that Committee were, overwhelmingly, men of a new generation like Tom Amlie, La Guardia, Maury Maverick, and Senators Benson and Bone. And while it is natural that the membership should be largely new men, there were many surviving progressives of the old type who did not join—so many, in fact, that the progressive National Committee, while it may have represented a fair sample of existing reformism, cannot be said to constitute proof that the older progressives were with Roosevelt. By 1936, most of them were not.[12]

12. Other old progressives, not in the sample, who appeared as members of the Committee were Grace Abbott*, Frank Walsh*, and William T. Evjue* (hereafter, progressives not in the sample who appear in the narrative will be designated by an asterisk). Formation of the Committee was reported in *The New York Times,* September 11 and 12. Donald R. McCoy found that $35,000 of the PNC budget of $55,000 (1936) came from the United Mine Workers, a good indication that the word "progressive" now denoted reformers of a different type. See McCoy, "The Progressive National Committee of 1936," *Western Political Quarterly,* IX (June 1956), 454-69.

After the election of 1936, with its massive mandate for Roosevelt, some of his progressive opponents were to soften briefly (notably Albert Shaw), and some allowed themselves to be converted by the November display of national confidence and to become reconciled to the New Deal (notably Chase Osborn and Raymond Robins). But most continued to distrust the gay reformer, and to deplore what was being done in the name of reform. They found new reasons, in 1937 and 1938, to remain in opposition.

The secession and growth of the militant C.I.O. and the discovery of the technique of the sit-down strike were no part of the

11. See *The New York Times,* October 19, 1936. Seven of the eighteen appear in my sample: Henry J. Allen, Robert P. Bass, Amos Pinchot, Chester Rowell, Albert Shaw, Marshall Stimson, and William Allen White.

New Deal, but most Americans associated labor gains with Roosveltian design, and for many progressives the militancy of organized workingmen in that period was the natural fruit and probably even the intention of New Deal class consciousness. Hiram Johnson, for example, wrote to John Francis Neylan in February of 1937: "The power we are giving him, taken in conjunction with events that are occurring like the 'sit-down strike,' with which he is sympathetic, is mighty ominous, and frankly, I fear for my country." [13] That same month saw the beginning of Roosevelt's move to reform the Court, and the spring of 1937 must be accepted as the moment when he held the support of fewer old reformers than at any other time. Old Bull Moosers that spring and summer forgot T.R.'s attack on the judiciary, and feared the worst as the Court proposal was being fought out. E. A. Dickson wrote to Hiram Johnson that "it seemed as though the collapse of our country was impending." [14] Johnson matched his millenarian mood in writing to Neylan: "I felt seriously that it was the beginning of the end of the Republic." [15]

Those who disliked Roosevelt's attempt to increase the number of Supreme Court justices generally had an equal dislike for the Wages and Hours Bill, although they could not stop it. But by 1938 events in Europe and the administration's response to them were pushing ahead of purely domestic concerns. Progressives, most of whom had established, after perhaps some early vacillation, what was to be their attitude toward the changes Roosevelt made and allowed to be made at home, were in 1938 and afterward subjected to entirely different stresses and choices. Those years and those choices, dominated by international conflict, are beyond the scope of this study.[16] But before going back for an

---

16. I will not attempt to deal with what the coming of World War II did to these progressives, and the person who does so will not find it easy to generalize about their foreign policy attitudes nor to locate the rules which govern how various sorts of progressives would fall out when collective security confronted neutrality. There commenced in 1938 or so a highly complicated shifting of allegiances among progressives, as

13. Johnson to Neylan, February 26, 1937, Johnson MSS, Bancroft Library, University of California, Berkeley.
14. Dickson to Johnson, August 17, 1937, Dickson MSS, University of California, Los Angeles.
15. Johnson to Neylan, July 24, 1937, Johnson MSS.

among other Americans; the brew of progressivism contained pacifism of several shades, virulent nationalism that might turn either isolationist or globalist, a strong school of internationalism that inclined some to intervention, moral sensitivity to the plight of the European Jew, and other ingredients that made it highly volatile in the late 1930's. After 1938, with Roosevelt associated with intervention on behalf of the Allies, progressives began to regroup and change sides rather wildly, forgetting the old issues of NRA and an unbalanced budget. Men like Stimson and Chester Rowell and Gifford Pinchot stopped citicizing Roosevelt for the New Deal and began to support the administration, sometimes even taking posts within it. The opposite movement, more dramatic but not necessarily involving greater numbers, saw men who had been with, or to the Left of, Roosevelt in the 1930's move over into opposition. These new political alignments rearranged the membership of the Hate Roosevelt and Support Roosevelt groupings, and easily the most interesting aspect of these wartime realignments, from the standpoint of the student of the reform mind, is the way in which the isolationist tide that carried so many progressives into opposition to Roosevelt over the war also seemed to provide the occasion of, if not the partial cause of, a "souring" of progressives on the administration's *domestic* accomplishments. I suspect that the student of this process of "deconversion" (Richard Hofstadter's phrase, I believe) will find that the disillusionment with domestic liberalism among progressives such as George Creel, Hiram Johnson, Amos Pinchot, Villard, Senator Gerald Nye*, Senator Burton Wheeler* and others actually began much earlier than Roosevelt's move toward involvement in the European situation. As I have said elsewhere in this account, it will also probably appear that these progressives who after World War II kept the company of the Knowlands and the Brickers and even the McCarthys were not so changed as it might appear.

It should be noticed, however, that not all those progressives who became angry with Roosevelt and found themselves after 1939 in chorus with men who disliked the President for his domestic policies went on to despise what he had done at home. It was possible for a progressive to oppose Roosevelt after 1939 and still emerge from the war with an unimpaired commitment to the reform movement which Roosevelt had carried so far in the 1930's. I think especially of John Dewey, John Haynes Holmes, and above all of Charles A. Beard*, three who took part in the now-despised opposition to collective security but who were not headed for postwar reaction.

The logic of their course is more apparent to men who lived through the 1945-66 years, including the Viet Nam war, than it was to their contemporaries. Beard*, perhaps the best known of those reformers whose liberalism made no room for the war, saw war as the nemesis of reform, urged "continentalism" as an antidote to those pressures which have three times in this century pushed America, under reform Presidents, toward wars which ended by strengthening reaction at home. There were some unlovely characters in the isolationist camp, but in retrospect I am not at all sure that one would want to argue that Roosevelt was a wiser liberal than those few old reformers who went from a domestic liberalism that was considerably warmer than his own to the America First Committee.

---

analysis of the progressive responses I have sketched, two general reflections should be made, and they concern aspects of the New Deal about which the progressives said surprisingly little.

First, there is little evidence that more than two of the entire group of 168 recognized the celebrated shift, in 1935, from the New Nationalism to the New Freedom phases of the New Deal.[17] Louis Brandeis and Norman Hapgood had schooled themselves to measure all political developments by the test of New Freedom values and policy, and they welcomed—in Brandeis's case partially engineered—the abandonment of the planning efforts of the early New Deal. But I discovered no other cases of that recognition. Certainly no old Bull Moosers stayed with Roosevelt during 1933 and 1934 because he was emphasizing the familiar planning and co-operation features of Theodore Roosevelt's 1912 philosophy, only to break in 1935 because he shifted to antitrust and the denunciation of business leaders generally. Bull Moosers who broke with F.D.R.—the Pinchots, Hiram Johnson, and the rest—either became estranged earlier than 1935, or, if afterward, for reasons having no relation to what could be called New Freedom policies. Conversely, there were no old Wilsonians, leaving aside Brandeis and Hapgood, who veered sharply from opposition to support because they detected, in the spring and summer of 1935, that Roosevelt was moving away from the New Nationalism and toward the old Wilsonian policies.

There are a number of reasons why this was so. While historians, including myself (see the article just cited), have divided

17. See Otis L. Graham, Jr., "Historians and the New Deals: 1944-60," *Social Studies*, LIV (April 1963), 133-40, for a review of the literature on this shift.

the New Deal into two phases and labeled them the "first" or New Nationalism phase (1933-35) and the "second" or New Freedom phase (1935-38) after the progressive philosophies which seemed ascendant within the administration at the time, there are good reasons to believe that this has been overdone. *Time* magazine reported in 1935 that all signs indicated that Roosevelt had decided for the balance of his tenure to pursue Recovery and conciliation of business rather than Reform, an observation by contemporaries that is exactly the opposite of the way historians have reconstructed the events of 1935.[18] In all likelihood, William Leuchtenburg and William H. Wilson are right when they argue that this "shift" was either nonexistent or too clouded by contradiction to be of much analytical value.[19]

The failure of the old progressives to respond to the shift at all, much less with any philosophical consistency, does not in itself prove that it never took place, however. Very few progressives were close observers of the New Deal, and the contest of philosophies and personnel within its myriad agencies was hard enough to follow even for those who had the inclination. Watching an astute political journalist like Walter Lippmann grow more hostile to the planning features of the New Deal, and finally attack them in his *The Good Society* in 1937, precisely when the New Deal had almost entirely abandoned the few timid attempts at planning which it launched in 1933, reminds us that even the best informed contemporaries found the 1930's a difficult time for unclouded judgments.

But even if the change in administration policies and advisers in 1935 was less dramatic than some have said, why didn't more Bull Moosers follow those well known New Nationalism theorists such as Hugh Johnson*, Raymond Moley*, and Don Richberg* out of the ranks of the New Deal toward the end of the first term? These men provided criticisms of the New Deal from a New Nationalism point of view after drifting into opposition in the period 1935-37, giving us grounds to expect that most Bull Moosers would follow that same pattern.[20] It is not enough to say, I think,

---

20. Moley and Richberg, especially, were highly articulate and their retrospective criticisms of the New Deal aided historians

18. *Time*, XXV (February 18, 1935), 14-15.
19. Leuchtenburg, *Franklin D. Roosevelt and the New Deal, 1932-1940* (New York: Harper and Row, 1963), pp. 162-6; Wilson, "The Two New Deals: A Valid Concept?" *Historian*, XXVIII (February 1966), 268-88.

in seeing, perhaps too clearly, the philosophical shift which these New Nationalism theorists thought so disastrous. Actually, in all three cases the break with Roosevelt came in large part because of a deterioration of the individual's relationship with the President and the intense disappointment which it brought to their political hopes. The timing of their break with the New Deal owed as much to their political fortunes as to the course of New Deal legislation, and only later did it appear to all of them that 1935 was the year when Roosevelt committed the great philosophical error. Johnson expressed himself in speeches and occasional articles after 1936, Moley had his say in *After Seven Years* (New York: Harper, 1939) and in his *Today* magazine, and Richberg, in addition to a flood of articles and addresses, spoke of Roosevelt's errors in his autobiography, *My Hero: The Indiscreet Memoirs of an Eventful but Unheroic Life* (New York: G. P. Putnam's Sons, 1954); see also Christopher Lasch's perceptive Master's essay, "Don Richberg and the Idea of a National Interest," unpublished, Columbia University, 1955.

---

that Bull Moose survivors failed to break at the end of the first term merely because Roosevelt's change of mind was not clear even to the most intelligent observers. If we are surprised at the failure of Bull Moosers to act consistently, the reason lies to a large extent in the mistaken assumption that all or even most of those who participated in Roosevelt's Progressive party bolt did so because they "believed" in the "New Nationalism." On the contrary, many of those who joined Theodore Roosevelt had no sympathy with the idea that government should take on a broad interventionist role in behalf of less fortunate groups. The social welfare portions of the Bull Moose platform were urged on Roosevelt not by the convention but by a small group of social workers,[21] and there were many in the party who joined it not because of its humanitarian goals but for more prosaic reasons, such as a dislike of Taft or Wilson, or by a bandwagon political gamble that Roosevelt was the vehicle to offices now held by regular Republicans. The platform may have expressed a very advanced social philosophy, but it had to support not only Jane Addams but men of the most suspect reformism, such as William Flinn of Pennsylvania, Walter F. Brown of Ohio, or the industrialist

21. See Allen F. Davis, "The Social Workers and the Progressive Party, 1912-16," *American Historical Review*, LXIX (April 1964), 671-88.

George Perkins. "Think of me and Jane Addams," exclaimed Medill McCormick, "on the same platform!" [22]

We should not forget that the Progressive party combined these disparate elements, and that while it unquestionably did attract most domestic radicals in 1912, it was also well supplied with less visionary types, such as those two dedicated proponents of things-as-they-are, Herbert Hoover and Alfred M. Landon. Even its ideologists were not in agreement; under the Bull Moose standard with T.R. as he stumped for the acceptance of corporate size restrained by a potent government, one could find New Jersey's George Record, the influential philosopher of the restoration of competition. With such a diverse membership, the Bull Moose contingent could hardly be expected to have reacted as a group to Franklin Roosevelt's shift away from something resembling the "New Nationalism" in 1935.

But even for those Bull Moosers who did associate themselves with the New Nationalism, it turned out that a later generation was to misunderstand what they had meant when they spoke of blending aid to underprivileged groups with planning in the national interest. One of the differences, for example, between the New Freedom and the New Nationalism, as the standard interpretation goes, arises out of the question of public policy toward special interests, the extent to which government was to intervene and whether that intervention was to be—to utilize inadequate but popular terminology—"positive" or "negative"; i.e. whether government was to deal with interest groups and apportion rewards, or police a fair start for all and ignore the result. As Wilson saw it, "paternalism" was not what was wanted, but simply the restoration of an open field to enterprise. That view of the progressive task was congenial to many men, most of them within Wilson's party. Theodore Roosevelt was supposed to have stood for the shouldering, by government, of the duty to dispense favors where wrongs had accumulated ("social legislation"), and those attracted to the Bull Moose standard presumably endorsed that view.

22. Quoted in Donald Richberg, *Tents of the Mighty* (New York: Willett, Clark and Colby, 1930), p. 36. McCormick thought that incongruous, but in that same army that marched to Armageddon with T.R. were two who were never again to agree on anything, Dean Acheson (*A Democrat Looks at his Party*, New York: Harper, 1955, p. 15), and H. L. Hunt of Dallas (interview in *Playboy*, August 1966, p. 51).

But there does not seem to have been any concentration among Bull Moosers of a tolerance for social legislation, or a monopoly of dislike for it among Wilsonians. Wilsonians like Newton Baker and Carl Vrooman were very critical of special laws which singled out certain groups for favors, it is true, but so were Marshall Stimson, Irvine Lenroot, and Jonathan Bourne, all of whom had voted for Roosevelt.

The truth is that the social welfare aspects of the Progressive platform and ideology have often been exaggerated at the expense of another and a partially contradictory imperative—the National Interest. While not above a favor here and there to women or children at work, the average (non-social work) New Nationalist could never be in accord with a policy which saw reform primarily in terms of the parceling out of material favors to clamoring groups. Such a policy would be profoundly divisive, and anyway was at odds with the deepest Croly-Roosevelt suspicions of mere material concerns. Unity was what was wanted, and an end to conflict would come only when some leader of national vision lifted all eyes to goals which none need seek at the expense of others. That concept of the national interest and how to foster it was to set many New Nationalists against the New Deal. Marshall Stimson, for example, a good Bull Mooser, appealed in the 1930's for the time when "men will think of the national welfare rather than increased wages or profits. Expenditures for luxuries and trifles will cease. Labor will quickly depose leaders who advocate strikes. . . . The country will strip for action." [23] Frederick Morgan Davenport, another Bull Mooser, was fond of recalling that T.R. had quoted Garibaldi whenever men seemed too fixed upon mere material gains. The Italian patriot said: "I promise you battles, hardships, toil, weariness, difficult marches, hard bivouacs!" Compare this sort of appeal, Davenport said, with the politics of the present Roosevelt! [24]

23. From an article in the *Los Angeles Herald*, dated only 1942; Marshall Stimson MSS, Box II, Huntington Library, San Marino, California. Stimson (1876-1951) was a Los Angeles lawyer and civic reformer who was active in the statewide progressive movement in California and in the Progressive party in 1912.

24. Typed manuscript, no date; Davenport MSS, Box 6, Syracuse University Library. Davenport began his career as a teacher at Hamilton College, served intermittently in the New York state senate from 1909 to 1925, and then in the United States Congress from 1925 to 1933. In New York he associated himself with the reform element, first with the Hughes group and then with

The misunderstanding was as great where the concept of "planning" was concerned. While some younger intellectuals like Rex Tugwell took the teachings of Croly and Charles Van Hise and Theodore Roosevelt to mean that the economy was to be directed toward productivity and efficiency by Veblen's engineers, the bulk of New Nationalists who spoke to this problem made it clear that businessmen were to do the planning while sympathetic governmental officials assisted by gathering national trade information and maintaining a healthy business climate. "Heaven knows," wrote Donald Richberg*, "that the progressives of recent years have devoted a great deal of time to planning what things should be done! But I regret to say that they acted on the assumption that this planning should be done by government, which really means by politicians. . . . Let me submit that this is a totally different method of planning progress from what I had in mind." [25] With these ambiguities at the heart of the New Nationalist creed itself, and remembering that by no means all Bull Moosers were New Nationalists, we can understand why there was no concerted flight of old Progressives from the New Deal to conveniently mark off the administration's major philosophical turning point.

Second, these progressives rarely aimed criticism at the innovations embodied in Federal relief, public works, or social security programs. There was occasional complaint about the expense and the bureaucracy involved, but almost all progressives endorsed or acquiesced in the assumption of some form of Federal responsibility for the relief of Depression hardship. And, oddly enough, there was very little criticism of TVA. Progressives, in fact, did not follow the New Deal very closely, for the most part, and they generally spared measures and programs of a clearly humanitarian or social welfare nature. Their fire was concentrated on all attempts at economic planning, on the aura of class warfare and interest politics, and on the mushroom growth of the Federal establishment in general. But where conservatives like James M. Beck had much to say about high taxes and the awful waste of unemployment relief, very few progressives devoted much critical effort to these things. Their fear was chiefly of power, not of char-

---

Theodore Roosevelt, running unsuccessfully for governor as a Progressive in 1914.
25. Richberg, *My Hero,* p. 348.

ity; power, especially, in the hands of such unpredictable individuals as Roosevelt and his circle seemed to be. With the general idea of some form of federally initiated philanthropy in the Depression crisis, they had no quarrel; but if recovery must be bought at the price Roosevelt asked, a re-shaping of American institutions in the fire of angry majorities from beneath, they were not willing to pay it.

Finally, behind the baffling legislation and the disturbing new tone and the unknown advisers, there loomed Roosevelt himself: evasive, mercurial, powerful. For men such as these, whose distrust of power ran deep, it was absolutely essential to entrust power, if it must be concentrated at all, to a man whose motives were as steady and transparently selfless as they were loftly. Such a man was Woodrow Wilson, and many of the progressives, like George Creel or Ray Stannard Baker, cherished to the end a memory of Wilson's predictable idealism. Theodore Roosevelt, brusque and righteous, elicited almost the same degree of confidence.[26] When Oswald Garrison Villard, toward the end of his

26. Many, like Mark Sullivan and Frederick Morgan Davenport, adored and trusted T.R. But, possibly because of his impulsiveness and his obvious enjoyment of power, T.R. convinced a good many that even he was not to be trusted. Ray Stannard Baker, for example, was originally a Roosevelt man, but finally supported Wilson in 1912 simply on this matter of personality and the attitude toward power.

life, judged the greatest President of his era to have been Grover Cleveland as he went down to principled defeat in 1888, he was expressing in its most uncompromising form their view of political leadership. Power was a trust, not an instrument; the great leaders exercised a kind of moral negative over the shortsighted clamor of the crowd for some quick way to wealth or some martial adventure. Measured by those standards, the Roosevelt presidency must have appeared a public disaster.

It is true that the emergency of 1933 made almost everyone see the need for executive action of a broad sort. But most old progressives could not accept Roosevelt's actions for long, for they came to suspect his motives. If power were sought for personal reasons, the preachments and gestures of reform made no difference—were, in fact, the more evidence of a dangerous duplicity.

Power must be accepted with reluctance, borne with dignity, employed in a disciplined way through a clear program, aimed at achieving certain clearly stated ends. Some progressives distrusted Theodore Roosevelt, some Wilson, but virtually all of them had trusted one of these men with the augmented powers of the state. Franklin Roosevelt did not enjoy that trust among the majority of progressives.

They found it hard to state exactly why. Some were won by his charm when in the presidential presence (Carter Glass, for example, or Hiram Johnson), but when the distance was restored the flaws of Roosevelt's personality reappeared. They found something shifty about the man, some indefinable quality of ambition and excessive flexibility, amounting ultimately to expediency in all things. William Allen White expressed it well enough:

"He had the National Society of Editors at the White House, Thursday evening, April 19. . . . He talked for two full hours, sitting down, in the dining room which was cleared of tables and filled with chairs. I had not seen him for nearly ten years. I was struck by the change that had come over him. He shakes his head a good deal and gestures from the neck up when he talks. He is facile, and his facility under duress may become recklessness, but under normal conditions is somewhat the basis of his charm. He frankly confessed his currency tinkering had been a failure; . . . He complained about the silver group ganging up on him and in several instances when he was explaining the basis of certain actions and certain policies, he exhibited what to me seemed a dangerous tendency to reason from one to many. He has a habit of generalization and simplification which is not scientific and sometimes is disillusioning, at least to me. His mind is quick and superficial. Of this I am dead sure. He still smiles too easily for one who shakes his head so positively. I fear his smile is from the teeth out, though I am not sure how much the unconscious arrogance of conscious class is back of his smile. Away down in my heart I am scared. He is a fair-weather pilot. He cannot stand the storm." [27]

And more briefly to Ray Robins, "I don't trust Roosevelt." [28]

27. White to Allan Nevins, May 24, 1934; quoted in Walter Johnson (ed.), *Selected Letters of William Allen White, 1899-1943* (New York: Henry Holt, 1947), p. 345.
28. White to Ray Robins, February 10, 1936, White MSS, Box 172, Library of Congress.

In part, certainly, this was the product of their relative neglect. Roosevelt had many of them to the White House—George Creel, Frederick Morgan Davenport, Hiram Johnson, White himself— but nothing could mask the fact that they were not really consulted, not men whose advice made a difference as it had in the day of Wilson or Theodore Roosevelt.[29] In part, also, they were

29. A good example comes from a letter Richard Ely wrote to Wesley Mitchell in 1934, asking "why it is we have never had an opportunity to serve the present administration?" Ely to Mitchell, August 10, 1934, Ely MSS. Box 249, Wisconsin State Historical Society. Progressive era Presidents were, by contrast to the 1930's to say nothing of the 1960's, amazingly accessible. Irving Fisher regularly was granted interviews with both presidential candidates before he made up his mind how to cast his one vote (Irving N. Fisher, *My Father Irving Fisher* (New York, 1956), p. 201; and John Graham Brooks, when he sent T.R. books on two occasions, received from the President a long discussion of the issues raised and the implications for policy. These and other T.R. letters are in the John Graham Brooks MSS, possession of Lawrence G. Brooks, Medford, Massachusetts.

convinced that Roosevelt, unlike Wilson especially, sought power for purely personal ends. As Ellery Sedgwick wrote in his autobiography, "My race of heroes died with Wilson. It revived again in a brief but violent flame with Al Smith . . . and after him my line of heroes disappeared forever. . . . A hero is a man whose self is forgotten in his victories." [30]

30. Ellery Sedgwick, *The Happy Profession* (Boston: Little, Brown, 1946), pp. 186-7. A classic comparison of the motivation of Wilson and Franklin Roosevelt, invidious to the latter, is found in George Creel's autobiography, *Rebel at Large* (New York: G. P. Putnam's Sons, 1947), chap. XII. To the historian, of course, men like Wilson and Al Smith appear quite as dominated by egocentric drives as was Franklin Roosevelt, but it must be admitted that they projected a less unscrupulous image to the reformers who watched all these men so closely.

What made the difference in the end, perhaps, was the general unintelligibility of the New Deal itself. It was all the harder to trust Roosevelt because intelligent men, accustomed to following public affairs, could not tell where Roosevelt was going. "Roosevelt," Amos Pinchot wrote in 1935, "with all his kind-heartedness, is failing because he follows no consecutive line and apparently doesn't think things through to the end . . . No one knows what he thinks or what he will do tomorrow. He is the Great Uncertainty." [31]

31. Amos Pinchot to Felix Frankfurter, July 15, 1935, Box 56, Pinchot MSS, Library of Congress. For Amos, things were to get worse. By the end of the decade he was convinced of the existence of a tight little conspiracy of intellectuals, with a significant European representation, who had designs upon the country. His article, "The Roosevelt-Laski Scheme," published in *Scribner's Commentary* in October of 1941, saw Roosevelt as conspiring with Winant, Fred Rodell, Ernest Bevin, Hopkins, Keynes, Frankfurter, Cohen, and, especially, Laski—"a small, close corporation of internationally minded and exceedingly powerful men." (A copy of the article, unpaginated, is in the "Laski" file, Pinchot MSS.)

Added to the several twists and turns of the New Deal which often annoyed them in content, and always struck them as unnecessarily devious, came this final indignity, especially in the decade of Hitler, Mussolini and Stalin, of a President who received emergency powers in a spirit of arrogance, flippancy, and brazen ambition.

I I

Thus the New Deal made old reformers into anti-reformers, and in such numbers as to force us to decide whether we deal here with aberration or consistency, lest we misunderstand progressivism entirely. Reformers under one Roosevelt, the antagonists of reform under another; what accounts for that reversal of role? Is this simply a case of the conservatism of age? Had they purged themselves of all progressivism years before, out of personal ambition, greed of luxury or office, out of a loss of faith in "the people" after the war, out of that mysterious process of "reaction" which overtakes those who hope for too much?

Some of them lapsed into silence, and while we know they opposed Roosevelt, we shall probably never know more than that. A few, clearly, had gone through the Left-to-Right trajectory, had changed their minds substantially, and no longer identified themselves with liberalism.[32] But most insisted that they, and not

32. Ellery Sedgwick, for example, went from crusading editor of the *Atlantic Monthly* and an ardent Wilsonian to being a Franco sympathizer and self-confessed conservative. "In any journey of three-score years or more it is the practice of thinking people to travel from Left to Right. Along that path I have trudged. I was cradled about the middle of the Left wing, and my grave will be about the middle of the Right." (*Harvard Class of 1894*: Fiftieth Anniversary Report, Norwood: Plimpton Press, 1944, p. 475.) I think it can be said that Sedgwick, and perhaps Reginald Wright Kauffman, were the only progressives who underwent a fundamental change of mind. One might add those socialists—Max Eastman, Robert Hunter, and John Spargo—who wound up as great admirers of capitalism, as Republicans, and, in Eastman's case, a frequent contributor to the *National Review*. Some progressives, such as George Sheldon, Hiram Johnson, George Creel, William Randolph Hearst, and even Oswald Garrison Villard, finished their lives talking the language and keeping the company of the Tafts, Knowlands, Brickers, and even the McCarthys of postwar America. But none of them saw this as a change of principles or values, but only as a shift in emphasis. One can see their reasoning; the objective was a certain sort of America, and if for a time the chief threat to it was the corporation, they were alert enough to respond when the threat came from welfare state liberals or from international communism.

Roosevelt, had kept the faith.

In that, many of them were outspoken. "Now as to age causing a conservative growth," Chase Osborn wrote to Frank Knox in the year he came out against the New Deal, "I think not if the heart and soul grow with the belly and the intellect. . . . I am more liberal than ever before." [33] And Irvine Lenroot: "I was for old Bob La Follette and I have not changed in any way my views that I held then concerning abuses in our economic life." He then added, as if to explain his long struggle against the New Deal: "But I have always believed that a thing that was wrong when committed by capital and industry did not become right if committed by large groups who were able to swing elections." [34]

33. Chase Osborn to Frank Knox, January 29, 1935, quoted in Robert M. Warner, "Chase Osborn and the Progressive Movement," unpublished Ph.D. dissertation, University of Michigan, 1957, p. 368.
34. Lenroot to E. D. Parsons, August 28, 1943, Box 4, Lenroot MSS, Library of Congress.

Or consider the remark of Mark Sullivan in a letter to Albert Shaw: "I am on the same side now that I was back in the old *Collier* days. The fight was for individualism then and is for individualism now. The enemy was regimentation attempted by big business; the enemy now is regimentation attempted by the government." [35] Examples could be multiplied.[36] Most of the progres-

36. For example, Hiram Johnson: "In all my political life, I have pursued one course, and at my present age I could not if I would, and I would not if I could alter that course." (Johnson to H. L. Baggerly, September 24, 1937, Johnson MSS.) Or Burton K. Wheeler: "My own feeling is that while the times, the issues, and the leaders have changed, my basic outlook has remained the same." (Wheeler, *Yankee From the West*, Garden City: Doubleday, 1962, p. 428) Wheeler wrote this late in life, when he had been for a number of years what the casual observer would call a staunch conservative.

sives opposing Roosevelt continued to identify themselves with the best and most idealistic in American life, and resented the implication that their politics in the 1930's amounted to a backsliding from youthful ideals. How reformers, after taking thought, could reject a reform movement apparently so akin to their own, and do so largely in terms of familiar progressive principles—this is the central question to be put to the anti–New Deal progressive.

If age had brought a conservative apostasy, as it did in a small number of cases, the inquiry would illuminate little but the mental world of their old age, and the action of the years upon early intellectual positions.[37] But according to most of them, they spoke

37. The notion that the old are necessarily the primary custodians of conservatism was wounded even more, for the 1930's at least, by James Patterson's paper read before the American Historical Association on December 29, 1964. Patterson indicated that the average age of the conservative coalition in the Senate in 1937 was exactly the same as that of those who supported the New Deal. For Patterson's findings, see James T. Patterson, "A Conservative Coalition Forms in Congress, 1933-39," *Journal of American History*, LII (March 1966), 759.

35. Sullivan to Shaw, January 2, 1935, Box "1934-36," Shaw MSS, New York Public Library.

for progressivism to the end. To the extent that this is so, we learn much about the reform movements of both periods through attention to these progressives who would not be liberals. They were conscious of the paradox, acutely so whenever the New Deal appropriated the word "progressive," and they left behind a rich literature in explanation of their collision course with what passed as the extension of progressivism in the 1930's.

To begin with, the situation had altered rather fundamentally. Historians are generally in agreement that America crossed from one century to another at about the onset of World War I, and this meant moving from a period of buoyant hopes and familiar, stable values into a time marked by disappointment and pessimism, by the collapse of certainties. This transformation is the subject of Henry May's *The End of American Innocence*,[38] and May sees it as coming at the end of the progressive era. The American future, simple and full of irresistible promise, had been clouded as the country came out of the war, and the aging progressives were acutely aware of it. "Those were the wonderful days," recalled William Randolph Hearst, thinking back on the prewar period, "and happy achievements of youth. . . . Life was not 'one damn thing after another' then. It was one adventure after another. The competition of journalism was a glad sport. We were young. As Kingsley sings:

> When all the world is young, lad,
> And all the trees are green,
> And every goose a swan, lad,
> And every lass a queen;
> Then hey for boot and horse, lad,
> And 'round the world away.
> Young blood must have its course, lad,
> And every dog his day." [39]

What Hearst memorialized with this banal verse was more than just the normal nostalgia of an old man. Youth, for men who were of the progressive generation, coincided with the years when America did not doubt her mission nor the soundness of her economic and political institutions. "How wonderful was 1907, when

38. (New York: Alfred A. Knopf, 1959).
39. William A. Swanberg, *Citizen Hearst* (New York: Charles Scribner's Sons, 1961), p. 496.

I began my ministry in this city! That was the golden after-glow of the nineteenth century, which itself outdid in splendor every thing since Periclean Greece," John Haynes Holmes remembered. He went on to add: "Those of you who did not live in that period before 1914, or are not old enough to remember it, cannot imagine the security we enjoyed and the serenity we felt in that old world." [40] For Irving Cobb, it had been "the jubilee age of this earth." [41] Mark Sullivan simply quoted Goethe: "When I was eighteen, Germany was eighteen." [42]

One deals here not merely with routine nostalgia, I think, but with a clue to the limits of progressive reformism. It was precisely because they assumed the stability of their society and the reliability of its promise that reckless adventure and social reform were psychologically possible. Compare their memories of youthful adventure and rebellion with their sense, in the 1930's, of the disasters awaiting the unwary and the incautious. Compare the absence of a concern for lurking social disaster in the 1898-1914 period with the perils they saw in the 1930's, and you encounter the relationship, noted by Stanley Elkins,[43] between a loss of room

43. The idea of "room to manuever" as a prerequisite for reform is developed in Stanley Elkins, *Slavery* (Chicago: University of Chicago Press, 1959), chap. IV (.3).

The progressive generation had a strong appetite for adventure, more so, it seems to me, than one would take to be usual. This association of progressivism and an almost compulsive drive to perilous personal adventure has not been sufficiently explored. Teddy Roosevelt embodies that chest-thumping, buffalo-hunting element within so many men of that generation, and perhaps an urge for great "male" exploits was not confined just to the reformers. But reformers certainly did not take second place. One thinks of the exploits of Francis Joseph Heney, who was expelled (like Wallace and Will Irwin) from college for fighting and who killed a man in a gunfight in an Arizona town long before he entered the tranquil battles of Boss Ruef's San Francisco; of Chase Osborn, reform governor of Michigan, who prospected alone in the upper Great Lakes region, discovered the Moose Mountain iron deposit and cov-

40. Holmes, "Forty Years of It," delivered in Community Church, February 9, 1947, and privately printed (pp. 14-15).
41. Irving S. Cobb, *Exit Laughing* (New York: Bobbs-Merrill, 1941), p. 544.
42. Mark Sullivan, *The Education of An American* (New York: Doubleday, Doran, 1938), p. 238.

ered 2200 miles a season on foot; of Napoleon Bonaparte
Broward *, who before becoming governor of Florida worked
as a deck hand on the St. Johns River, in Newfoundland and
Boston, and regularly ran arms to Cuba on his own ship; of
Ray Robins, who left home in Florida to work his way to San
Francisco as a cowboy and miner, turned up in Alaska as a
prospector and minister to the Eskimo, made a fortune in gold,
and returned to spend most of it in a Chicago slum.

---

to maneuver and the reform impulse. Radical men pursue reform
undeterrred, perhaps encouraged, by increasing signs of social
revolution. For the conservative reformer, reform should be attempted with great caution, if at all, when society is in deep trouble. The 1930's struck the old progressives as such a time.

Prior to World War I, democratic political systems, our own
pre-eminent among them, seemed firmly in control of the desti-
nies of the leading Western states. There were no threats to
American democracy from without, and the progressives were
confident that they could cope with those within. There were no
signs that progressive democracies, here or abroad, were in a stage
of transition to something else. But developments in Europe after
the war darkened the future of democratic governments generally, and especially undermined the progressive faith in the ultimate tractability of the state, which was, after all, the chief progressive instrument. The writings of the progressives are strewn
with worried references to Mussolini and Hitler and Stalin, to the
emergence of malignant totalitarian regimes. The progressive
American, never entirely at home with the state because he was
an American before he was a progressive, saw in Europe's conversion to totalitarianism a case of history teaching by negative example that those who proposed to grant further power to government in the cause of social reform were headed in the wrong direction. Reformers, apparently, had overestimated the amiability
of government—that was the lesson of 1917 in Europe, and of
1922, and of 1933.

It is possible to convey by quotation only the average form, but
not the frequency, of references to European disasters as seeming
to prove that the state should be given no more power in America. Oswald Garrison Villard cited what he had seen in Europe,
especially in Germany, as his reason for opposing the Court Plan:
"We know that the Supreme Court has been tinkered with before, but we also know that those changes took place, or were

attempted, in what might be called the piping times of peace, compared to the grave hour in which we live today. . . . I share Dorothy Thompson's feelings that this proposal opens the way to a dictatorship." [44]

Amos Pinchot's letter to Roosevelt in 1937 put these fears in perhaps their clearest form: "What has happened in Europe makes it clear enough, that, if a leader pursues the path of bureaucratic regimentation of industry and agriculture, he must go forward into dictatorship, whether he wants to or not. . . . We are familiar with the kind of coercion Stalin has had to use in order to control the farms and industries of Russia. We have seen almost the same coercion used by Hitler and Mussolini." [45] Walter Lippmann's *The Good Society,* conceived in fright at the planning state, might have been their tract for the times:

"To the reader of the current newspapers such deeds and such views [the absolutism, in practice and theory, of Richelieu's France] are no longer the curiosities of polite learning. For him they are virulently alive once more and his world is turbulent with the violence of men who really do such deeds and really hold such views. He is perforce reminded that the struggle of his forefathers continues, that even the rudiments of the good life have still to be wrested daily from the earth in sweat and trouble and defended against implacable enemies. If he is of middle age and, therefore, a survivor from the age of temporary peace and plenty, he is compelled to realize that he was misled by the sheltered thinkers of that age—by men who did not apprehend deeply . . . the imperatives of human existence.

"The certainties they taught him to take for granted are in ruins." [46]

History, European history, had ruined those certainties, and

44. U. S. Senate, 75th Congress, 1st Session, Hearings on Reorganization of the Federal Judiciary (March 1937), IV, 1029. James Paul Warburg, author of *Hell Bent For Election* and a prominent critic of the New Deal after 1934, later regretted that he had used this sort of European analogy in opposing the President. He came to realize, as he put it in his autobiography, that "the rise of totalitarian governments in Western Europe had not resulted from too much exercise of governmental power. Totalitarian governments had come to power in every instance through the failure of democratic governments to do enough." (Warburg, *The Long Road Home: The Autobiography of a Maverick* (Garden City: Doubleday, 1964), p. 162.)

45. Pinchot to Franklin D. Roosevelt, April 26, 1937, PPF 1677, Roosevelt Library, Hyde Park.

46. *The Good Society* (Boston: Little, Brown, 1937), p. 370.

the chief casualty was a confidence in melioration through government. Reform of society, which in another sense meant running experiments on a sick patient, now seemed inadvisable, especially since reform had expected to accomplish its ends through the use of the state. Considering the demonstrated dangers, "room to maneuver" had abruptly narrowed. As Tugwell remembered Brandeis saying, in April of 1933, life in modern America was like Poe's room where the walls constantly converged.[47] A healthy economy, the Western world confident of its political stability and peaceful future, America in the care of reformers on the verge of great and permanent cures—these were the circumstances in which progressive criticism and experimentation were carried out. Circumstances had changed by 1933, and that change was part of the reason why the New Deal had more enemies than friends among the old reformers.

But a changed historic situation, especially since it surrounds all progressives, friend as well as foe of the New Deal, can be only part of the answer. A great deal is explained by their personal situations, what might be called their sociological profile. Progressives who thought the New Deal too radical outnumbered those who were glad to support it, and by a substantial margin. A comparison of these two groups suggests some reasons why.

As far as age is concerned there is no correlation between age and conservatism *within* the progressive group itself and there was a considerable variance in age within that group. The median year of birth for 168 surviving progressive reformers was 1867; for the 60 conservatives it was 1867, and for the 40 New Deal supporters, 1867. The mean year of birth tells the same story (1868, 1868, 1867); there was no appreciable difference in their ages.

The next likely factor would seem to be wealth. Wealth, social standing, and style of life, are hard to define and as hard to measure. A man's fortunes change, and in the case of these progressives this generally meant going from a modest birth and upbringing

47. Related in A. M. Schlesinger, Jr., *The Politics of Upheaval* (Boston: Houghton, Mifflin 1960), p. 234. A powerful lament for the passing of a world in which individual adventure was still possible is Newton Baker's essay, "The Decay of Self-Reliance," *Atlantic Monthly*, 154 (December 1934), 726-33. Baker's yearning for the recapture of "wide spiritual spaces" and "room beyond all horizons" transforms this "Equality is conquering Liberty" polemic into a poignant protest which is only half-heartedly aimed at the New Deal.

to an economic situation of comfort or affluence. They were, on the whole, successful people. Still, fortunes varied even in maturity; witness Irving Fisher, the Yale economist, who was "worth" perhaps $10 million in the 1920's and who was imploring Yale for a pension or for an advance on his library in 1939. It is rarely possible to be quite sure of the financial standing of these men and women. But, working with five categories (from "Lower" to "Wealthy") and with 84 progressives whose political response was known, it appears that those opposing the New Deal had a slight tendency to have been born in better circumstances, and to have been in better circumstances in the 1930's.

The difference is rather slight on this scale of personal wealth, and both groups (those for and those against the New Deal) are bunched in the "Upper-Middle" category. For every Henry Stimson or Bainbridge Colby whose visible affluence seems to account for an equally visible conservatism, there was likely to be a George Foster Peabody or a J. Lionberger Davis, well supplied with both wealth and enthusiasm for the New Deal. I do not wish to appear to discount economic factors entirely; the New Deal activated economic fears among the comfortable, and progressives were not entirely proof from these concerns, as the taxation complaints of Albert Shaw and William Randolph Hearst, for example, attest. But neither the struggling nor the affluent always voted their "interests."

If neither age nor wealth seem to have varied closely with political attitude among surviving progressives, the geographical origins of progressives, as well as the rural-urban identification, might be of striking importance. Table 3 of Appendix I reveals that regional origin, taken by itself, had little to do with political attitude. But whether a man had a rural or an urban upbringing seems to have made a difference. The urban progressive was as likely to be a supporter of the New Deal as not (of 26, 13 were for Roosevelt), whereas progressives of small town and rural regions were more strongly conservative (29 to 16 among those of small-town rearing; 14 to 7 among those raised on farms).

There is no way to be sure that other things, such as ethnic or religious factors, are not being measured within the circumstance of urban or rural rearing, of course. There are some obvious reasons why the New Deal, with its celebrated urban tinge—its voting base, its pragmatic and non-puritan value orientation, the welfare and labor aspects of its program—would appeal more strongly to the urban progressives, and one would need to present a much closer analysis of the components of the urban experience and personality in order to account with any confidence for political preference among the urban reformers. But the positive effect of urban origin and rearing on attitude toward the New Deal is clear enough.

A certain amount of the progressive opposition to the New Deal stemmed from party—i.e. Republican—loyalties. It is true that most of the progressives had an avowed and fairly consistent (in a few cases, fervent) party identification: 97 out of all those surviving, in fact. It is also true that most of these (56 per cent) were Republicans, and, more important, of the 60 progressives opposing the New Deal, 32 were Republicans with only 6 Republicans supporting Roosevelt. A man who was Republican and had been a part of the progressive movement, then, was better than a five to one bet to oppose the New Deal.

That ratio conveys little surprise, but it does suggest that opposition to the New Deal among progressives may have simply been a matter of predictably regular voting habits and party loyalties. A closer examination, however, makes it clear that party loyalty was by no means always decisive, but was only one of the factors shaping political attitudes in the upsetting 1930's. In the first place, not all Republicans went into opposition, and those who did made up only slightly over half of the progressives on the Right. They were joined by Independents, by some ex-socialists, and by 15 Democrats. That group of Democrats is the best evidence that party loyalty was often overborne by other factors.[48]

---

48. For a Democrat to oppose the New Deal, after years of political drought since Wilson, the provocation had to be considerable. The economic crisis of the 1930's created something of a national front psychology, and it was far easier for Republicans to cross over than for Democrats.

Just as Democrats bolted the President, many Republicans had bolted Hoover in 1932, openly or covertly, rupturing at least once the ties of political inheritance. In fact, few of these men could show, at the end of long lives, an unbroken record of party loyalty. For the occasional William S. Bennet, who never voted any but the Republican ticket, there were many more like Hiram Johnson or the Pinchots, who voted the other way once or twice, and others like Chase Osborn and Harold Ickes, for whom party label exercised little pressure. And there had been a good bit of shuffling around as these men reached their twenties, with sons leaving the party of their fathers. In short, most progressives had an occasional party irregularity in their past, and when they voted for a Democrat in 1936 it would not have been the first time. It therefore seems that party identification, while undoubtedly a factor in the opposition of some old progressives, operated with less force than the data might suggest, and may have itself been a reflection of other and more controlling circumstances.

But if party was not inevitably the determinant of political attitude, its force must not be dismissed. It was very hard for Republicans with continuing political ambitions—men like Borah, Gifford Pinchot, or Robert Perkins Bass, all of whom found the New Deal at least partially appealing—to make more than a temporary peace with Franklin Roosevelt. The case of Gifford Pinchot is instructive. A leading conservation advocate in Theodore Roosevelt's administration, Pinchot was a man of vocal social sympathies and an insurgent temperament, and as governor of Pennyslvania during the Depression (1930-34) he had inaugurated a program of welfare spending and reform which was the beginning of Pennsylvania's " little New Deal." [49]

In the early days of the New Deal in Washington, Pinchot made strenuous efforts to be friendly to the administration, and made it clear that he remained a Bull Moose Republican, as fond of executive responsibility and social welfare measures as Roosevelt himself. The President did not respond to overtures for a bipartisan alliance, and threw the weight of the administration behind Joseph Guffey in the Senate race of 1934, while directing Ickes not to appear to support Pinchot in the Republican senatorial primary against David Reed. The Gifford Pinchot who backed Landon in 1936, and who openly denounced WPA and other unspecified sins of the administration between 1935 and 1940, was less the humanitarian gone sour than the ambitious Republican politician taking the only course open to him. Only the existence of parties, the opportunities they alone can offer and the loyalties they come to inspire, can satisfactorily explain the anti–New Deal stance of a few of the old progressives. Among

49. See Richard C. Keller, "Pennsylvania's Little New Deal," unpublished Ph.D. dissertation, Columbia University, 1960.

these, Gifford Pinchot is the best documented example of the power of party, although as often as ambition we find simple institutional loyalty.[50]

It might be argued, in fact, that an uncalculating loyalty, buttressed by suspicion of the enemy, counted for more than career ambitions where party and its attachments are concerned. Whatever the reasons for joining the party in the first place, once the association was made, the institution received from some of them the devoted attachment of men for whom vital institutions come few and far between. David Hinshaw, in his biography of William Allen White, tells of White informing his mother by long-distance phone in 1912, "in a voice breaking with emotion," that "he had decided to leave the party of his mother, of his boyhood, and his young manhood." [51] Even the Bull Moose bolt, which most anti-Taft Republicans considered less rash than actually joining the Democrats, was a wrenching experience. The Democratic party, despite Cleveland and Wilson, remained to many Republicans an almost totally unfit body of place-seekers, the party of woolly Bryanism and—never far out of mind—secession. In the 1930's, as earlier, nothing good could come out of it; so, at least, thought a significant number of Americans who happened to be Republicans and old progressives. Walter Lippmann was acquainted with the tenacity of such loyalties: "I know how bogeys are made. I was a child of four during the Panic of '93, and Cleveland has always been a sinister figure to me. His name was uttered with monstrous dread in the household. Then came Bryan, an ogre from the West, and a waiting for the election returns of 1896 with beating heart. And to this day I find myself with a

50. See James A. Kehl and Samuel J. Astorino, "A Bull Moose Responds to the New Deal: Pennsylvania's Gifford Pinchot," *Pennsylvania Magazine of History and Biography*, LXXXVIII (January 1964), 37-50, and M. Nelson McGeary, *Gifford Pinchot: Forester and Politician* (Princeton: Princeton University Press, 1960). Both convincingly demonstrate how Pinchot's course in the 1930's was shaped by the collision of his progressivism with the realities of party politics and his own powerful presidential ambitions.

51. *A Man From Kansas: The Story of William Allen White* (New York: G. P. Putnam's Sons, 1945), p. 24. White, Robert Bass, and both Pinchots continued to hope for the nomination of a Republican progressive who would conduct a reform movement along acceptable lines, and the history of their party from 1901 to 1916 encouraged them in that hope. As they saw it, progressivism had been born of their party, and no safe or far-sighted reform could be expected outside it. They hoped for the nomination of Borah, or La Guardia, and eventually accepted Landon's brief progressive credentials.

subtle prejudice against Democrats that goes deeper than what we call political convictions." [52]

The New Deal was the professor's delight, and while it was accomplishing the permanent attachment of Negroes, Labor, and the urban masses to the Democratic party, it added intellectuals to that coalition in sufficient numbers so that the terms intellectual and liberal became almost synonymous. Whether that mutual attraction came of the great openness to novelty among highly educated people, their estrangement from the business community, their boredom at having no national use for their expertise, or from other sources, it seems reasonable to inquire if among the old progressives there might be some positive relationship between the amount of formal study and an acceptance of the New Deal.

I was especially interested in the possibility that study in Europe might show up consistently in the backgrounds of those favoring the New Deal, in view of the oft-remarked contribution of men who had studied abroad (especially in Germany) to what came to be called Reform Darwinism. The data derived from surviving progressives shows no such relationship. Neither college degrees, nor graduate work, nor European study appear to have had any simple correlation with political attitudes in the 1930's. [53]

---

53. The only reliable way to measure education is to take account of formal education, measured generally in terms of degrees or years completed. There is no way to measure self-education from books, outside a few cases like those of Ray Robins or Charles Stelzle, who reported on their reading habits. Naturally, education in its broader sense, including experience, could not be measured.

When, however, graduate study was examined as to discipline, it was clear that those with law degrees were much more likely to oppose the New Deal (about four to one), while those who held Master's and Doctor's degrees tended to support it (about nine to seven). Thus, while years of formal education seem in themselves to have made no difference in political attitude, the type of graduate education did bear a strong relationship to subsequent political habits.

Harvard University was the undergraduate or graduate home of an amazing 24 per cent of the 117 college graduates among

52. *Drift and Mastery* (New York: Kennerly, 1914), pp. 240-41.

these progressives, a dominance which, to the best of my knowledge, has never been remarked before.[54] This underlines again the

54. Except by Richard B. Sherman in his "The Status Revolution and Massachusetts Progressive Leadership," *Political Science Quarterly,* LXXVII (March 1963), 59-65, but any study of
Massachusetts would reflect the influence of Harvard. There is,
however, considerable evidence that Harvard was the sort of
place in the late nineteenth century—when most progressives
were in college—that awakened young men to social issues, becoming, along with New York City and such places as Toynbee
Hall, one of the cradles of progressivism. Men like Homer
Folks, Hutchins and Norman Hapgood, John Haynes Holmes,
Ellery Sedgwick, and Oswald Garrison Villard paid tribute, in
autobiographical accounts, to Harvard's teaching staff and general atmosphere for alerting them to their responsibilities in
the transitional times facing the nation. Laurence Veysey
writes, concerning this period: "Heterogeneity did not of itself
suffice to liberate intellectual ferment. For this to happen, students of diverse means and temperaments not only had to live
side by side in comparative toleration; it was also essential that
the non-conformist receive inspiration and sustenance from at
least some of his peers and elders. This peculiar combination.
. . . Harvard alone possessed." Veysey, *The Emergence of the
American University* (Chicago: University of Chicago Press,
1965), p. 291. For a sketch of some of the greats on the Harvard faculty at the turn of the century, see Rollo Walter
Brown, *Harvard Yard in the Golden Age* (New York: A. A.
Wyn, 1948). Samuel Eliot Morison wrote of Harvard in 1886
that "the abolition of compulsory prayers, the influence of Dr.
[Francis Greenwood] Peabody's new courses in Social Ethics,
and the example of Toynbee Hall . . . enhanced the religious
interest in Harvard College, and gave it a definite turn toward
philanthropy." Morison, *Three Centuries of Harvard* (Cambridge: Harvard University Press, 1936), p. 367. On the other
hand, most of us are familiar with the complaints of men like
John Reed (Class of 1910) and John Dos Passos (Class of
1916) that Harvard was smug and stultifying, and even Franklin Roosevelt (Class of 1904) wrote that "from a reformatory
for the aborigines, the University has become the resort of
thousands of Lilliputians. . . . Many of the inmates indeed
come, not to study, but for the experience—the finishing touch,
which in many instances seemed indeed the finishing touch!"
(*Harvard Advocate Centennial Anthology.* Cambridge: Schenk-
man, 1966, p. 55.) Morison himself estimates that the student

body did not become radicalized in significant numbers until about 1910, at which time the progressive leadership had emerged and begun its final campaigns.

fact that this sample of progressives is a sample of leadership, of well-educated and talented people for the most part. It is tempting, also, to add the hypothesis that a form of educational ferment was taking place at Harvard from about 1885 through the first decade of the twentieth century, but one could turn to the simpler explanation that men who went to Harvard were, by nature and after association with the nation's oldest university, more likely to become conspicuous in whatever they attempted. The eighteen Harvard graduates for whom there is reliable information on political attitude in the 1930's were almost exactly as conservative in the 1930's as the sample as a whole.

More effective in shaping political attitude than any other factors, however, were occupation and type of reform activity. The relation of the two is often obvious—as when journalists took part in the muckrake movement—but is just as often not evident when only occupation is known. For example, a lawyer like Raymond B. Fosdick followed a career that touched New York politics, social work, and the publication of an occasional article in the popular magazines. If we then separate occupation and reform activity and consider them in that order, we find that lawyers and the journalist-editor group were strongly opposed to the New Deal (the ratio was about three to one), and that the same was true of those whose reform careers had been predominantly in the areas of politics or serial publishing.[55]

55. Lawyers went about two to one against the New Deal, but the proportion would have been higher if only practicing lawyers had been counted. Of the 10 lawyers known to favor the New Deal (out of 28 whose views were known), most were judges, such as John Burke or Ben Lindsey, or, like Raymond B. Fosdick, had gone into other lines of work. This sample contained relatively few men from business and banking (for a discussion, see Appendix II, pp. 205-6), too few to generalize from. It is highly probable that such men, even when they were old progressives, predominantly opposed the New Deal, although Roosevelt had his friends in banking (J. Lionberger Davis), finance (George Foster Peabody), and industry (Rudolph Spreckels, Merle D. Vincent).

Because men voted their class so often in the New Deal years, there are those who would see nothing but naked self-interest behind the conservatism of those in the occupations of law and publishing, where corporations rewarded them so amply by fees and advertising rates. The resistance, in 1930, to Charles Evans Hughes's appointment to the Supreme Court arose from just such suspicions, and few would be surprised at the hostility toward the New Deal among lawyers in the service of corporations. William S. Bennet was code counsel to the Chicago Retail Lumber Dealer's Association; Newton D. Baker's Cleveland firm had a blue-ribbon clientele; Joe Tumulty was retained by utility interests to lobby against Roosevelt's Public Utilities Holding Company bill —such activities made New Deal sympathies unlikely. But it is a restrictive view of human nature that leads us to search only for who paid the piper when we try to account for the selection of the political tune. These men, long before Roosevelt's presidency, had taken up the associations and the rewards of large urban practices and successful editing and publishing, and well before the New Deal years their social aspirations, their circle of friends, and, yes, their savings, had disposed them against rocking the boat. And it seems likely, going back further, that men of more conservative stripe would be attracted to politics, law, and publishing in the first place, making these occupations strongholds of resistance to extensive social change for reasons which are at least as much psychological as financial.

Some of the muckrakers argued, late in life, that their movement had never been really directed toward radical changes. Ida Tarbell insisted that she should never have been called a reformer, and Will Irwin recalled in his autobiography that, with the exception of Lincoln Steffens, "few of the muckrakers . . . were then or later political or social radicals." [56] As for the lawyers, there is even stronger evidence that the same mental qualities that led them into the law and guided them in their progressive activities inclined them later on to disapprove of the New Deal. The frequency of the criticism that the New Deal was intellectually incoherent hints that a sort of mental tidiness, a desire to think carefully and have the theory straight before acting, was common among men of the law and as much as anything else set them against the intellectually chaotic program of Franklin Roo-

56. Will Irwin, *The Making of a Reporter* (New York: G. P. Putnam's Sons, 1942), p. 151.

sevelt. The files of Newton Baker, Amos Pinchot, and Robert Bass, for example, are filled with little essays which carefully worked out the meaning of "Liberalism" or "Reform," or which presented some "Platform" or "Statement of Principles" to re-orient on paper the ideas of men so perilously—and understand-ably—close to confusion. One could multiply almost indefinitely remarks such as this one made by the lawyer Newton Baker: "The Administration seems to me to have no philosophy or prin-ciples." [57]

It is true of the progressives as a whole that they were men of ideas—recall Tom Johnson's determination, extending to the re-tention of an attorney to read *Progress and Poverty*, to learn the truth about the Single Tax—and many of them would follow no reform until they were satisfied that it pursued a clear and logical program. This seems to have been especially true of the lawyers, and the best example of this characteristic and its consequences for political preferences is probably George Record.

Record comes as close as anyone to being that unlikely person, the typical progressive. Born in New England to a struggling law-yer and his wife, Record worked his way through Bates College and took up the practice of law in Jersey City. He was in the center of the "New Idea" movement in New Jersey politics, and served as the midwife to reform in that state for over ten years, much as William U'Ren had done in Oregon.

Record's program was a model of deductive logic. In brief, it assumed that reform meant the elimination of special privilege, and it proposed a relentless attack upon the sources of monopoly, to include public ownership of certain railroads, the Chicago stockyards, and one oil pipeline, open patents to all, antitrust action against the steel, oil and coal trusts, a limit on excess for-tunes, and the Single Tax on land. It was pure New Freedomism before Wilson, but Record and Amos Pinchot carried that philos-ophy into the Bull Moose camp in 1912. Record was a purist where progressivism—which meant his program—was concerned, and although he supported La Follette in 1924, he knew that neither La Follette nor Roosevelt nor Wilson ever announced or applied anything close to it.

This was emphatically true of the New Deal, which Record lived to see, at least in part. From the first the New Deal had

57. Baker to Walter Lippmann, January 27, 1936, Box 149, Baker MSS, Library of Congress.

believed in the impossible, in the regulation of business; from the first it had enlarged the state, the last thing Record wanted. "This Roosevelt experiment is pure socialism," he had told Pinchot, "and will sink beneath a million details." [58] Its central flaw seemed to him its intellectual confusion, born of the attempt to arrive at truth by combining all available social theories, when truth yielded only to hard, lonely thought: "Roosevelt . . . . could never make good until he fired nine-tenths of his advisors and worked things out on his own hook." [59]

But reform had miscarried before, and Record died confident that the education of the people was going forward, and that one day they would reason their way to the means of liberation. Pinchot said of Record that "in a sense, he belonged to the Golden Age of American politics which formed its tradition in the first decade of the Republic, to the time when men cared passionately for ideas and believed in their power and practical bearing upon a nation's life." [60]

Add this quality of mental orderliness, so strong among lawyers especially, to the wealth and social position and associations of legal practice, and the resistance of lawyers to a social movement so disdainful of theory becomes easier to understand. While its operation was complex, what might be called occupational insurance was a potent force working against the acceptance of the type of intellectual open game played by the New Dealers.

The progressive who was likely to be a critic to the Right of the New Deal was most typically a man like Cleveland's Atlee Pomerene: born in a small town (Berlin, Ohio) to a comfortable family, graduated from college (Princeton) in the late 1880's or early 1890's, unaffected by the rural radicalisms of that decade, entered law practice briefly in a small town and then moved to the nearest city where opportunities were greater, was swept up in the local municipal reform movement (Tom Johnson's Cleveland), went on in the Taft years to the Congress (United States

58. Quoted by Amos Pinchot in a typescript essay on Record, File 100, Pinchot MSS.
59. George L. Record, *How to Abolish Poverty* (Jersey City: George L. Record Memorial Association, 1936), p. 19.
60. Pinchot, quoted in Helen M. Hooker (ed.), *The History of the Progressive Party, 1912-16*, by Amos Pinchot (New York: New York University Press, 1958), p. 78. See also Pinchot's Introduction to Record's *How to Abolish Poverty*, and Ransom E. Noble, *New Jersey Progressivism Before Wilson* (Princeton: Princeton University Press, 1946).

Senate), where he stayed through the Wilson period and voted for the New Freedom reforms but parted company over the nineteenth Amendment and the Plumb Plan for the railroads, and finally left public life in the 1920's for a lucrative law practice in Washington or back home (Cleveland). Like Pomerene, this progressive critic of the New Deal had entered politics to defeat the machine and to raise the moral tone of public life; he had always been considered safe on fundamental matters, had never mixed socially with any but the best elements of his profession and his class, and left politics with a reputation for honesty and moderation. Such a man, with such a life pattern, would almost certainly have been in angry opposition to the New Deal by 1936.[61]

The reasonably alert reader will recognize at once an anomaly in this emerging portrait of the typical figure on the progressive "Right." Specify a good middle-class if not a genteel upbringing, a college education, law school, and legal practice in one of the larger cities; specify an entry into politics and, rather quickly, identification with the "Good Government" reforms being confidently and energetically pushed by the best elements of the young man's party. Note the nature of this reform commitment— opposition to the corrupt old gang at city hall or state house, to the trusts, and perhaps even to uncompensated industrial accidents and other unfair handicaps to the work force. Note also its limits—uncertainty about woman suffrage and about a Federal approach to child labor, ambivalence about the rights of labor, uneasiness over union power in shop and politics, and an almost total lack of concern with the life of the Negro and the ghetto immigrant. These qualities describe a progressive who almost certainly drifted, as he prospered politically and financially during the 1920's and 1930's, into sufficiently cautious social attitudes that his reformism would not stand the demands of New Deal liberalism. But they also describe Franklin D. Roosevelt.

Although Roosevelt participated only in the final stages of the progressive movement, he was undeniably a progressive. His background is familiar: Hudson River gentry, Groton, Harvard, Columbia Law School, New York state politics of the "Good Government" reform variety, steady New Freedom attachments, and, after political misfortune ended the episode of progressivism, a

61. See Philip R. Shriver, "The Making of a Moderate Progressive: Atlee Pomerene," unpublished Ph.D. dissertation, Columbia University, 1954.

return to law and business.[62] But we know a good deal more about Franklin Roosevelt after his short progressive period than before, and any student of his mind and career could tell us that the more novel experiments in Federal action that he guided in the 1930's—that is, the eye-catching bulk of the New Deal—were somehow and importantly rooted in what Roosevelt saw and felt and learned in the 1920's and 1930's. His progressivism had been unexceptional and his mind platitudinous before World War I; after polio, after New York politics, where he learned from Al Smith and met the social workers and intellectuals who were eager to help New York's Depression governor, and, above all, after finding himself with presidential power in a nation desperate for national leadership—after he had passed through these experiences and met these men and women—Roosevelt was substantially transformed as a political thinker.

But if it is true for the central figure of the 1930's that his early reform activities and personal background equipped him to play a conservative role in the 1930's along with many other progressives of his class and sort, but that he went beyond the limits of this background under the influence of people and events encountered after the end of progressivism, it might be argued that I have concentrated unduly upon early influences affecting the progressives considered here. For while I have tried to take account of individual and group situation in the 1930's—including party loyalty, political ambitions, social class, and so forth—the main emphasis has been upon early factors of upbringing, education, and progressive activity and their enduring influence upon habits of thought. This may seem to be too static a view, one that allows too little room for growth and change in attitude during the war years and beyond.

I can only say that we need a comprehensive study of the progressive collective mind from America's entry into the war to 1933, but this is not that study. I have been led to go back beyond the political expression and personal situation of these progressives in the 1930's only out of a desire to understand the basis of their attitudes, and my own thought and researches have led me

62. For Roosevelt's early political life and progressivism, see Frank Freidel, *Franklin D. Roosevelt: The Apprenticeship* (Boston: Little, Brown, 1952), pp. 91-133, and Daniel R. Fusfeld, *The Economic Thought of Franklin D. Roosevelt and the Origins of the New Deal* (New York: Columbia University Press, 1960), chapter iii.

to emphasize factors which were substantially in being by 1916 or thereabouts. We do not have a comprehensive view of the evolution of progressive political thought from Wilson to F.D.R., despite some recent work on certain individuals and groups. Nonetheless, and I emphasize the tentativeness of my argument here, while no one would want to minimize the impact of the war and the years of disillusionment that followed, I think the attitudes of progressives in the 1930's are to be understood principally with reference to the events of the 1930's themselves and the situation of individuals in those years, taken against the stubborn persistence of social attitudes and a social education begun and largely completed many years before.

This is not to say that the years between 1916 and 1932 are of no importance at all, for we know that they brought a waning of hopes to many, a deep complacency to some. But they rarely stimulated in an old reformer a change in basic ideals—as so many of them were later to insist. And, with the exception of those few who were involved in the War Industries Board and other coordinating agencies of government during World War I, the progressives did not catch a glimpse of new methods by which to wage the old fight, largely because they, along with the public, had lost their zeal and turned, sometimes reluctantly, to private affairs. Because of the temper of the 1920's and their general lack of involvement in public life, the experiences they had rarely led, as did those of F.D.R., toward New Deal liberalism and its bolder employment of Federal power. It is a rare autobiography from one of these reformers that reveals a restless search for other and more effective measures of social reconstruction in the postwar years because it was a rare career line which forced such a search. Outside of those involved in social service, for whom the 1920's *were* a time of modest but significant intellectual advance, very few men found themselves, as did Roosevelt in Albany and Gifford Pinchot in Harrisburg, under insistent pressures to move gradually leftward onto new tactical ground. Without executive responsibility during the Depression, first at Albany and later in Washington, Roosevelt would not have stood so squarely at the focal point of public distress, interest group pressures, and new ideas about what the state could do to insure a better life in America. Not in a law office, nor in the Congress nor on the bench, not publishing a magazine nor writing for one, could these pressures be met with such intensity, if at all. For this reason most of these progressives had largely the same attitude toward American government and what decent men ought to be for and against in the 1930's as they did twenty years before.

There is support for this interpretation in the strong statistical association between youthful education, occupation, reform activity, party choice, and so forth, and later response to the New Deal. In addition to the patterns I have mentioned, it turns out that the very timing of these progressives' entry into reform affords a good basis upon which to predict attitudes toward the New Deal.[63] Taken as a whole, the progressive generation dis-

---

63. The reform wave that has been called progressivism might be described as follows. It originated as early as the 1880's and 1890's, a substantially new reform movement, distinguishable from the Mugwump or the Populist efforts by, among other things, its issues and its urban locale. Its earliest recruits were likely to enter settlements or social work, but here and there a city—Chicago, Detroit, Boston—would be the site of a citizen's movement to clean up city government or the public utilities. The movement in the nineteenth century, however, was insubstantial, and most of those who later came in were at this time either finishing college or were deploring the unrest of the 1890's. After the turn of the century municipal and state reform spread, was described widely in the "muckrake" press, and became something the better sort of young man often did. Theodore Roosevelt, followed by the congressional Insurgents of Taft's day, made reform respectable at the national level. The press was by now generally friendly; more young men entered politics as reformers or turned into reformers in office, and by 1912 it was clear that reform was the mood of the nation. If this account is generally accurate, a man or woman coming to reform before roughly 1900-1902—the latter year seeing Steffens's first muckraker article and the launching of the Northern Securities Case—had done so in the face, usually, of either public opprobrium or apathy, and was likely to be more deeply committed to the job than those who came later. One perhaps sees here the operation of Charles Péguy's rule, *tout commence en mystique et finit en politique;* as the cause of Dreyfus attracted a different type of man with different goals as it grew more popular, so it may have gone, to some extent, with progressivism. The pre-1900 progressives seem to have been a different sort, and the later phases of the movement swept up a large number of more conservative types.

To give this hypothesis a rough test, I secured information

on the date of entrance into reform for a number of these progressives. There are many reasons to be tentative in interpreting this data; not only was this information hard to find, but the year an individual joins an organization or adopts a reform platform would often be later than his actual "conversion." Further, some were simply too young to enter reform in the 1890's whatever their ultimate commitment, and the small towns and more remote states naturally came later to an awareness both of social wrongs and the possibility of a successful rebellion. But even with these cautions, the results compel attention: Of 31 pre-1900 reformers, 16 supported the New Deal, 11 opposed, and 4 were to the Left; of 48 coming to reform later, 11 supported the New Deal, 36 opposed, and one was to the Left. Thus, even admitting the many exceptions and the poor quality of our information, it seems that a rough rule applies: the earlier in the course of the progressive movement that a person decided to become a reformer, the more likely he or she would still be pulling for reform of the rich and relief for the poor in the 1930's.

---

played, as they aged, the most remarkable tenacity of belief. Leaving aside the few enormously interesting instances of real intellectual change in the war years and the 1920's, such as with Lincoln Steffens or John Dewey or the journalist Reginald Wright Kaufman,[64] most progressives came through to the 1930's with values and programs pretty much intact. The mood changed, certainly, but their mood was so responsive to contemporary events that whatever subtle changes the war and the New Era had made were overwhelmed and superseded by the shock of 1929 and the excited hopes of the spring of 1933. But the continuity of political philosophy is there, for the vast majority. At the end of the progressive era, an observer could have guessed with fair success the subsequent course of most progressives, for by then he had available most of the data about the components of established political personalities. He would often be wrong, of course; he would be surprised to find John Burke and Josephus Daniels

---

64. Dewey's changing ideas may be followed in Sidney Hook, *John Dewey: An Intellectual Portrait* (New York: John Day, 1939); see also pp. 133-5 below, and the works cited in the Bibliographical Essay. For Kauffman's shift, see his remarks in the *Twenty-Fifth Anniversary Report: Harvard College Class of 1900* (Cambridge: Harvard University Press, 1925), pp. 417-18, and the *Fiftieth Anniversary Report* (1950), pp. 379-21. For Steffens, see the widely read *The Autobiography of Lincoln Steffens* (New York: Harcourt, Brace, 2 vols., 1931), and pp. 139-41, below.

and Peter Dunne and George Norris among the New Deal's friends, surprised at the dislike it engendered in men like John Graham Brooks, George Creel, Robert Hunter and John Spargo, all of them at one time on the Left edge of the early reform movement. But given only a knowledge of education, voting habits, occupation, and reform involvement as of Wilson's second term, and adding to this some grasp of the forces exerted in individual cases in the 1930's by political and financial prospects, the response to the New Deal may in most instances be anticipated and generally accounted for.

Thus the New Deal was finally to be measured by these progressives against the intellectual and moral standards of their own triumphant era before World War I—standards which were still substantially unaltered, and which they considered still viable—measured in terms of its immediate effect upon personal ambitions and hopes, political or economic. In the end, the progressive experience provided more than the rhetorical storehouse for the attacks that the majority were to launch against Franklin Roosevelt and his works; revived and intact, the old progressive doctrines prevented an accommodation to the new reforms of the 1930's by most of those for whom the word reform had been both a label and a high calling.

III

For the majority of surviving reformers, there was no way to reconcile progressivism and the New Deal, and, as they had never ceased to believe in the long-run wisdom of the former, there was nothing for it but to fight the Democratic Roosevelt as they had once fought corruption and the trusts. Most of them chose to do so in the language, not of the outraged constitutionalism of the James M. Becks and Herbert Hoovers of the era, but of the principles of true progressive reform.

Their first and most frequent complaint was that the New Deal was unforgivably coercive, and far from entering upon that role with hesitation, apologies, and promises of early retrenchment, it gave all the signs of a permanent Federal paternalism. Without question it was NRA that most embodied this trend toward statism (with AAA corroborating evidence), but even after the death of NRA these progressives perceived signs enough that the New

Deal could be summed up as a drive toward a permanent collectivism, which even after the *Schechter* decision would find ways enough to work its ends. This sort of fear—the indispensable words here were "loss of individual initiative," "collectivism," "socialism," and the like—was to be repeated in the 1930's by the economically and politically wounded, repeated so often that these words are virtually ruined for serious political uses, and their very hysteria becomes boring.

Progressives, in choosing to use the language of the Liberty League to any extent, were in strange company, but most of them did not find it an entirely new vocabulary. Theirs had been an effort to free the individual, and when it came time to choose between individualism and social reforms that could only be reached through unprecedented legal coercion, their choice merely reminds us of the original priorities. The Edgar Lee Masters who had loved Bryan and Tom Johnson, whose law practice had suffered for his radicalism ("I was full of passion for Democracy and for the glory of the Republic," he summarized his early views),[65] wound up as angry with the New Deal as he had been with the corporations of an earlier day, and his political principles had not budged. In *The New Star Chamber* of 1904, where he defended the right of labor to strike, he went on to deplore the "monarchical" tendencies of Theodore Roosevelt, and to write: "In proportion as the functions of government are multiplied, individual liberty is decreased." [66] He had always been a Bryan-Tom Watson Jeffersonian, opposed to war and to the industrial assault upon the early yeoman Republic. Lois Teal Hartley, in a review of his early poetry, found there all the opposition to centralization, all the individualism, that naturally predisposed him against the New Deal.[67] Masters is only one example of the individualistic focus that marked most of the early progressives. Their faith had always been in private exertion, in moral suasion, and in the lonely virtues of the self-reliant character. The fight had always been against restraint. When Ida Tarbell wrote in 1935

65. Masters, *Across Spoon River: An Autobiography* (New York: Holt, Rinehart and Winston, 1936, 1964), p. 172.
66. Masters, *The New Star Chamber and Other Essays*, (New York: Macmillan, 1904), pp. 37-8.
67. Hartley, "Edgar Lee Masters: A Critical Study," unpublished Ph.D. dissertation, University of Ilinois, 1949.

that our hope lay in "discipline and the education of the individual to self-control and right doing," she was not reporting any fundamental change of mind.[68]

For many of the progressives their attitude in the 1930's was predictable on the basis of positions early taken; they rejected the New Deal on behalf of the original hope, for a reform which released, not bound. William S. U'Ren was never very widely known, even after Lincoln Steffens included an essay about him in his *Upbuilders*. But if any man was the progressive at his most exemplary, it was U'Ren—self-made, optimistic, honest, indefatigable, self-effacing, advocate and political leader in a stunning series of electoral reforms in his native Oregon.

The New Deal aroused U'Ren, still the humanitarian, the dreamer of a better world through conscious change, to propose to Frederick Morgan Davenport a progressive alternative to the New Deal. His plan called for an "American Industrial Army . . . for voluntary co-operation and self-supporting employment," a force where any man could find employment to tide him over the temporary hardships of the 1930's, a force costing the public nothing, run without bureaucracy, governed by the enlistees, paying its own way. "The plan I offer," U'Ren wrote Davenport, "is an attempt to provide for nation-wide permanent and unlimited opportunity . . . and at the same time fully preserve . . . that rugged individualism which is the very heart and soul of government by the people." [69] U'Ren cared less for the details than for the progressive principle; even when an emergency forces men to act as a group, the association must be entirely voluntary. No plan that transferred private economic decision-making to a distant center of power, he thought, could be squared with what they had been struggling for. Coercive collectivism as a general operating principle, with the attendant atrophy of private

68. *All In the Day's Work*, p. 393. See also her article "Is Our Generosity Wearing Thin?," *Scribner's Magazine*, XCVII (April 1935), 235-9, for a restrained opposition to the New Deal. She had always been a fundamentally conservative woman, whose admiration for the titans of business predated even her muckraking days, and, despite her series on Standard Oil, it continued undiminished to the end of her life. She apparently voted for Roosevelt in 1936, but with deep reluctance.
69. U'Ren to Davenport, August 4, 1934, Box 15, Davenport MSS, Syracuse University. See also Lincoln Steffens, "U'Ren," in *Upbuilders* (New York: Doubleday, Page, 1909).

strengths, was to U'Ren and many of his fellow progressives the primary sin of the New Deal.

This sin was to be accompanied by others as the New Deal plunged ahead. The incitement of class against class, hard enough to avoid in any reform effort which moved against some forms of privilege, had been accepted by Roosevelt as a legitimate political weapon. His legislation conferred special favors (NIRA, AAA, the Wagner Act); his campaigns were marked by open appeals to class hatred (the acceptance speech at Philadelphia, 1936); and it was Roosevelt who succeeded in the unwanted but deliberate class realignment of the major political parties. The New Deal did not deplore special interests—it encouraged them in their demands, yielded, and combined the interests, through the apportionment of favors, into a political machine at the national level. The nation was thus to become permanently and publicly divided as a result of Rooseveltian policy.

This is what moved the veteran Insurgent Irvine Lenroot to write, in 1936, "I believe our greatest danger today is the division of our people into classes, each seeking its selfish ends without regard to the welfare of others." [70] It is what caused Carl Vrooman, Wilson's Assistant Secretary of Agriculture and a lifelong Democrat, to leave his party in the 1930's. To beat F.D.R., Vrooman wrote, the Republicans must not make the same selfish appeal to the top one-third as Roosevelt was making to the bottom one-third, but must simply announce a call to self-sacrifice and the general interest. Vrooman came reluctantly to the conviction that the abandonment, in politics, of moral issues in favor of unabashed economic bartering constituted an unforgivable betrayal of the older progressive purpose.[71]

Their concern, at least verbally, was not so much with the fear of class warfare, with the actual despoliation of the rich by the poor, but rather with the erosion of what had taken so long to build up, politics as the forum for moral questions. A central idea of progressivism had been to bring to public life the example of selfless men engaged in public service. What progressives had

70. Lenroot, speech of January 16, 1936, copy in Box 10, Lenroot MSS, Library of Congress.
71. See Carl Vrooman, *The Present Republican Opportunity: By a Democrat* (Chenoa, Illinois: Carl Vrooman, 1936).

worked to reduce and even to eliminate were questions of merely material advantage. It had not been easy; but the moments they valued were those when, led by Roosevelt, Wilson, or La Follette, they had driven divisive material questions from politics and replaced them with moral—that is, general—concerns. This had been a job worth mighty efforts, worth the disillusionment of occasional failure, worth the dereliction of private affairs. Note that the moral and the general were synonymous, and that which was unworthy turned out to be the private, the partial, interest. This, if a great number of old reformers may be believed, was an essential part of the progressive concern.

But Franklin Roosevelt did not reduce the squabble of competing economic interests, did not even seem to frown on it. The result was a lowering of the tone and a demeaning of the substance of public debate. Lenroot wrote in 1935, "We are largely a nation of groups, with little thought of the general welfare. Organized capital, organized labor, organized farmers, organized wets and organized drys. . . . I would not, if I could, be a Member of Congress . . . because of the pressure of organized minorities today." [72] And Newton Baker, whose dislike for the New Deal almost matched Lenroot's, wrote in the same vein to his close friend John H. Clarke. "When the idea is erected that government is a universal insurance society, competition for the benefit of its protection ceases to be on the basis of deserts and comes to be a mere question of organized pressure for minority preference." [73]

When this materialistic and interest-group oriented focus of New Deal politics did not turn an old reformer against it, as it did with Lenroot and Baker and others, it spoiled the initial joy of many in a resurrected reformism, and made their support of Roosevelt dispirited and lifeless. Ray Stannard Baker wrote in his diary in 1936, even as he prepared to vote for Roosevelt, "In this dreary campaign there was almost no call to any kind of unselfish service; everywhere group demands for special favors, and career politicians promising to grant them." [74] Thus Roosevelt's broker state, whatever its benevolence (and even of this some of them were not convinced), bore no fundamental relation to the earlier progressivism.

72. Lenroot, speech of July 4, 1935, Box 10, Lenroot MSS.
73. Baker to Clarke, May 15, 1936, Box 60, Baker MSS, Library of Congress.
74. Notebook 53, Entry of November 3, 1936, Baker MSS.

Another persistent theme among progressives opposing the New Deal was an invidious comparison between the urban spirit of the New Deal and the outlook and values of small-town–rural American from which most of them derived. This was a rather general complaint, alleging few specific offenses, a complaint ignoring efforts at farm resettlement, for example, and based upon an urban image composed of electoral strength, city intellectuals, and a vague feeling that the New Deal was doing nothing to return America to the village culture she had unaccountably departed. Innocent though it may have been of having undermined the serene small-town society of Cleveland and McKinley, the New Deal seemed nonetheless somehow culpable. If it was not directly responsible for the demise of the small town, the New Deal reserved its principal favors for the cities, entered into unsavory alliances with their political machines, and presided over even if it did not engineer the sudden arrival of new ethnic groups to social and political potency.

Because this was so, it ran afoul of the mounting nostalgia among countless progressives for a way of life which was now in tragic eclipse. "The town," wrote Mark Sullivan of West Chester, Pennsylvania, in reproaching the present by raising a finer standard, "was ancient, secure, serene. Its economic base was the leisurely trade of an incomparably well-tilled fertile farming country. . . . There were no factories to speak of. Nobody was poor, nobody rich." [75] Sullivan was a foe of the New Deal. "I would like to live," said Topeka's Reverend Charles M. Sheldon, "in a town of not more than 15,000 people. The big cities have never attracted me." [76] Sheldon voted for Landon. Albert Shaw decided, in 1938, to write one last book, and his subject would be rural life in America; in essence, the book would be a final lament for Iowa: "It could be said of Iowa at any given moment that there were no paupers and no millionaires. Every neighborhood could . . . take care of any family or individual who through illness or other misfortune needed assistance. . . . The typical citizen was a farmer." [77] Shaw, farming in Virginia in be-

75. Mark Sullivan, *The Education of an American* (New York: Doubleday, Doran, 1938), p. 119.
76. Charles M. Sheldon, *Doctor Sheldon's Scrapbook* (Topeka: Christian Herald Association, 1942), p. 44.
77. Albert Shaw, memo to himself, October 22, 1937; Shaw MSS, New York Public Library.

tween trips to New York when he wrote these words, was consistently opposed to the New Deal after 1934.

The memory of the small town had provided part of the vision
which guided their work from the first, and it came through in
the 1930's with undiminished emotional force. Its complement
was often the strongest sort of dislike for cities. "It is when I go
to the city," Ray Stannard Baker wrote in his Notebook, "that I
am afraid for America. Thousands and thousands of faces with no
light in them!" [78] And the progressive Senator from Kansas, Arthur
Capper, pleaded in 1936 that we "clean up and disinfect the great
cities. . . . They seem accursed." [79]

Ironically, this was the generation that voluntarily left the small
town for the greater opportunities of the city, as hundreds of their
career lines show. The city exercised for the progressive a fascina-
tion which their letters and memoirs do not adequately disclose.
In the real conduct of life, as distinct from autobiographical rhetoric, the city and progressives were inseparable. Not only did they
flock to Chicago and New York and Cleveland as young men in
search of a wider scope for their talents, but they almost invariably remained there for the rest of their lives. It would be interesting, for example, to see how many progressives who served in
the Congress and Senate actually returned to the small town after
electoral defeat or retirement. Most, I would estimate, lingered
like Henry Fountain Ashurst in the Fairfax Hotel in Washington, practicing a little law and basking in the reflected glory and
energy of the center of things. But this, of course, is a part of a
larger American ambivalence, and is not confined to progressives
or their generation. For our purposes, it is enough to understand
that, whether an old progressive wrote from rural retirement or a
New York office, he frequently indicted the new Democratic party
for the demise of the lost world of wide streets, vacant lots, and
easy neighborliness, a foremost casualty of the twentieth century.

The word for their response, of course is *conservative*. To resist
power not in their (i.e. private and familiar) hands, to invoke the
virtue of a unified nation against awakenings of division, to ele-
vate moral considerations over material ones, to indulge a nostalgia for a lost harmonious localized condition, this was all de-

78. Notebook 53, Ray Stannard Baker MSS, Library of Congress.
79. File "1936," Arthur Capper MSS, Kansas State Historical Society, Topeka,
Kansas.

signed to protect the present against the revolutionizing New Dealers, and no self-professed conservative could have bettered that intellectual arsenal.

Some of them applied the word conservative to themselves: Brandeis, John R. Commons. Hutchins Hapgood, William Randolph Hearst, Joe Robinson, Albert Shaw, William Allen White, to mention only those committing the sentiment to paper. It was White who suggested to Landon that he mention Edmund Burke in his campaign speeches in order to identify himself with the right kind of conservatism, and who wrote to Congressman E. H. Rees: "As you know, Ed, I am supposed to be one of those impulsive scatterbrained liberals. But I hope you know that in serious matters I am as conservative as wisdom need be." [80]

I V

Some reformers underwent an alteration in basic political outlook, usually veering toward a greater conservatism, under the pressure of the war and postwar disillusionments, the successes of middle life, or age and its encroaching cautions. But, as I have said before, many of those opposing Roosevelt hotly denied that their position was an apostasy from reform, and insisted that their roles as critics of selfish power and of attacks upon true democracy had not been relinquished. If this is true, we should find in the years of progressive ferment the same impulses and purposes that later led them against the New Deal.

Many students of reform have argued that, despite the exaggerations of nervous contemporaries, there was very little radicalism generated within progressive circles, and this has seemed especially true of the areas of state and national politics, and of journalism. Most progressive proposals were severely limited in scope, it is true, and projected no fundamental alteration of wealth or political power. There is no need to posit a change of heart to account for so much opposition to the New Deal. I propose to use certain representative careers to illustrate the essential conservatism of the predominant forms of progressive action, and to demonstrate the consistency between reform in the first decade of the twentieth century and anti-reform in the fourth. Four careers that

80. White to Landon, August 9, 1936, Box 191, White MSS, Library of Congress. White to E. H. Rees, January 19, 1937, quoted in Walter Johnson, *Selected Letters,* p. 372.

demonstrate this are those of the lawyer Amos Pinchot, the politician Morton D. Hull, the economist Richard T. Ely, and the journalist Mark Sullivan.

No one who is at all familiar with Amos Pinchot would want to advance too carelessly with the use of Pinchot as a type. He was a complicated man, and acted out his rather unusual political career on the periphery of several radical movements. Yet Amos (I adopt this nomenclature not out of familiarity but to differentiate one Pinchot from another) did represent a certain type of progressive whose deeply conservative reformism easily—and usually—passed for a very radical variety. Only in the 1930's was it possible to discern how little he had ever merited Theodore Roosevelt's "lunatic fringe" remark.[81] For Amos and several others,

81. Roosevelt, who had liked Amos and worked with him from about 1910 forward, had some grounds for saying that. Amos's progressivism survived World War I (which was unusual), extended to a real friendliness toward labor, to involvement with *The Masses* and the group that formed the American Civil Liberties Union, and to membership on the "Committee of 48" which tried to keep progressivism alive after the war. Nonetheless, all Amos wanted was a return to old style competitive capitalism. The best study of him (there is no biography) is the Introduction to Pinchot's *History of the Progressive Party, 1912-16* (New York: New York University Press, 1958), by Helen M. Hooker.

certain radical but strictly limited reforms were the only way to salvage the system. In the progressive period, the accent fell upon the "radical." Only in the 1930's did the limits appear in their true perspective.

Amos wanted what most progressives wanted—restoration of competitive conditions in the American economy. Through the death of monopoly, he reasoned, would come a cure for America's major ills. But Amos was not content with resentment of monopoly and a vague determination to smite it with an antitrust law; he armed himself with a thorough program that went directly to the root of the problem. That the program was originally that of George Record is not important. Amos was not concerned about its originality but about its effectiveness, and he adopted it because he thought that only such measures would defeat monopoly. Monopoly, his argument ran, was fostered by control of transportation facilities and by the patent laws. He therefore advocated public ownership of at least the major railroads, and at least one oil pipeline; seizure of a part of Standard Oil and United States Steel and their lease to competitors; open patents to all after a brief period of waiting; the limitation of huge fortunes through inheritance taxes; finally, and he did not push this very hard, the Single Tax on land. Privilege would not survive another day, and the race would be open to all.[82]

To the intellectually careless, it sounded like socialism. For Amos, it was the only way to "preserve free competitive industrial conditions" and to prevent the entrance of government regulatory probes and institutions into business enterprise.

He was a Bull Moose Republican, an associate of the New Nationalists, yet here is the New Freedom in uncompromising form, government policy designed to devastate monopoly without increasing the discretionary and regulatory powers of government.[83]

83. Amos was for Wilson in 1916, but not before he attended the Progressive convention of 1916 and did all he could to keep the movement alive. Considering his views of government and the economy, his presence in the Bull Moose group of 1912 merely emphasizes its heterogeneity and the futility of talking about Bull Moosers as if they "believed" in the New Nationalism. Amos, of course, was one of those Republicans who came over to Theodore Roosevelt only after La Follette faltered.

Nationalizing railroads was strong medicine, but once taken, he was sure, it would prevent the patient from falling into the hands of socialist quacks. The program was brief, clear, limited—and there was no other way. It should not have been hard to see, behind the public image of the proponent of one great innovation, a counterattacking conservative. "I am," he wrote in 1934, "one of the old breed of individualists. I don't want to see the railroads taken over as a step to socialism, but as a means of keeping equal opportunity, Billy Sumner's 'equal chance,' alive." [84]

What Amos represented was a special sort of progressive, the

82. For his early views, see A. P. to George Thompson, August 31, 1910; A. P. to W. K. Brice, September 1, 1910; A. P., "The Cause of Industrial Unrest" (1915), typescript in Amos Pinchot MSS, Library of Congress; Amos Pinchot, "Two Revolts," *McClure's Magazine*, 35 (September 1910), 581-90.
84. Amos Pinchot to Joseph B. Eastman, April 11, 1934, Box 55, Pinchot MSS, Library of Congress.

radical conservative. For the few like him, the situation was too serious for the timid improvements of the political machinery so popular among the Good Government types. Men like Amos were intellectuals by habit, liked to analyze thoroughly and as thoroughly to outline the appropriate relief. More acutely aware of undesirable social changes at work, they were driven to more ambitious, almost surgical cures. Often, in an effort to make their instinctive caution and their acquired sense of urgency more compatible, they came to believe in the single, quick, drastic solution. For Amos Pinchot and George Record, public ownership of transportation facilities; for Irving Fisher, public ownership of the Federal Reserve banks and public control of the volume of checkbook money; for Louis Brandeis, a determined use of the taxing and licensing powers of government to restore little business units.[85] It is easy to say that their radicalism was all in their

---

85. Brandeis was not in the anti–New Deal group, but he staunchly and for the most part successfully opposed the planning features of the New Deal, and most of its centralizing tendencies.

---

tactics, not in their ends, but that too is misleading. Radical as some of these proposals were, all stopped short at, and were designed to prevent, the growth of government.[86]

---

86. The prototype of the Misunderstood (or Disguised) Conservative is Henry George. The Single Tax proved compelling to men who preferred one sweeping reform, especially one promising a reduction of taxes and of the size of government, to the awful choice between socialism and plutocracy. Ransom E. Noble has recognized the influence of George on many progressives in his article, "Henry George and the Progressive Movement," *American Journal of Economics and Sociology*, VIII (April 1949), 259-70. If anything, Noble understated that influence. The number of progressives who were persuaded by *Progress and Poverty* is astonishing, and most of them remained half-convinced to the end of their lives. There was a good bit of open profession of Single Tax sympathies during the progressive era, but as the century wore on there was less open avowal of what was one of the most heretical economic proposals abroad in America. The Single Tax ranked just to the Right of socialism and decidedly to the Left of the silver schemes of the Bryanites, and for this reason few of them openly identified themselves with the Single Tax as their ca-

reers took hold. But the Single Tax never lost its most appealing quality—its nice combination of social justice with a remedy both simple and not unfriendly to capitalism. The appeal of the Single Tax was enhanced by the fact that it was the only popular progressive thought dealing with economics.

When the New Deal arrived and men like Amos bolted, they were, as Helen Hooker argues about Amos himself, quite consistent. They had appeared to be on the left wing of progressivism, for they had not feared to talk of such things as a public claim on private property. But, from the first, it was remote power Amos had feared, and he came eventually to see that government had the same possibilities to work evil as business monopoly. "The longer I live and the more I study," he wrote in 1935, "the harder, as it seems to me, it is for government, and especially 'strong government,' to do good." [87] He had always meant to achieve reform without enlarging the state, for reform itself meant the diminishing of those aggregations of power which threatened the isolated human unit. Having worked out, with George Record, a theory of reform sufficient to the task, he was predictably bitter when Franklin Roosevelt, leaving the trusts unharmed, asked for compensatory powers undreamed of and potentially uncontrollable.

Thus Amos emerged in the 1930's as what he had always been, a courageous individualist for whom reform meant a battle against size. At first reluctantly, then with mounting determination, he took up the battle again—with F.D.R. on the other side of the barricades.[88]

88. Paul Kellogg, in a perceptive letter to Amos in 1936, suggested that reformers of his type—men whose central concern was a restoration of the competitive order, and whose instruments were likely to be antimonopoly laws, monetary reforms, and occasionally a dose of Henry George—not only constituted a distinct school of reformers but were tending now to fall into alliance with their old enemies, the comfortable and conservative. This was so, Kellogg went on, because the school of reformers Amos represented (and of which George Record was the archetype) would not go along with what the more modern type of reformer found it necessary to do. "I think there is a split in method, if not in purpose," Kellogg wrote, "in process between the Single Taxers, the anti-monopolists, the money

87. Amos Pinchot to Will Eno, May 29, 1935, Box 5, Pinchot MSS.

reformers, the municipal ownership people and those who would unlimber government in new ways to bring greater order and democracy into production and distribution. They may not pin their faith, as you do, on free competition as the corrector of all the ills of American life and labor; but it is bunk to charge that because they want to resort to forethought, planning and controls strong enough to keep privilege and exploitation in leash, and get the good out of this continent for its people, that they are hell bent to destroy freedom. They want to give freedom a chance." (Paul Kellogg to Amos Pinchot, October 21, 1936; File 768, Survey Associates MSS, Social Welfare History Archives Center, Minneapolis.)

Kellogg comes as close here as anyone has in formulating categories which will clarify the basic division among early twentieth-century reformers—a division which almost all scholars have sensed, and for which we have adopted such essentially unsatisfactory labels as New Freedom and New Nationalism. Kellogg, unfortunately, neglected to add the labels to his accurate insight.

Richard T. Ely, the University of Wisconsin political economist who had come to the Social Gospel and the interventionist state by way of graduate study in Germany, probably had as much impact upon his generation as any other thinker of the progressive era. One of the founders of the American Economic Association (in 1885), the author of books and articles advancing the idea of state interference to Christianize American economic life, Ely was thought of then and later as one of the more radical men of his time. Yet he made his torturous way, in the 1930's, to an anti–New Deal position, even as his former students were carrying out what they took to be his political philosophy in the offices of New Deal agencies.

It was a complicated intellectual and financial journey for Ely, and he awaits a biographer.[89] Revered by countless young men who had been guided by him into liberal political views and creative work in the social sciences, Ely was not comfortable as an antireformer and made gallant but futile efforts to adjust to the changes that had come in his ninth decade. He eventually took up a position, shaped for the most part by lifelong social attitudes

89. One hopes that the brief doctoral dissertation by Benjamin Rader, "The Professor as Reformer: Richard T. Ely, 1854-1943," University of Maryland, 1965, may be expanded and published.

and to a lesser extent by age and financial distress, which his lais-sez-faire enemies of a lifetime could easily approve.[90]

It is not hard to square the conservative Ely of 1935 with the young economist who subscribed, fifty years earlier, to the American Economic Associations' statement of principles, which began: "We regard the state as an agency whose positive assistance is an indispensable condition of human progress." He had changed his mind in only one particular, that of the public ownership of natural monopolies.[91] In all else, the Ely who had written sympathet-ically of socialism, extolled state interference, and condemned laissez-faire had not fundamentally changed.

He had talked all his life of the end of individualism and the need for "trained intelligence" to direct our "social operations," and he did not retreat from that. In 1931 he proposed that the state set up a "peacetime army" to provide work for the unem-ployed, the venture to be financed through a government bond issue.[92] In 1935 he was still calling for "new ways" and for public direction to replace private drift.[93] Yet when the time was ripe for

93. See Ely and Bohn, *The Great Change*. Ely's half of this book is a frustratingly ambivalent performance, and indicates how hard he found the task of keeping his social attitudes and his reform reputation in harness. A part of his essay is prag-matic, bold, full of the desire to control social change—and vague. The rest is a catalogue of moral preferences, all of them redolent of rural, Calvinistic, conservative America. Yet Ely was always capable of startling receptivity to innovation; at one point he called for one year of compulsory factory service for youths of both sexes. Ely seemed oddly attracted to ideas such as this, which would recruit civilians into quasi-military organi-zations, giving them a much needed "discipline" and a new sense of the superiority of the national interest. He perhaps

90. Ely's autobiography, *Ground Under Our Feet* (New York: Macmillan, 1938), only hints (see esp. p. 263) at the hostility toward the New Deal which he revealed more fully in *The Great Change*, written with Frank Bohn (New York: T. Nelson and Sons, 1935), and at several places in his private cor-respondence. The young Ely was very prolific, but a good representative statement of his early views may be found in Richard T. Ely, "Fundamental Beliefs in My Social Philosophy," *Forum*, XVIII (1894), 173-83; see also Sidney Fine, "Richard T. Ely: Forerunner of Progressivism, 1880-1901," *Mississippi Valley Historical Review*, XXXVII (March 1951), 599-624.
91. Ely, *Ground Under Our Feet*, pp. 252-61.
92. Richard T. Ely, *Hard Times: The Way In and the Way Out* (New York: Macmillan, 1931), p. 112.

acquired a fondness for such arrangements in Germany, for he often alluded with admiration to the solidarity of the German people under the Prussian state. This strain in Ely's thought found many counterparts in the country at large and even within the New Deal in the early 1930's. See William E. Leuchtenburg, "The New Deal and the Analogue of War," in John Braeman, Robert Bremner, and Everett Walters, (eds.), *Change and Continuity in Twentieth Century America* (Columbus: Ohio State University Press, 1965).

such departures under Franklin Roosevelt, and some of Ely's students saw themselves as putting Ely's ideas into practice in Washinton, Ely himself was making clear the limits of his reformism. Involved in 1933 and early 1934 in a study group which wrote and talked as if the New Deal were not radical enough, Ely nevertheless worked out by 1935 a guarded but unmistakably conservative criticism of the New Deal.[94] His autobiography of 1938, *Ground*

94. This study group, which called itself "The Committee of '76," was based in New York, and hoped to provide through discussion and position papers a reasonable reform program against which the New Deal might be measured. Its activities may be followed in the papers of Amos Pinchot and in the "Amos Pinchot" File (#768) in the Survey Associates papers; its history is short and fascinating, and it is enough to say here that it had substantially dissolved by late 1934. For Ely's views during this period, see "Suggestions for Mr. Amos Pinchot's Sub-Committee," typescript in File 768, Survey Associates collection.

Under Our Feet, allowed that criticism its freest expression.

In the light of all that he had written, the objections he felt toward the New Deal represented no change of heart. Even as he proposed "planning" and something akin to deficit financing in 1931, he was cool to Foster and Catchings' idea of a redistribution of wealth to boost purchasing power, uninterested in old age security, and actually hostile to unemployment insurance.[95] He

95. Ely, *Hard Times*, pp. 48-52, 130-32. Ely expressed interest in a suspension of the antitrust laws to let businessmen combine to rationalize their operations. Actually, with his friendliness to paternalism, his interest in the disciplinary aspects of the "Peacetime Army" he was urging, Ely was very much in the Herbert Croly–New Nationalism tradition, and resembled no one so much as Raymond Moley or Hugh Johnson. There is no

evidence, however, either in his published opinions or in his private papers, that his dislike of the New Deal, even though it surfaced in about 1935, coincided with Roosevelt's 1935 break with New Nationalism approaches.

was not inclined to use the words "Social Justice," nor to blame businessmen or a businessman's administration for what had happened in 1929. In his book of 1935, *The Great Change,* which carried a bold demand for public action, he still insisted on a balanced budget, a state rather than a Federal focus for reform, recovery through hard work and thrift and character rather than through regimentation. Ely, who had always recognized the need for an end to laissez-faire, had never entertained the idea that the public leadership of the future need spring from the blue-collar classes, nor that it should adopt a tone which threatened and condemned the owners of capital. Without being in any way close to the administration, Ely perfectly reflected the mood—Tugwell excluded—of the first New Deal.

It should not have been surprising, then, that when the New Dealers, especially after 1935, called for new public action in words reminiscent of his own, Ely urged delay and the need for "more research." [96] It is here that Ely, like most of his generation,

96. "If we are going to find the way out, we must have a great deal more independent, fearless research," he told a Wisconsin legislative committee in 1934, admitting the intellectual bankruptcy of fifty years of progressive effort. (See his address to the Wisconsin Legislative Interim Committee on Taxation Problems, May 2, 1934, Box 278, Ely MSS.) The planning he suggested at that time was a combination of tighter zoning regulations and the Single Tax (not called by that name). In this fashion, Ely manfully worked his way through the Depression years, still no further along than Henry George had been, tentative in all else, instinctively cautious, hoping and working in his final years for the answer which he knew a lifetime of study had not produced.

revealed how poorly some of his earlier talk expressed his essential caution. He had always been a gradualist, and had hoped to prevent revolution through sermons on social solidarity and a touch of safe German state socialism. His willingness to use the state, and his evolutionary attitude, both derived from European precept, may have pointed his students toward the welfare state of Franklin Roosevelt; Ely himself lived long enough to see the beginnings, and in finding it offensively radical he clarified the limits of his original reformism. Nothing better illustrates the antiquity of his social goals than his dogged advancement, as an alternative to the New Deal, of a mass return to the land and the adoption of the Single Tax. He had never dreamed of a determined attack upon holders of private economic power by a favor-dispensing, powerful state, and those who thought him a radical in the 1930's were as wrong as those who had arraigned him in 1894 at Wisconsin for socialistic views, and for the same reasons. His defense in 1894 should have made this clear.

"A writer's whole nature may be that of a conservative: he may love the old ways; he may to some extent draw his social ideals from a past which he considers, with respect to feeling about wealth, saner than the present age, and yet, because he would, by social action, endeavor to change certain tendencies, and to conserve the treasures of the past which he feels threatened by new and startling forces, he is still a radical in the eyes of those men whose one and sole test is money. . . .

"I may say that I am a conservative rather than a radical, . . . an aristocrat rather than a democrat. I have in mind . . . an aristocracy which lives for the fulfillment of special service." [97]

Morton D. Hull came of one of those moderately prosperous Midwestern families whose roots went back to Massachusetts Bay. His upbringing and education both fitted him for, and caused him to expect, that combination of personal success and public service found in the careers of so many progressives. He wrote to his parents from Harvard in 1890, "If America is to remain a representative government and fulfill the destiny which its past history has given us reasonable ground to hope for there must exist among its citizens a strong healthy moral tone." [98] He was to bring that strong moral tone to Illinois politics.

The story of Chicago's corruption in the late nineteenth century has been told many times, usually as a preface to a description of the efforts of a small group of awakened citizens toward

97. Ely, quoted in Theron Schlabach, "An Aristocrat on Trial: The Case of Richard T. Ely," *Wisconsin Magazine of History,* XLVII (Winter 1963-64), pp. 146-59.
98. Denison B. Hull, *The Legislative Life of Morton D. Hull* (Chicago: privately printed, 1948), p. 16.

clean-up and correction. Morton D. Hull, along with better known men such as Walter Lowrie Fisher, Harold Ickes, William Kent, George Cole, and Lyman Gage, was active in the Legislative Voters League and the City Club from the beginning. He was elected to the Illinois House in 1906, and was counted as a spokesman of those "better elements" who were urging reform. Hull played an important role in the passage of a law increasing public control over state funds, for example, and a direct primary law.

But his progressivism showed its limits quite early. He was cool to the initiative and referendum as being too close a flirtation with mob passions. Exhibiting the same sort of elemental caution, he stayed with Taft in 1912 on the ground that Roosevelt "would not proceed in an orderly way." [99] Hull's influence in the legislature increased. He was largely responsible for a series of measures increasing the efficiency of state government, and for a "loan shark" control law. He was cool to woman suffrage, but by 1917 had decided to back both the vote for women and a child labor law. His record, nevertheless, seemed sufficiently conservative for Harold Ickes to oppose his candidacy for governor in 1916 with the remark that Hull seems to have maintained a very moderate progressivism throughout, with about an even number of enemies to the Right and Left. His progressivism was of a familiar type, confined to the proposition that honest men with no special interests to serve must enter politics to insure that, through judicious reforms followed by vigilance, the system operated as it was intended. Reform for him meant efficient, honest, and impartial government, and late in his Illinois career included assistance to working children and voteless women. Such was the agenda of progressivism as he saw it.

"A true conservative," as Charles Merriam wrote in an introduction to Denison Hull's study of his father, Hull was a conservative who would rather reform than stand idly by while society blindly transformed itself for the worse. This sort of progressivism, busy with reopening the channels of political expression and with a close scrutiny of the public purse, brought many men to local and even national attention as reformers. [100] Cordell Hull had a similar

---

100. Hull eventually won election to the Congress, and served without special distinction from 1923 to 1933. It was his view,

99. Ibid. p. 62.

in the 1930's, that Hoover could have brought America out of
the Depression under the program he presented in 1932 (letter
from D. B. Hull to the author, April 5, 1964).

career, and the same reform intentions, as did Carter Glass, James
A. Reed, A Mitchell Palmer, Arthur Capper, and literally hundreds of others. They were known as progressives, and accepted
the designation. But they were never radicals, never ventured far
into social justice movements where God's poor were to be encountered. There was thus no incongruity between their progressivism and their dislike of Franklin Roosevelt. "I didn't have a
very wide program," said Frederick Morgan Davenport of his reform days in New York: "The liquor traffic was one thing to fight,
so for a while we fought for [sic] it. . . . I was interested in having things done in a decent way within the political parties, and in
fighting for the right things." [101] The bulk of those progressives

101. "Reminiscences of Frederick Morgan Davenport," Colum-
bia Oral History Collection, p. 36. Among anti–New Deal progressives, the following seem to me to have pursued reform
careers of this type (usually from law into politics and eventually back into law): Cordell Hull, Morton Hull, Reed, Glass,
Capper, Palmer, John M. Nelson, Hiram Johnson, Jonathan
Bourne, Robert Perkins Bass, Charles Evans Hughes, Henry J.
Allen, William S. Bennet, Joseph Bristow, A. S. Burleson,
Bainbridge Colby, Coe Crawford, James R. Garfield, Irvine
Lenroot, William E. Borah, James H. Kirkland, Atlee Pomerene, George Sheldon, both Stimsons, William S. U'Ren, Carl
Vrooman, and Davenport. They had almost no contact with
settlement house, social work, Negro, or other social justice
causes. See also the discussion of Southern progressives, Appen-
dix II.

who opposed Roosevelt in the 1930's had, like Morton Hull, been
involved in the modest Good Government forms of progressivism,
and "didn't have a very wide program." They stopped short of
welfare legislation in the progressive era, and from the same general position condemned the welfare state twenty years later.
Their progressivism made little contact with the New Deal, and
in fact easily permitted the crossover from Left to Right which
characterized so many.

The risks of utilizing a representative figure for progressivism
are especially great when dealing with reform journalists. They

were surely the most individualistic and refractory members of a generation of self-conscious individualists. Still, I think it possible to use Mark Sullivan as an example of how a combination of pugnacity, the love of adventure, and a certain resentment of privilege—a combination rather general among young editors, journalists, and free-lance writers of the muckraker era—passed at the time for a serious commitment to social reform among men who were actually quite fond of the existing system and who meant all along to enter rather than to radically alter it.

Sullivan was born into a large Irish family in the rich farming country of the Brandywine region of Pennsylvania, and was working on the West Chester *Morning Republican* before he was out of high school. At nineteen he bought the Phoenixville *Republican,* but realizing how poorly his education supported his ambitions, went to Harvard and graduated in the Class of 1900. A brief experience as a reporter with E. A. Van Valkenberg's Philadelphia *North American* proved confining, and he returned to Harvard to take a degree in law (1903). While in law school he wrote aritcles on conservation, travel, and politics for the Boston *Transcript,* and wrote what he later called the first muckrake article, "The Ills of Pennsylvania," which appeared in the *Atlantic Monthly* in 1901. He was to write for Bok's *Ladies' Home Journal* (1904-6), *McClure's* (briefly), and *Collier's* (1906-19), where he was Editor after Norman Hapgood's resignation. He became a muckraker at least as early as any of the others, and built a reputation as a prominent reformer through his patent medicine series for the *Ladies' Home Journal* and his column, "Comment on Congress," for *Collier's.* He was a Progressive in 1912, and recalls that he "may have joined" a socialist group at about that time. Yet the Sullivan who damned F.D.R. and thought the 1936 election "the last election we will ever have" was intellectually the same man as he had been in 1912—wealthier, dignified by fame, momentarily hysterical, perhaps, but unchanged in his views of what America ought to be, and ought to do toward that end.[102]

102. The quotation is taken from A. M. Schlesinger, Jr., *The Politics of Upheaval* (Boston: Houghton Mifflin, 1960), p. 500. The only book on Sullivan is his autobiography, *The Education of An American* (New York: Doubleday, Doran, 1938). For his political views in the 1930's, see his regular column in the New York *Herald Tribune,* which started in 1923 and ran until his death in 1952. His early views may be followed in his scattered essays in *Ladies' Home Journal* (1906-9) and *Collier's* (1909-15). There are collections

Sullivan, like most of the muckrakers, had never been attracted to deep social problems nor demanded much more than a clean politics.[103] His widely read column on the Congress for *Collier's*

103. There were exceptions, such as Marie Van Vorst, whose chief work was a series on working women; Robert Hunter, who wrote *Poverty;* Ray Stannard Baker, who wrote about the plight of the Negro. But most muckrakers proposed to warn the middle class that its food was adulterated, its insurance funds misused, its stock watered, and its government full of graft.

Of the 60 anti–New Dealers, 20 were publishers, editors, or journalists. They were Cobb, Creel, Dickson, Hard, Hendrick, Irwin (Wallace and Will), Kauffman, Hearst, Lippmann, Hunter, McClure, McCormick, Pillsbury, Rowell, Sedgwick, Shaw, Spargo, Sullivan, and White. Bristow, Capper, and Glass doubled as politicians.

sparked the fight against House Speaker Cannon and continued the fire against Senator Aldrich, but this was hardly revolutionary. Sullivan, as his early articles reveal, was thoroughly conventional in his values, and his picture of what needed to be accomplished through reform would have been familiar to the Mugwumps. Twice, in the *Collier's* period, he opened his editorials with a picture of a log house (that of Grant, and then that of J. Sterling Morton) and argued that this time-honored goal of American life was still within the grasp of patient individuals, "granted the willingness to work with their hands, and granted that education and city life have not made them effeminate. . . . Much so-called social reform is governed by a spirit which puts the mark of intolerable burdens upon those conditions which call out initiative and hard work." [104]

The Insurgents appealed to him because they were rebellious individualists, but he was not much concerned with the substantive issues that might be raised as a result of a more democratic politics. Charles A. Lindbergh's flight, he wrote in his autobiography, was evidence of that same fine spirit of individualism that caused Lindbergh's father to become an Insurgent. Thus Sullivan

of his private papers in the Library of Congress and in the Hoover Institution on War, Revolution and Peace, Stanford University, Stanford, California.
104. Sullivan, *Education of an American*, p. 279. Sullivan gives no date for this particular editorial, but it was written during the *Collier's* years.

early equated progressivism with individuals defiantly seceding from institutional restraints.

The wonder is that many of these journalists and editors became reformers at all, and indeed Ida Tarbell always argued that most of them never had been. Like so many others in his profession, Sullivan came to journalism in search of adventure, not of a fulcrum for social change. In this respect he was a paler copy of the unruly Hearst, or the Irwin brothers, who were both thrown out of Stanford for their brand of "rugged individualism." With the frontier "closed" and a business career ruled out either by distaste for commercial routine or by the feeling that the adventures there were all over, journalism offered one of the last vocations for the young man who loved to travel, to be independent, to make a quick reputation, to move mountains.[105] Around the turn of the century, journalism recruited a new college-bred generation of men spoiling for exertion against the odds.

Once in journalism—and again like most of his peers—Mark Sullivan came to *reform* journalism more out of youthful pugnacity than any deep social sympathies, or any long-matured social criticisms. He recalled that when he and his partner decided to put their little Phoenixville paper editorially behind the "kickers" (the outs of the local Republican party), they did so because their own temperaments dictated the side of the underdog and the rebel, not because of any understanding of the political issues involved—if there were any. Sullivan joined Roosevelt in 1912 out of personal admiration, not New Nationalism principles, and was able to say of himself that, in the same year he flirted with socialism, "I was a sheer individualist. . . . I believed in self help."[106] He *had* helped himself, and when the poor Irish boy found himself in middle life moving as a social if not quite a financial equal among bank and corporation presidents, and American Presidents as well, he took that as a vindication of those principles which led him into reform: keep the race free, open to all, and the best man would win.

A time came, of course, when Sullivan, like so many progres-

105. For a taste of the special flavor of newspaper life in the early years of this century—a mixture of Bohemianism, war reporting (during two wars), hard drinking, urban politics, and lusty circulation battles—see the biographies of Hearst and Joseph Medill Patterson, George Creel, Hutchins Hapgood, Will Irwin, and Mark Sullivan. For a composite picture, see George Seldes, *Lords of the Press* (New York: Julian Messner, 1938).
106. *Education of an American*, p. 278.

sives whose social philosophy was composed of a mixture of Jefferson, Sumner, and Alger, realized that he was rubbing elbows inside the movement with men who had no love for individualism and the competitive race and who dreamed of a more collective life. When he realized this he denounced them as false liberals, and when in the postwar years they gradually purloined the word for a philosophy he hated, Sullivan with remarkable consistency followed his brand of progressivism into the camp of Roosevelt's enemies. We see him becoming aware of this division among progressives in a letter to Josephus Daniels in 1922.

"Now, it happens that this is just the point [Daniels had been complaining about excessive bond issues for road building] as to which I felt troubled in my mind about some of our progressive friends. Some of the leaders of this new progressive movement in the Republican Party think of progressivism largely in terms of taking more money out of the taxpayers and spending it more widely. I am decidedly disturbed by a conception of progressivism which includes high taxation and prodigal expenditures with the public money. Some of our progressive friends think of the income tax not merely as a device for raising the necessary revenues for the government, but really as a device for social leveling. They want to take as much money as they can out of the rich and the near-rich, and in an obscure way their notion is to deprive the rich and the near-rich of the power that goes with wealth. But you and I know that the taking of this money in the way we now take it is really a matter of taking it out of productive private enterprises and putting it into public improvements which we don't need—certainly which we cannot afford. I cannot help but be gravely disturbed by a system of taxation and by a point of view on the part of some public men which puts a penalty on saving—makes saving less possible; and stimulates expenditures, both private and public. It is because this new progressive movement within the Republican Party is so touched by this conception of the public revenues, that I hesitate to go along with them as wholeheartedly as I did with the old insurgent and progressive movement in 1912." [107]

Thus it was progressivism which changed, moving away to the Left, while Sullivan manned to the end the position he had held in the day of William Howard Taft.

107. Sullivan to Josephus Daniels, December 8, 1922; Box 1, Sullivan MSS, Hoover Institution on War, Revolution and Peace.

Progressivism in journalism had been half a good fight against heavy odds, it could be said, and half the simple joy of ferreting out the truth—the whole encouraged by the discovery that muckraking increased sales. For only a few of its practitioners did it have the direct aim of threatening the gains of the successful in the effort to relieve the miseries of the urban lower classes. Reform journalism did sound a tocsin, but what was contemplated was not some drastic alteration of existing arrangements, but merely a good fight to throw out tenured rascals. The same qualities which made men like Mark Sullivan reformers—dogged insistence upon honesty and efficiency in government, and a psychological preference for opposition—led them to that other, final fight against the ins and the odds in the person of Franklin Roosevelt.

V

It is evident that their opposition to the New Deal stresses the nineteenth-century roots of progressive thought, and underlines the intellectual, political, and social changes that overtook America after World War I. Their reaction to the changed mores and manners of the postwar period frequently called attention to the fact that it was not only their political views that were becoming obsolete. Somehow one is not surprised to find that Carter Glass distrusted automobiles, that William Allen White would not allow smoking in the offices of the *Emporia Gazette,* that James C. McReynolds left the Supreme Court chamber when a woman lawyer came to the bar, that Oswald Garrison Villard was decidedly uncomfortable with the new poetry his younger staff members ran in the *Nation,* or that Mark Sullivan found F.D.R.'s first-naming of the Press intolerably poor taste. They were born and educated in the nineteenth century, and were flexible enough, under the provocation of swarming social ills, to lead a nationwide political revolt. But what guided that revolt was less a utopian vision than a memory, and most of them were quick to detect in the New Deal's combination of centralism and unfamiliar faces and arrogant tone the lockstep of an evil century.

George Creel, crusading editor and muckraker in Kansas City, Denver, and New York, spelled out the differences they had with the new liberalism in his autobiography, *Rebel at Large.*

"If I have dug far back into the past, it is for the purpose of drawing a comparison between the progressive movement of other years and the so-called 'liberal' movement of today. As nothing else, it shows how far we have fallen from the heights. Whatever its faults, the progressivism preached and led by Theodore Roosevelt, La Follette and Woodrow Wilson was intensely American, its core a love of country and pride in our free institutions.

"Present day 'liberalism,' as it has the impudence to call itself, is anti-American; . . . 'Liberalism!' Not in all history has a word been so wrenched away from its true meaning and dragged through every gutter of defilement. Where once it stood for the dignity of man—the rescue of the spirit from the debasements of materialism—it now stands for the obliteration of individualism at the hands of a ruthless, all-powerful state. . . . The progressive movement of other days was self-supporting, its campaigns made possible by the sacrifices of devoted men and women. The new 'liberalism' derives its income from forced contributions . . . and the largess of rich addlepates who seek to hide their futility behind the pretense of Bold Thinking.

"Old-time progressives were instinct [sic] with patriotism, and what they fought for was not a change in the democratic ideal, but the remedying of wrongs and perversions that shamed the ideal. 'Liberals' sneer at patriotism as old-fashioned and talk of 'revolution' as calmly as though they were ordering a sundae.

.   .   .

"My whole life has been devoted to criticism of the barnacled faults of the American system; yet never once have I doubted the wisdom and rightness of the system itself." [108]

---

108. Creel, *Rebel At Large* (New York: G. P. Putnam's Sons, 1947), pp. 370-71 and 375-6. Creel was enthusiastic at first about the New Deal. He joined NRA as a member of the West Coast District Board, but found the confusion intolerable, and resigned to work for *Collier's* as Washington correspondent. He ran, unsuccessfully, for governor of California (1934), and had one more brief New Deal job under Harry Hopkins (National Advisory Board to WPA) which he liked even less than the first. As a *Collier's* reporter and an old Wilsonian who had known Roosevelt since the first World War, Creel saw a good bit of the President and was considered the chief presidential intimate among the press. But it was clear that he was disenchanted with New Deal liberalism when his autobiography

came out in 1947, and his papers indicate that he began to sour about 1936, with the Third Term issue the occasion of an open break. Creel is a good example of the classic Left-to-Right trajectory; he wound up after the war close friends with Richard Nixon, Karl Mundt, and Harry Byrd. In 1951 he preferred Taft to any other Republican (and any Republican to a Democrat), and wrote when he sent a check to Joseph McCarthy in 1952 that McCarthy's work "stems from the same sturdy Americanism that led plain men to risk all at Lexington and Concord." (Creel to "Editor," dated only 1952, Container 4, Creel MSS, Library of Congress.)

It is clear that whatever it was about the New Deal that put the progressives off, it turned out to be those parts, if their language be any guide, which most contradicted long-held *progressive* beliefs. Whatever the shaping power of age or fatigue, it was to progressive principles that they repaired in the final battle against hostile power.

The resentment of so many progressives to New Deal measures suggests that it is easy to understimate the social changes that had occurred in the early decades of this century. Even as these spokesmen of the best conscience of an older era were mobilizing to clean up America, Americans were moving to the cities, the immigrant was coming of political age and starting to vote, Protestant churches and rural areas were declining in influence, and men like Rex Tugwell and Gardner Jackson and Harry Hopkins were emerging from American universities with an irreverence for the old truths. From the Adamson Act of 1916 to the "Hundred Days" was only seventeen years, but the impression given by these old reformers was that the country had raced many generations in that time. Their resistance to the New Deal thus does a double duty, underlining the flux in demography and technology that had altered the situation and made their political ideas seem quaint, and forcing also a recognition that values and beliefs have a tenacity that resists the determined erosion of time. It was precisely this intellectual tenacity that brought most progressives up on the "wrong" side of reform, despite the price of loss of influence, of reform identity, and of public favor.

V I

Others have been struck by the conservatism of the progressive era reformers, and wondered why the battle for their reforms was so hard, and why more men were not progressive in those days. What seems to require explanation is that America has been so thoroughly conservative, the battles being invariably fought between standpat conservatives and other conservatives who, through a combination of decency and fear that inaction might hasten revolution, propose slight structural changes. When a society falls in arrears, as it must in a time when unco-ordinated social revolution accelerates each day, even conservative men are drawn into reform. Their work is uphill, and is apt, even when successful, to be quickly outdated. By the time they were finished, the progressives were falling behind again. The next reform was to be only seventeen years, but for them a sea change later.

But in stressing the conservatism of so many, one is in danger of missing the tenacity of another social belief they held; that a decent man was a reformer almost by definition. It was a role not easily shrugged. Not only did many progressives line up with the New Deal, but even among those who did not like it there were some who equally did not like, would not rest content in, the negative role of the conservative. After all, they were charter reformers, men who had known the bluff Tom Johnson, the incorruptible George Record, Governor Altgeld and Senator La Follette, and two progressive Presidents. It was they who had awakened the public from its self-centered slumber. Remembering this, when principle and conviction enjoined a battle against the reform impostor from Hyde Park, few were entirely without qualms in that stance, and most did not easily give up association with reform.[109]

---

109. Of the 60, the only ones who can be said to have become reactionary without regrets or apology would be James A. Reed, Ellery Sedgwick, Carter Glass, James McReynolds, Bainbridge Colby, and Burton Hendrick. None of these had gone very far with reform even in their most reckless days. The others seem generally to have worried about being in opposition, and often either made some effort to explain it or expressed the nagging doubts natural to reformers who find themselves amid plutocratic company.

One way to occupy both positions—that of opposition to the New Deal and at the same time that of the citizen who still believes that America could be improved—was to formulate a middle position, a substitute reform proposal clothed in the traditional rhetoric of reform but without the disturbing adventures in Federal power associated with the New Deal. Ideally, this took the form of programs for recovery which were shorter, briefer, clearer, cheaper, less coercive, and less dependent upon bureaucracy than the New Deal.

It was that sort of plan that the Oregon reformer, William S. U'Ren, sent to Frederick Morgan Davenport in 1934, proposing a voluntary citizen's army to provide pay-as-you-go work projects as insurance against the hardships of unemployment. U'Ren's plan was four pages long, and he had worked hard on it. He had not fought the laissez-faire forces for years just to retire to a sterile do-nothingism in the 1930's. Others, along with U'Ren, worked on plans of their own which would allow reformers a less noxious alternative than the bewilderment of bureaus and Thou-Shalt-Nots of the New Deal.

If they were Republicans, they continued to believe in and struggle for a reformed Republican party. "I still believe in fairies," William Allen White wrote to Carl Sandburg in 1936, "and I still hope the Republican Party will have enough sense to know that it can't go back to McKinley." [110] This meant that the party must nominate in 1936 a man with a progressive past, and not a reactionary acceptable to the Hoover wing of the party. Most of the progressives finally threw in with the Borah boomlet, and when Borah faltered several prominent Republican progressives like Robert Perkins Bass, White, and Chester Rowell urged the party to select a man and an image of sensible reform.[111] They insisted that the party of Lincoln was the only party capable of safe policies, although many of them were quite willing (mostly in private) to denounce the G.O.P., as they had in Taft's day, as reactionary and greedy. Once Landon was nominated—and he was a plausible reformer if one were in a lenient mood—most tried to convince themselves that progressivism had returned to its Republican home.

110. White to Carl Sandburg, quoted in Walter Johnson, *Selected Letters*, p. 361.
111. See Chester H. Rowell, "A Positive Programme for the Republican Party," *Yale Review*, XXV (March 1936), 443-52.

Robert Bass sent a memo to the nominee during the campaign reminding him that theirs was the party of humanitarian reforms as well as of caution, and, when the campaign was over, Bass wrote Styles Bridges, "If we are to escape class alignments in this country, the permanent minority party must present a sufficiently liberal constructive program to meet the needs of the average citizen in the light of present day conditions. . . . Our failure to take such action while we were in power, and the manner of our opposition in Congress to this administration has placed us in a particularly weak position." [112]

As Republican progressives, including Landon, discovered, developing a Republican program that would be cheaper and simpler than the New Deal was easier said than done. But a progressive did not have to be a Republican to make the effort. Old progressives who were Democrats were extraordinarily imaginative at devising plans to substitute one simple, controlled alteration for the bewildering changes Roosevelt was making. Old Wilsonians like Albert Sidney Burleson urged a vigorous drive to institute Free Trade; Herbert Seely Bigelow, for one, trusted in the Single Tax; Edgar Lee Masters even proposed that the country be cut in half to reduce bureaucracy, Federal expense, and the possibility of tyranny. Bull Mooser Amos Pinchot urged on the President the old George Record program of public ownership of key railroads and pipelines. Yale's Irving Fisher, an Independent, and former Democratic Senator Robert L. Owen begged the President and the Congress to achieve recovery through public control of checkbook money.

As they offered these alternatives they were manifestly still reformers, still engaged in the thankless task of prodding the public to do what was necessary—and only what was necessary—in the general interest. Owen kept hoping that Roosevelt, who, after all, had gone off the gold standard and shown a remarkable financial open-mindedness, would respond to his letters and personal entreaties and, after securing Federal control of checkbook money, proceed to a deliberate inflation. When it became clear that the New Deal would not extend its banking reforms to include the abolition of the fractional reserve system, but was wasting those golden years of opportunity on a melange of costly and futile projects, Owen's disappointment broke through in a letter to the

112. Robert P. Bass to Styles Bridges, February 25, 1937, Box 46, Bass MSS, Dartmouth University.

President: "My poor efforts to serve you . . . have been deeply disappointing, because in five years you have only had time to give me twenty-nine minutes." [113]

For Owen, the struggle for reform had not ended with progressivism, but the New Deal, so tantalizingly unorthodox on money questions, brought America no nearer to what he wanted. The control of credit remained in private hands; the monetary path to recovery, so simple and quick and vastly more conservative than production controls, remained unused. Another monetary reformer, Irving Fisher, was even more bitter than Owen at the thought of Roosevelt building wasteful bureaucracies and his own power, when all he needed to do was to transfer the issuance of money from private to public hands. Once having converted, through government purchase of the entire debt by means of a greenback issuance, to what Fisher called a 100 per cent reserve plan, the nation need never again experience a contraction like that of 1929-33. Private bankers would no longer create money, nor destroy it; beyond that one modification we need not go, and with the supply of money not tied to banker's confidence, the entire capitalistic economy would flourish unimpaired.[114]

113. Robert Owen to Franklin D. Roosevelt, October 29, 1937, Box 2, Owen MSS, Library of Congress. Owen was not categorized as an anti–New Dealer, but as one of those who had to be put in an indeterminate status. He never openly broke with the leader of his party, deluged him with respectful, pleading letters, and right up until the end of the period (1938) expressed a sympathy with Roosevelt's objectives—including the plan to reduce the obstructive power of the Court. But Owen did not like any of the New Deal beyond its objectives—and the gold decisions—and he thought of it as a series of lost opportunities. See Edward M. Keso, *The Senatorial Career of Robert L. Owen* (Nashville: George Peabody College Press, 1937), and Robert L. Owen, *The National Economy and the Banking System of the United States* (District of Columbia: Government Printing Office, 1939). The Owen papers are in the Library of Congress.

114. On Owen, Fisher, and other monetary reformers during the Depression, see Joseph E. Reeve, *Monetary Reform Movements: A Survey of Plans and Panaceas* (Washington: American Council on Public Affairs, 1943). For Fisher's monetary views, see *After Reflation, What?* (New York: Adelphi, 1933), or *100% Money* (New York: Adelphi, 1935). Fisher did not originate the 100 per cent reserve plan, but he probably gave it its most forceful expression during the 1930's. In support of the plan, see Frank D. Graham, "Reserve Money and the 100 Per Cent Proposal," *American Economic Review*, XXVI (September 1936), 428-40; for a critical analysis, see Rollin G. Thomas, "100 Per Cent Money—The Present Status of the 100 Per Cent Plan," *American Economic Review*, XXX (June 1940), 315-23, and L. L. Watkins, "Commercial Banking Reform in the United States," *Michigan*

Fisher explained in two separate statements the certainties within which he operated—i.e. that it was conservative to be a monetary reformer, as a simple change in the rules governing money would make unnecessary all the other disturbing and far-reaching alterations that made up the New Deal:

"Money stable in purchasing power is inherently conservative. . . . Unstable money is behind . . . our great booms and depressions, . . . our political upheavals, the radicalism which conservatives so much deplore. To hang doggedly onto the chief cause of our upsets is not true conservatism. True conservatism will take us back to John Adams . . . who thought it an outrage that private banks should issue money and so usurp a federal function." [115]

"I think it would be wise to sit back and see for some years what comes out of Russia before following her any further than the New Deal has done. In fact, I think the New Deal has been rather rash in this way. . . . It seems to me we should go slowly and begin nearly or chiefly with monetary reform. In another generation, after experience with sound money properly managed by the government, we can see more clearly as to what further changes need to be made, if any. . . . I feel we have done too much now." [116]

---

116. Irving Fisher to R. A. Lester, November 25, 1936, Box 18, Fisher MSS, Yale University. Fisher opposed NRA, public works, AAA, the Court Plan, the Third and Fourth Terms—everything, in fact, except the CCC and inflation (see, for example, his letter to *The New York Times,* November 10, 1934). "I agree," he wrote to J. A. Farrell in 1936, "that probably 90% of the administration's experiments were wrong." (Fisher to Farrell, April 23, 1936, Box 18, Fisher MSS.) He saw Roosevelt early in the New Deal period, valued the prospect of becoming an influential adviser, and his public comments on the New

---

Business Studies, VIII (1938). The conservatism of the monetary reformers may be seen in the continuity of membership between the Committee For the Nation of 1932-33, interested in monetary reform, and the Committee to Uphold Constitutional Government of 1937-38, formed to fight the Court Plan and the Wages and Hours bill. Irving Fisher and Amos Pinchot, to name only two, were associated with both committees. See Richard Polenberg, "The National Committee to Uphold Constitutional Government, 1937-1941," *Journal of American History,* LII (December 1966), 582-98.

115. Index Number Institute Release, June 29, 1936, Box 2, Owen MSS.

Deal were, until the very late 1930's, generally moderate. Toward the end of the decade, and continuing through and after
World War II, his private correspondence reflected a deep distaste for the New Deal. "I am actively associated with a movement to try to safeguard private enterprise," he wrote Baldwin
Sawyer in 1944; he referred to Gannett and Rumely's Committee To Uphold Constitutional Government. This letter, re-
printed in Irving Norton Fisher, *My Father Irving Fisher*
(New York: Comet Press, 1956), pp. 326-30, represents the best
statement of the elder Fisher's final views.

Predictably, whether these old progressives tried to pull the
Republican party to a sound progressive program, or to work out
progressive alternatives to the New Deal, the result was the same.
The Republican party would not reform, Roosevelt would not
listen, and the New Deal, unimproved by their pruning, was the
order of the day. There seemed to be no way to locate oneself, as
in the past, on the simple side of right and honesty—and also
action.[117] One is struck, on reading through their literary de-

---

117. There was at least one exception. Frederick Morgan Davenport, a Republican congressman defeated in 1932, would
seem to have lost what little opportunity he had to moderate
the New Deal or to activate the conscience of his own party—
and he was committed to both. But Davenport, who had taught
government at Hamilton College, did not stand on the political sidelines long and criticize. He founded the National Institute of Public Affairs to train young men for public service,
and was instrumental in recruiting and training a political bureaucracy until the Civil Service Commission took up the task
in 1947. This was a constructive idea that Roosevelt could use,
and Davenport ultimately became friendly toward the President, if never entirely happy with the New Deal. Roosevelt
named him Chairman of the Federal Council on Personnel Administration upon its establishment in 1939. (See "Reminiscences of Frederick Morgan Davenport," COHC; Louis Brown-
low, *A Passion For Anonymity* (Chicago: University of Chicago
Press, 1958, 2 vols.), II, 462-3.

---

posit, by the frequent note of sadness, of bewilderment at the
absence of acceptable prospects, of distress at the loss of intellectual and moral clarity.
    One cannot read through Richard T. Ely's letters, for example,
and follow that gallant struggle to discover through "more re-

search" or through the establishment of the abortive School of Land Economics the answers to economic depression, without being aware of how hard it was for Ely's optimism to conquer his dismay that he had no answers. Here, as so often, William Allen White offers the most illuminating and articulate statement of their bankruptcy.

White had not liked much of the New Deal, and despite some poorly concealed doubts, backed his old friend Alf Landon in 1936. Throughout the New Deal, White struggled to reconcile his instinctive sympathy for the underdog with his middle-class fears of the social revolution Roosevelt was guiding. To make the ambivalence worse, the Depression caught White intellectually unprepared, facing intricate economic problems armed only with the moral homilies and futile individualism of younger days. A comment to Congressman Rees on the Wages and Hours bill of 1938 captures this dilemma: "I don't know what is right. I don't like the bill. . . . On the other hand, something should be done to establish a standard of living in industry below which no one willing to work need fall. . . . You and I are just pumpkin busters from the wide open spaces and we don't know much about industry. . . . I'm not as smart as I used to think I was."[118]

Again, in a 1934 letter to Allan Nevins, White expressed the same confusion at being faced with two unacceptable choices—the New Deal, dangerous and without consistency, and Wall Street, the ancient plutocratic enemy—and could only close with, "Lord, I don't know." [119] And in a 1936 letter to Harold Ickes: "It is so hard to know what a man ought to do." [120]

Not all the old reformers found that their continuing progressivism not only ruled out both the New Deal and the G.O.P. do-nothing alternative, but failed to provide them with an understanding of or remedy for our economic collapse. But many did, and, while there is manifestly no typical progressive, the old reformer in that no man's land between the New Deal and laissez-faire remains a major terminus of the progressive movement. The half-dozen finished and unfinished essays on "Liberalism" and "Individualism" found in the papers of Amos Pinchot provide traces of this struggle for orientation. These are essays of indomi-

118. White to E. H. Rees, August 5, 1937, Box 191, White MSS.
119. White to Allan Nevins, May 24, 1934; quoted in Walter Johnson, *Selected Letters*, p. 346.
120. Ibid. p. 366.

table idealism, morally crisp but programmatically vague; they are the well-meaning but largely futile efforts of an old reformer to reconstruct, if only on paper, the clear purpose and accurate diagnosis of earlier days.

Inevitably, such men envied those few veterans of progressivism who were still able to fight on the side the public recognized as the side of the People. "I suppose," White wrote to Oswald Garrison Villard, "in looking at the wisdom and consistency of your life, in seeing how right you are and have been upon the great problems facing the world, I have a wistful longing, possibly inspired somewhat by regret that my course has not been so true as yours."[121]

121. White to Villard, July 24, 1936, Box 191, White MSS. White, worried by the threat of war and unhappy with the New Deal, but too much the progressive to wish for a return to Coolidge-ism, permitted himself the wistful hope in 1939 that salvation might come by learning to get more power out of our fuel. See his liberal, pessimistic, and confused book, *The Changing West: An Economic Theory About Our Golden Age* (New York: Macmillan, 1939). Actually, Villard was by this time at least as confused as White, and was moving from his early qualified approval of the New Deal to a deep suspicion of Roosevelt's motives and the sinister possibilities of the Federal establishment, bureaucratic and military.

But Marshall Stimson gave the most candid statement of the bewilderment that some of them expressed, and more of them must have felt, at the impossible situation they were in. Writing to Freda Kirchwey in 1944, after hearing of a dinner honoring her for a lifetime of unswerving devotion to liberal causes, Stimson reviewed his own checkered party record, freely confessing his unhappiness at his inability to discover just where an old Progressive belonged.[122] He concluded, "I suppose a person like my-

122. Stimson was a Republican, bolted and became a Bull Mooser in 1912, was back with his party in 1916, bolted again in 1920 to vote for Cox as inheritor of Wilsonian internationalism. He went back to the G.O.P. thereafter. Stimson was for Landon in 1936, and in 1944 went over to Roosevelt after much soul-searching.

self has to make choices, as I have done, but it [my career] is far from satisfactory. I have great admiration for women who, like yourself, have pursued a thoroly [sic] consistent course for a long period of time. . . . I wish to be a true liberal. I have always fought hard for the things I believed in and I am not laying down on the job."[123]

And so the old men, veterans of another campaign to reform America, spread across the political expanse to the Right of the New Deal during the 1930's. And to those willing to reread their rhetoric and their history with an ear more attuned to preferences and values than to the literal sense of their bold demands for reform through the use of government, it is not surprising that Franklin Roosevelt's New Deal did not carry them forward, with it, into the complex world of the welfare state in urban America.

123. Marshall Stimson to Freda Kirchwey, May 23, 1944, Stimson MSS, Huntington Library.

III

The Culmination of Progressivism:
II   The Progressive as Liberal

> It is perfectly clear to every man who has any vision of the
> immediate future, who can forecast any part of it from the
> indications of the present, that we are just upon the thresh-
> old of a time when the systematic life of this country will be
> sustained, or at least supplemented, at every point by gov-
> ernmental activity.
>
> WOODROW WILSON

The rumpled figure of George Norris, veteran of every liberal
cause since the fight over Speaker Cannon in 1910, served in the
seventy-third congress as irrefutable evidence that the progressive
impulse, revived and militant, was a major support of the New
Deal. Norris was not alone, for a sizable minority of progressives
connected the New Deal to earlier reform by their political sympathies and activities after 1932. For some reason they were not as
voluble as those opposing the New Deal, and they left a much
smaller deposit of reflective and explanatory material. They
wrote fewer autobiographies, and their personal papers, where
preserved, are oddly devoid of political soul-searching. The William McAdoo papers, for example, are quite arid; the autobiographies of Josephus Daniels and Lillian Wald are kindly but
shallow; the sermons of Stephen S. Wise and Bishop McConnell
are affirmations of steady altruism and little else. Intrepid reformers like Peter Witt and Rudolph Spreckels left no written
explanation for their devotion to progressive causes. The various
ways the New Deal struck them, their reasons for coming to its
support, these are hard to discover on the record they left.[1]

Perhaps they were too busy in those years when most progres-

1. The chief exception that comes to mind would be Harold Ickes's little
volume, *The New Democracy* (New York: W. W. Norton, 1934). For a list
of those progressives who consistently supported the New Deal, see Appendix I.

sives had retired and were putting to paper the results of years of work and thought—too busy, in many cases, because in one way or another they were drawn into the New Deal. Perhaps, since they remained reformers, they were spared that goad to published self-justification, public opposition to a popular leader. Whatever the reason, we must reconstruct and understand their response through a combination not only of what they said and did but what they did not say and do, noticing always the apparent fit of their social and intellectual backgrounds with the reform thrusts of the New Deal.

Unfortunately, even when they wrote, they were no more inclined to close analysis and systematic thought than those progressives who were angry with Roosevelt. Men who were actively involved in the New Deal—Harold Ickes, Josephus Daniels, Fred Howe, Henry Hunt, Merle D. Vincent—were entirely taken up with pressing bureaucratic routine, were Harry Hopkins's "doers," not "talkers." Those in the Congress—Senators McAdoo, Costigan, Norris, and Robinson, Congressmen Eagle and Bigelow—were of course expressing an opinion on the New Deal each time they voted, but a Yea vote is a poor reflection of political attitude. Others who were at greater distance, like George F. Peabody or Rudolph Spreckels or Peter Dunne or Mary Simkhovitch or Lillian Wald, had rarely followed politics very closely. Those few outside government who followed national politics closely, such as John B. Andrews and Paul Kellogg, were not much given to editorializing, either privately or through their respective journals. In summary, the comments of these friends of the New Deal were intermittent and cursory, revealing few of its crucial philosophical or political decisions and as little of their own. Yet if their recorded responses are thin, still they sketch in a collective attitude of unusual consistency.

Speaking generally, these progressives went along enthusiastically with all of it. The Court Plan, and before that the NRA, occasionally appear in their writings as dubious ventures, but on the whole the tone is one of affirmation. There was certainly no sense among them of any internal shift in 1935, which presumably committed the New Deal to a course more congenial to Wilsonians. Their acceptance was inclined to be total, and the New Deal emerges as a more unified reform experience than subsequent historical analysis has revealed. But from their comments we learn what in the New Deal most gladdened old progressive hearts and seemed most obviously the fulfillment of years of their effort.

Principally, they welcomed those programs—relief, public works, public housing, social security—which meant that the federal government was now committed to intercession against want. This was especially true of the social workers such as Homer Folks, Mary Simkhovitch, Paul Kellogg, Graham Taylor and Lillian Wald, whose contact with the urban poor made their progressivism come down essentially to a demand for Federal minima. When the New Deal offered relief, jobs, and old age insurance, it was apparently satisfying the most deeply rooted desire of these older reformers.

There was no talk among them of the erosion of character that presumably attended Federal relief. John B. Andrews, for thirty-two years the editor of the American Association for Labor Legislation's *Review,* quoted with approval an early answer to the "undermining of intitiative" argument,

"Many earnest people are afraid that social insurance will take away from the workingman his independence, initiative, and self-reliance, which are so celebrated in song and story, and transform him into a mere spoon-fed mollycoddle. This would be a cruel calamity. But if the worst comes to the worst, I, for my part, would rather see a race of sturdy, contented, healthful mollycoddles, carefully fed, medically examined, physically fit, nursed in illness and cared for in old age . . . than to see the most ferociously independent and self-reliant super-race of tubercular, rheumatic, and malarial cripples tottering unsocialistically along the socialized highways, reclining self-reliantly upon the communal benches of the public parks, and staring belligerently at the communal trees, . . . and at last going expensively to rest, independently and self-reliantly, in a socialized or mutualized graveyard full of little individualistic slabs erected to the memory of the independent and self-reliant dead." [2]

For those progressives who preferred the risks of character damage through Federal relief to the very real miseries brought by the Depression, whatever else the New Deal did or failed to do could not alter its assumption of this ancient progressive concern. Lillian Wald was able to write in 1935, "I . . . see many things

2. From a speech delivered by Royal Meeker in 1916, and quoted in the American Association for Labor Legislation *Review,* XXVI (March 1936), 6.

developing that I feared we would live a long time to see throughout this country." [3]

If the New Deal enacted a primary progressive agenda when it assumed responsibility for the victims of the Depression, it was again in the progressive tradition when it attacked the leaders of industry and finance. "We love him [F.D.R.]," George Norris wired a convention of progressives who had come together to support Roosevelt in 1936, "for the enemies he has made." [4] Even if the New Deal was in places unfamiliar, the familiar faces of its enemies—the banker, the industrialist, the corporation lawyer, the man of wealth generally—testified to its legitimacy among some progressives who might have doubted. Thus Gustavus Myers, who had written *The History of the Great American Fortunes* in 1910, was revived by the New Deal assault upon the rich to write a book which announced with only slightly restrained satisfaction that 1939 saw the completion of the essential work of redistribution begun under the progressive Presidents. [5] With the objections to reform coming from the same old quarter—the wealthy—the kinship of the New Deal to earlier reforms was patent. For a group of the surviving progressives, the New Deal was a last chance to pull down the tories, and they were glad to be alive to see it.

Finally, they welcomed the New Deal as a revival of the adventure they had set out upon thirty years before, an adventure upon the frontiers of social action at the national level. Of course there was a list of specific reforms which they hoped would achieve legal embodiment: abolition of child labor, conservation, old age security, Federal wage standards, securities regulation, and so on. But in their reflections it was not so much these cherished reforms they spoke of as it was the experience of working again in a cause above self. Paul Kellogg thought of the entire reform tradition since the Civil War as being an attempt to regain the heights of the Lincoln years, and rejoiced at the New Deal as bringing national unity again, with the capital as the energetic center of long-deferred social action. Progressivism, he wrote, had been above all

3. Lillian Wald to Ben Lindsey, November 9, 1935, Wald MSS, New York Public Library.
4. Norris to Conference of Progressives, September 11, 1936, Box 5, Norris MSS, Library of Congress.
5. *The Ending of Hereditary American Fortunes* (New York: Julian Messner, 1939).

else a renewal of the same pioneering spirit that drove the New England overflow along the Erie Canal route to the Midwest. The New Deal was accompanied by that same sense of a journey resumed.[6] "Not au revoir," exulted Homer Folks on his seventieth birthday in 1937, "but come on." [7]

II

Given their continued interest in reform, and their acceptance of the New Deal as a renewal of progressivism, one is not surprised that many of them, age permitting, took some part in it. A good number of progressives had united behind Roosevelt in 1932, forming the National Progressive League, under Norris's leadership.[8] The 1936 campaign produced another group of progressives for Roosevelt, and again Norris was prominent. It is true that the 1936 group, the Progressive National Committee, was peopled by a new type of reformer—men like Fiorello H. La Guardia, John L. Lewis, Sidney Hillman, Tom Amlie, and Senators Benson and Bone—and the older type of progressive was outnumbered. This was partly because of the defection among older progressives from what was frequently an early enthusiasm, and partly the natural consequence of the rise of a new generation. But many of the older group, among them Norris, Costigan, Paul Kellogg, Peter Witt, and Grace Abbott*, still remained.[9] Further, others worked in that campaign as members of the Good Neighbor League, headed by Lillian Wald and George Foster Peabody, and devoted to Roosevelt's re-election.[10]

Between campaigns, many continued to act within the New Deal as appointed officials or legislative supporters. In the cabinet, the Wilsonian Cordell Hull and the Bull Mooser Harold Ickes; as Ambassador to Mexico, Josephus Daniels; on the Social

6. See Kellogg's interesting reflections in the journal he was to edit for forty years, "Twenty-five years of *Survey Graphic*," *Survey Graphic*, XXV (December 1937), 15-38, and his "A Century of Achievement in Democracy," *Proceedings*, National Conference of Social Work (New York: Columbia University Press, 1939), pp. 1-29.
7. "Addresses: 1937," Folks MSS, New York School of Social Work.
8. Other prominent progressives in that group were Ickes, Fred Howe, Felix Frankfurter*, Donald Richberg*, and Amos Pinchot.
9. *The New York Times*, September 11-12, 1936.
10. Organizational lists may be found in the Good Neighbor League files, Franklin D. Roosevelt Library, Hyde Park (PPF 3435).

Security Advisory Board, John B. Andrews; and on the Advisory Council to the Committee on Economic Security, Paul Kellogg (along with Grace Abbott* and Molly Dewson*). Frederic C. Howe worked in AAA as Consumer's Counsel, Henry T. Hunt worked in PWA, and Merle Vincent in NRA. In the Senate, Costigan, McAdoo, Norris, and Joe Robinson voted and talked as if the New Deal were what they had been working for all along. In the House, Herbert Seely Bigelow and Joe Eagle dated back, in this sample, to the earlier period. Thus a sizable contingent came together, within the administration or rallying to it as advisers or campaign workers, testifying to the continuity of goals between the two periods of reform.

III

That some progressives feared and others welcomed the New Deal, in both cases in the name of progressive values, invites an analysis of the sources of that divergence. The comments that survive express dissent or approbation, but rarely illuminate the reasons for choosing the one over the other. But just as was the case with the anti–New Deal progressives, those supporting Roosevelt generally had much in common. At least a partial explanation for their continued attachment to reform is etched in their occupational and political situations, their experiences as citizens and as reformers, and in certain mental characteristics ranging from belligerency to pragmatism.[11]

Very little influence upon attitude toward the New Deal was brought to bear, so far as one can tell, by the individual's age, religion, or years of formal education taken singly. But the examination of the careers of these progressives suggests that one decisive factor *was* education, education in the broadest sense— formal schooling to begin with, supplemented by the equally important matter of where one came to live and what sort of people and problems one encountered. We shall see that a prominent feature common to those favorable to the New Deal was extended experience in cities, the post-graduate schoolhouse of the New Deal.

After college, or after graduate work in sociology, economics, or

11. The reader may wish to refer to Appendix I, pp. 195-204, for the data upon which the following generalizations are based.

other areas where contemporary society was the focus of attention and which did not lead to jobs in or related to business, the progressives who later welcomed the New Deal typically entered careers which required or at least permitted occupational and / or residential proximity to the urban lower classes. The city had been a shock to progressives of all shades,[12] and there seems to

12. A classic example of the shock effect of working in a large city—in this case, on a reporter—would be that of Ray Stannard Baker. Baker was oblivious to all social problems when he came to the *Chicago Record* in 1892 (he was raised in a small Michigan town), and was interested only in writing the Great American Novel. But successive assignments to cover Coxey's Army (Baker walked all the way to Washington with them), the arrival in Chicago of the British reformer William T. Stead, and the Pullman Strike, followed by the rise of Debs—all of this against the background of the Depression of 1893—turned Baker into a worried American who read Bellamy, George, and Robert Owen in search of social remedies to problems his professors had not hinted at. See Baker, *American Chronicle* (New York: Charles Scribner's Sons, 1945), pp. 1-38.

The effect of environment one can readily estimate, given sufficient biographical information. Whatever psychological factors that may be at work to bring a person to the city in the first place, or to shape his reaction to what was actually a fairly common exposure, one can only guess at. It may be that the sort of person who was inclined to place humanitarian values over constitutional or procedural scruples gravitated naturally into social work—or sociology, or public health, or an urban parish—rather than into law or politics. Probably the historical record does not and cannot provide the materials for a group psychoanalysis of this sort, however promising it might be for the study of politics.

have been a rough correlation between the length of one's exposure to it and the breadth of his or her tolerance of Federal approaches to all sorts of problems.

This persistent association of a certain type of urban reform experience with subsequent support for the New Deal is nowhere borne out as thoroughly as in the case of the social work group within progressivism. "Social workers," actually, is probably a misleading designation for these progressives, for it invites the conclusion that all social workers were social reformers with political views to the left of center. Social work as a profession is an extraordinarily diverse calling, including settlement workers, voluntary association staff, and all sorts of case workers and staff of welfare organizations, private and public. Further, not only has the commitment to reform varied from sector to sector within "social work" as a profession, but the entire profession has gone through successive changes in its general attitude toward society's casualties. The progressive era saw a shift that has been described as one from palliation (charity) to prevention (social reform), but in the 1920's the preventive function gave way increasingly to a return to individual and family service and relief—substantially free, however, from the paternalistic spirit of late nineteenth-century charity work.[13] And while the 1930's saw a revival of interest in broader preventive measures through state action, it was probably not true even then that the majority of social workers were also social reformers. We have reliable testimony that the rank and file, case workers and others attached to welfare agencies, were conservative or apathetic politically.[14] The figures whose names dot this study, social reformers in both periods, should perhaps be called something other than "social workers," and a number of substitutes have been suggested: "advanced progressives" (Arthur Link), "social engineers" (Clarke Chambers), "social progressives" (Irwin Yellowitz). Whatever they are called (and I shall lamely continue to call them social workers), they were the heart of the settlement house and voluntary association

13. These shifts are described in Robert Bremner, *From The Depths;* Clarke Chambers, "Social Service and Social Reform: A Historical Essay," *Social Service Review,* XXXVII (March 1963), 76-90; Amos G. Warner *et al., American Charities and Social Work* (4th ed., rev., New York: Crowell, 1930). For a discussion of differences in political attitude between "charity workers" and settlement workers, see Robert Hunter, "The Relation Between Social Settlements and Charity Organizations," *Journal of Political Economy,* XI (1902), 75-88, and Allen F. Davis, "Settlement Workers in Politics, 1890-1914," *Review of Politics,* XXVI (October 1964), 505-17.

14. Harry Lurie felt that most of his profession was "in general tied up with the reactionary rather than with the advancing forces of social change" even in the 1930's; see Harry Lurie, "The Part Which Social Workers Have Taken in Promoting Social Legislation in New York State," *Proceedings,* National Conference of Social Work (1935), p. 503. A similar view is expressed in Daisy Lee Worcester, *Grim The Battles* (New York: Exposition Press, 1954). Marvin E. Gettleman demonstrates the conservatism of the "charity workers" of the late nineteenth century in "Charity and Social Classes in the United States, 1874-1900," *American Journal of Economics and Sociology,* XXII (April 1963), 313-29, and Part 2, *AJES,* XXII (July 1963), 417-26.

component of modern social service, a small ascetic fraternity, the visible saints of twentieth-century reform.

The number of those reformers who were gladdened by the New Deal includes most of the great names in the social work tradition: John B. Andrews, Homer Folks, Paul Kellogg, Mary Simkhovitch, Graham Taylor, Lillian Wald, Jane Addams (who died in 1935), Grace Abbott*, Molly Dewson*, Julia Lathrop*, and many others.[15] The people of the slums were their constituency, and the New Deal, the first administration to bring Federal relief, represented the fruition of their most essential hopes. Public housing, relief, a minimum wage, an end to child labor, old-age security, maximum hours, unemployment compensation, "these, then, were objectives a Republican Roosevelt wanted mightily to come back and work for," wrote Paul Kellogg. "They are objectives a Democratic Roosevelt has helped mightily to set in motion. These are objectives which social workers, close to the ground, have espoused for thirty years."[16]

Close to the ground; and so they were, encountering daily, at Henry Street or Greenwich House or Chicago Commons, the human casualties of a broken economy. As Clarke Chambers has shown, social workers kept progressive thought and action alive after World War I while other groups dissolved into individuals in search of rest or private satisfactions.[17] When the time came, the social work element rallied almost to a man behind the New Deal. "People must understand," announced Lillian Wald, "that President Roosevelt thinks as Jane Addams and Lillian D. Wald think." [18]

15. Clarke Chambers has compiled a lengthy list of those social work reformers who played important roles in the New Deal. See *Seedtime of Reform*, pp. 254-9.
16. Kellogg, *Proceedings*, National Conference of Social Work (1939) p. 14.
17. *Seedtime of Reform: American Social Service and Social Action, 1918-33* (Minneapolis: University of Minnesota Press, 1963).
18. Lillian Wald to Felix Warburg, July 24, 1936, Wald MSS. Robert Bremner agrees: "Without minimizing the importance of the social reforms inaugurated during the 1930's, it may be said that the measures then adopted were largely implementations, amplifications, and—in some instances—but partial fulfillments of the program of preventive social work formulated before World War I." *From the Depths*, p. 261. See also Irving Bernstein, *The Lean Years* (Boston: Houghton Mifflin, 1960), pp. 463-5, who describes how the testimony of social workers before the La Follette Subcommittee in 1931-32 brought the extent of unemployment before the eyes of the Congress and thus hastened the breakthrough to Federal relief.

In addition to social workers of a preventive turn of mind, the old progressives who stood with Roosevelt tended to derive disproportionately from the municipal reform sector of progressivism. The category "municipal reformer" lacks precision, of course, for men and women of many interests and outlooks located their activities in the American city: settlement workers, urban clergymen, interested citizens who served in municipal governments and citizen's committees, city planners, public health officials, housing reformers, and so on, many of them acting on several fronts at once. But let us, without proposing any permanent clarification, separate city-based progressives into two groups: on the one hand, those who took time off from private careers to campaign for the restoration of honesty or efficiency in government, or lower taxes, or an elevation of the moral life of the community; on the other, those who, briefly or permanently, took up paying jobs (inevitably low-paying) in city governments, planning commissions, regulatory or investigatory bodies, or in one of the public or private welfare agencies which dotted the poorer neighborhoods—people whose concern was not with honesty or morals but with such matters as housing, transportation, or health. If we may for the moment make these rough distinctions, then on the basis of this sample it can be said that the latter sort of municipal reformer was far more likely to support the New Deal than the former.

Of course, we could wish for more information on municipal progressives, especially more biographies that would tell us what became of them. Of the Ohio urban reformers mentioned in Hoyt L. Warner's study of Ohio progressivism, most who survived through 1936 joined or applauded Roosevelt.[19] One thinks here of Peter Witt, Fred Howe, Herbert Seely Bigelow, Henry T. Hunt, and the moderately sympathetic James Cox*. Newton Baker and Brand Whitlock, however, were conspicuous in their dislike of the New Deal. Perhaps close studies of surviving municipal reformers from other cities would show a similar result, with progressives like Edward A. Dickson of Los Angeles, a typical Good Government reformer, usually disliking the New Deal, and men like Raymond B. Fosdick of New York, much more deeply involved in city administration and in welfare and philanthropy, happy to see Roosevelt and Hopkins at work. Rexford Tugwell, in a recent article, has argued persuasively that the urban re-

19. *Progressivism in Ohio, 1897-1917* (Columbus: Ohio State University Press, 1964).

formers generally were among the first to see the inadequacy of "clean government" progressivism, and thinks that their municipal ownership schemes were an important intellectual start on the pilosophy which eventually informed the New Deal.[20] Tugwell cites at length those city reform groups and individuals who were ready for a more positive reform movement when Roosevelt was elected: Ickes and Merriam among the Chicago group, La Guardia and others from New York, William F. Ogburn, Roosevelt's uncle Frederic A. Delano, and the entire city planning movement. My sample of urban-reform progressives certainly does not contradict that judgment.

Clergymen who took up the social gospel and became prominent in the progressive movement, if this small sample is to be credited, generally did not lose their sympathy for the lower third. Charles Sheldon is here the exception, and Stephen S. Wise, Herbert Seely Bigelow, John Haynes Holmes, Bishop Francis McConnell, Charles Stelzle, and the clergyman turned social worker Graham Taylor are the rule.

The feature common to these reformers appears to have been contact with urban poverty, a contact which was no part of the sealed-off existence of the corporation lawyer (James R. Garfield, Amos Pinchot), or the politician in Washington (Carter Glass, Hiram Johnson, or Charles Evans Hughes). Social worker, urban clergyman, urban reformer, these were the progressive types most likely to accept gracefully the clumsy interferences of a liberal government.

Turning from social or occupational group traits to apparent characterological ones is an inter-disciplinary step which I take reluctantly, and only because the evidence of characterological

20. Tugwell, "The Sources of New Deal Reformism," *Ethics*, LXIV (July 1954), 249-74. As strong as Tugwell's argument is, two books by Roy Lubove encourage a caution about granting too much vision to the early urban reformers. His *Progressives and the Slums: Tenement House Reform in New York City, 1890-1917* (Pittsburgh: University of Pittsburgh Press, 1962) demonstrates that the restrictive law of 1901 and the zoning law of 1916 marked the limit to which they were willing to go for the slum dweller; they would not hear of public housing. In *Community Planning in the 1920's: The Contribution of the Regional Planning Association of America* (Pittsburgh: University of Pittsburgh Press, 1963), Lubove not only traces the New Deal debt to this creative group, but allows us to see that men like Clarence Stein and Charles Whitaker of the RPAA were by age and ethnic origin, to mention only two tests, not "progressives" at all.

regularity seems to demand some sort of exposition. The pro-New Dealers demonstrated certain traits that seemed to incline them toward acceptance of the New Deal, and we might denote two of them as Flexibility and Proletarian Pugnacity.

A man like William Gibbs McAdoo represents a type of progressive whose most prominent characteristic was a deep and instinctive mental flexibility, a disinclination to believe anything too firmly.[21] Traditional in matters such as dress and family life,

---

21. Others would be Finley Peter Dunne, Raymond B. Fosdick, Homer Folks, E. A. Ross, Mary Woolley, and Lillian Wald, to mention only those who most clearly fit this characterization. All were moderate to conservative in political opinion, but were preserved from alarm at Roosevelt's erratic path by (among other things) their great tolerance of new methods and ideas. This, plus an enduring sympathy to humanitarian projects, made them all comfortable in the New Deal camp.

I think Mary Simkhovitch was describing this sort of personality in her *Neighborhood: My Story of Greenwich House* (New York: W. W. Norton, 1938, pp. 100-101), when she distinguished between "reformers" and settlement workers. Unlike the reformers, she and her associates did not turn in the local criminals, and in politics, where she had strong feelings, she refused to condemn anyone, for to do so would require a moral judgment which was alien to her temperament. Fosdick's autobiography, *Chronicle of a Generation* (New York: Harper, 1958), is the handiest example of this pragmatic humanism at its most appealing.

McAdoo nonetheless followed a very flexible political and ideological course from the beginning of his career. He was always thought of as a very moderate progressive, and his record as lawyer-promoter, and later as Wilson's Secretary of the Treasury, was marked by a restless (and generally successful) search for solutions with no discernible political or economic theories to hamper him. He stood with the more radical progressives during the struggle to enact the Federal Reserve Act, for example, but was later to anger most of them by proposing to finance World War I by a regressive tax bill—and in this, as always, McAdoo was following a path unmarked by deep constitutional or social convictions. If anything, his economic ideas sounded very much like Theodore Roosevelt's New Nationalism, despite his long and easy association with Wilson. "I do not like ideas that are suspended in air," he wrote in his autobiography. "There is not much metaphysics in my temperament." His support of the entire New Deal, including the Court plan, was virtually forecast in *Crowded Years*, his 1931 autobiography. In its briefest form this forecast read: "I like movement and change." [22]

Reading McAdoo's story, or Fosdick's *Chronicle of a Generation*, is to meet a sort of restless intellect, disinclined to occupy the old fortified defensive philosophical positions, eager for movement, for forays into new terrain.

Fosdick wrote, "Generally speaking, our social operations need motive power rather than brakes, imaginative action rather than an excess of caution. . . . Man is instinctively conservative. . . . Each progressive spirit is opposed by 1,000 men appointed to guard the past. The least that the most timid of us can do is not to add the immense dead weight which nature drags along." [23]

---

23. *Chronicle of a Generation,* p. 291. Fosdick's extraordinarily productive career began with service under John Purroy Mitchell in New York (in the Division of Accounts, before Mitchell's mayoralty), and included social work, a brief career with the League of Nations, some legal work in New York, and the presidency of the Rockefeller Foundation. He thought the Court Plan "unfortunate" and the London Conference "disastrous," but was a warm supporter of the New Deal generally. He was one of those touched early and decisively by the settlement movement: "The emphasis in my thinking, I suspect," he wrote, "went back in part to Miss Wald and my days at Henry Street." (*Chronicle of a Generation,* p. 292.)

Even when such a man had been a moderate reformer, this cast of mind gave his progressivism a staying power and a final open-endedness which allowed it to blend nicely into the liberalism of the 1930's.

One other type of progressive seems to have had a strong predisposition to continuing the fight from Left-of-Center: the angry man. Virtually every reformer, at some time or another, uttered an angry rebuke of some selfish interest. Yet there were those whose progressivism consistently took the form of a battle against heavy odds, and it took a certain native pugnacity to elect to endure it for very long. Most of those who fought for more than a

22. (Boston: Houghton Mifflin, 1931), p. 44, p. 291.

few years were those who relished it, who gladly identified themselves as combatants against the wealthy and the comfortable. They saw reform as a chance for combat, and while some of them may have left the fray after World War I, they rarely stopped hoping for another chance to fight again. It is this sort of progressive who rejoiced when Franklin Roosevelt gave a man a chance to battle against the old enemies, wealth and economic privilege.

One thinks, primarily, of men like Francis Joseph Heney, the California cowboy-gunfighter turned lawyer, the man who smote Boss Ruef and the Union Pacific with relish and without fatigue; of Judge Ben Lindsey, a gentle little man who may have preferred not to be forever in conflict, but whose entire lifetime was consumed in a bitter running battle with Denver and Los Angeles conservatives, until he learned to take an almost sad joy in civic battles; Peter Witt, the vituperative Cleveland machinist turned progressive, who provided the tent-meeting brimstone for the reforms of Tom Johnson and Newton Baker; Herbert Seely Bigelow, the pugnacious Ohio preacher who was in the front trench for every reform from Bryanism to the Court Fight of 1937; the acidulous Harold Ickes, self-styled curmudgeon, for whom politics had always been a series of delicious fights, and who found in Roosevelt's Interior Department a position from which to continue harassing the tories. Reformers engaged in struggle almost by definition, but what I am suggesting here is that the more bellicose among them, those who really enjoyed the rough-and-tumble of a battle against the comfortable and the influential, tended to resume the fight on the Left in the 1930's.

There is a clue to this pugnacity in the career of the North Carolina editor Josephus Daniels, who deeply relished a good fight with the enemies of the people (or his own, and the two usually coincided), Joseph Morrison, in a recent study of Daniel's early career, records the young editor's almost instinctive dislike of those in established political or social positions. "Josephus Daniels was, above all, a fighter," Morrison writes, "and the moneyed interests had a way of putting him in a fighting mood." [24] The young Daniels had written to his mother in 1886, "They all hate me now—I mean the fellows who have been accustomed to rule through their money or blood—and treat me cleverly only because it wouldn't

24. *Josephus Daniels Says . . . : An Editor's Political Odyssey from Bryan to Wilson and F.D.R., 1894-1913* (Chapel Hill: University of North Carolina, 1962), p. 124.

pay them to do otherwise. . . . I hate 'em with as holy a hatred as is possible." [25]

While there may have been other reasons for this social animosity, an animosity which more than anything else put Daniels into politics on the reform or "outs" side and made him an instinctive democrat, a possible explanation lies in his birth, which without being exactly obscure was at least to the broad yeoman rather than the gentry class. The others I have mentioned—Heney, Lindsey, Witt, Bigelow, Ickes, and more, such as Charles Stelzle, whom I might have mentioned—came from that type of social situation, were born to families in lower-middle circumstances or worse, often to ruined gentry (as, to cite an intriguing example, was Tom Watson). Their lifelong animus against the rich must have derived in some part from that fact.[26]

---

26. The political type I am describing naturally gravitated to the most exposed flank, and while this was generally the Left flank, the Right often served the same purposes. In the progressive era he was necessarily a reformer of one variety or another; in the 1930's, while he might be a staunch New Dealer, engaged with his customary gusto in assaulting the rich, he might be found in equally ferocious combat against Big Government led by Franklin Roosevelt. In either case, he liked to think of himself as thoroughly outnumbered, nobly and grandly alone. The political interchangeability of this sort of personality may be observed in the careers of Hiram Johnson and Burton K. Wheeler, who were strong for Roosevelt and against the old business enemies until about 1936, and then equally outraged and formidable in combat against the New Deal. In both cases, they had been miserable as they crossed the Center and temporarily lost their sense of righteousness.

To support the New Deal did not require open pugnacity, as the adherence of men like George Foster Peabody certainly proves; but it seemed to help. And while there are men of this temperament who preferred to battle Roosevelt rather than the Tom Girdlers—and one thinks here of Carter Glass, or of Hiram Johnson in his second phase—most of them apparently elected to support Roosevelt and to turn their guns on familiar redoubts. It is true that a few who were born to a certain amount of hardship, men such as Mark Sullivan or Ellery Sedgwick, found that their plebeian birth and attendant political attitudes could both be

25. Ibid. p. 25.

surmounted as they moved into the comfortable classes, and they remind us again that class is only one component of those factors affecting political attitude, and an erratic one at that. But a goodly number who were born to the economically embattled classes seem to have picked up in early life not only a lifelong identity with the people, but a congenital suspicion of the well-off —a suspicion which somehow resisted the oils of personal success. However it managed to survive, the sturdy populism of Daniels and Witt and the others has been at the core of all Left-of-Center political movements, and constitutes the most tangible thread connecting William Jennings Bryan to Franklin Roosevelt, whose personalities and political movements were other-so dissimilar.

The autobiographies of these reformers, in the very titles, often reflect this view of life as unremitting combat: George Norris's *Fighting Liberal,* Oswald Garrison Villard's *Fighting Years,* Ickes's *Autobiography of a Curmudgeon.* Judge Ben Lindsey, in his autobiography, *The Dangerous Life,* entitled the chapter on why he had become a reformer "Why I Fought." Rabbi Stephen S. Wise, glad antagonist of complacency and injustice from early days in Oregon politics through the honor roll of reform struggles—the Triangle Shirtwaist fire and investigation, the NAACP, the Jimmy Walker ouster, the Tom Mooney case, and on until one can hardly list them all—thought of calling his autobiography *My Twenty* (later *Thirty,* then *Forty*) *Years' Battle in the Ministry.* He settled for *Challenging Years,* but found other ways and occasions to express the pugnacity so often associated with liberalism. At his seventy-fifth birthday dinner at the Hotel Astor in New York, the firm-jawed old man listed the accomplishments and disappointments of a lifetime full of causes, and then brought the assembly to its feet with a closing "I'll Fight! I'll Fight! I'll Fight!" [27]

Occasionally, the reasons for attachment to the New Deal were reasons of individual circumstances which are readily discernible. In the study of politics, the most obvious of these is the political

27. Carl H. Voss, *Rabbi and Minister: The Friendship of Stephen S. Wise and John Haynes Holmes* (Cleveland: World, 1964), p. 347. The sense of conflict, for Norris, was not confined to the title of his autobiography, *Fighting Liberal.* He used the word "struggle" eight times in two and one-half pages of his Introduction.

interest of an individual, and it is most potent when there is a personal career involved. In the 1930's, especially, to be a Democrat was to know that the handwriting was on the wall, and it spelled Vote Left.[28] The decision to stand with Roosevelt often

28. Most students of the career of Gifford Pinchot, including his recent biographer, M. Nelson McGeary, would cite him as an example of personal ambition consistently overriding all else. In his case the shove was to the Right, where his party's presidential nomination perhaps awaited. Ickes thought that Pinchot's ambition was really that of his wife (*The Secret Diary of Harold Ickes*, New York: Simon and Schuster, 1953, vol. II, p. 77), and Ellery Sedgwick was apparently driven into conservative circles largely by his wife, a Cabot. Max Eastman thought that Lincoln Steffens's final move to the Left was a result of his marriage to Ella Winter (see Daniel Aaron, *Writers on the Left*, New York: Harcourt, Brace, 1961, p. 130). Political attitude may therefore sometimes be prosaically and rather selfishly determined, but the real source of the primary drive may be someone else entirely.

coincided not only with the rhetoric and ideals of a progressive past, party loyalty, and so forth, but also with direct political advantage. In the case of man like Senator Joseph Taylor Robinson, for example, there is no reason to look further.

Robinson, the Arkansas senator who piloted much of the New Deal legislation through the upper house and who had a near-perfect voting record as a New Dealer, was a man who disliked much of the New Deal, but who found sufficient reasons to ignore his own preferences in the principle of party regularity and in his ambition for a Supreme Court seat. He must be set down as a progressive who supported the New Deal, but he confessed to Baruch what was not hidden from very many, that he found much of it "distasteful." "I think I am what the public generally terms conservative," Robinson said in the spring of 1937, even as he led the fight to expand the Court, and he could have said the same thing with equal justice in 1896 when he fought the Populists, or during the Wilson years when he was an unobtrusive moderate in the Senate.[29] In Robinson's case, New Deal support was largely a setting aside of personal political convictions, such as they were, rather than their logical fulfillment.

29. Quoted in Nevin E. Neal, "A Biography of Joseph T. Robinson," unpublished Ph.D. dissertation, University of Oklahoma, 1958, p. 472.

To a certain extent, all the old progressives who held elective office in Left-leaning constituencies must have been influenced to a more ardent New Dealism than might otherwise have been the case. The political pressures were obvious: a popular President and a popular program; a heightened party loyalty due to the long period out of office; the memory of recent penalties meted out to the party of Hoover when it could not agree upon effective action. The effect must have been felt to some degree by all of those in the Congress, and probably also by those whose careers were associated with presidential appointment, men such as Ickes, Daniels, Howe, Hunt, and Vincent.[30] In the end there is no way

---

30. This could account for Cordell Hull's restraint just as easily, and for Borah's ambivalent course. In both cases the effect of political pressure was to hold conservative men from standing further to the Right, as they were inclined to do. Such pressures could push the other way, of course, as in the case of Carter Glass. His Southern Democrat principles prevented him from bolting his party, although many thought he would. Yet his safe constituency in Virginia allowed his vigorous toryism close to full play in voting and in public remarks.

---

to measure the force of personal ambition in most cases, especially as it operated within the context of a popular administration, but it must be judged real in all cases, and decisive in some.

There are gentler forms of ambition, and personal as well as party loyalties in politics. Josephus Daniels comes to mind, or a less well-known Democrat, J. Lionberger Davis of St. Louis. Davis, wealthy banker and former Wilsonian, appears among those who were staunch New Dealers, and his correspondence with the President goes a long way toward explaining his attitude.[31] He adored Franklin Roosevelt, sent him affectionate letters of advice and an occasional Roosevelt-inspired poem, and took a deep pleasure in dropping in on the President when other business took him to Washington. His political advice, when he offered it, was invariably conservative: restrict TVA to providing a yardstick, rather than allow it to compete with private lines extensively (November 22, 1934); avoid the indictment of classes of men, especially the leading financial classes (September 15, 1937); raise political discourse above controversial material issues to the

31. The Davis–F.D.R. letters are in the Roosevelt Library at Hyde Park, PPF 186.

"higher and deeper things in life" (November 5, 1940). Davis had been opposed, as he wrote "Missy" LeHand, F.D.R.'s secretary, to the lopsided margin of 1934, to the Court Plan, the "Purge," and the Third Term.

Yet the Roosevelt charm (Roosevelt cordially answered every letter) and the obvious pleasure Davis felt in spending occasional evenings in the White House to "advise" the President kept the cautious St. Louis banker, whose real sympathies were with the principles of Brandeis and Wilson, in the unfamiliar company of more radical Americans who hailed the New Deal. Personal affection such as Davis felt for Roosevelt was a factor of deep importance in many instances where a progressive knew the President or his wife, and for men like Davis, Daniels, or George Foster Peabody, it was decisive.

With the mention of Josephus Daniels, we encounter one of a small group of the forty whose political course in the 1930's was so unlike other reformers of similar background and experience as to discourage those who hope to reduce the study of political behavior to a science.[32] One thinks of Daniels, Edward P. Costigan,

---

32. Regarding Daniels, in addition to the sort of pugnacity which he habitually directed against some established interest, and in addition to the force of personal loyalty to Roosevelt, party loyalty meant a great deal to him. For him, Democracy and democracy were perpetually yoked, and one could and should be devoted to both. This sort of ironclad loyalty to the party, its nominee and program had been since the Civil War the most distinctive feature of Southern politics; this, almost without anything else, would probably have held Daniels to the New Deal. Still, it is hard to account for his unfeigned enthusiasm. He was an evangelical, a dry, and rather thoroughly provincial—a man, in fact, very much like Bryan. In the end, his ardent New Dealism is astonishing.

He does not explain himself at all in his rambling autobiography. The volume on the New Deal period, *Shirtsleeve Diplomat* (Chapel Hill: University of North Carolina Press ,1947) deals almost entirely with Mexico. E. David Cronon, "A Southern Progressive Looks at the New Deal," *Journal of Southern History*, XXIV (May 1958), 151-76, is a competent report based largely on the Daniels papers in the Library of Congress, but Daniels remains an inviting enigma. (Joseph L. Morrison's *Small-d Democrat: A Biography of Josephus Daniels* (Chapel

Hill: University of North Carolina Press, 1966) appeared too
late to be consulted.)

Francis E. McGovern, perhaps George Foster Peabody, and certainly George Norris. Four of them were from essentially rural
constituencies or areas, where New Deal liberalism was not originally nurtured and where it was not particularly strong. None of
the five had much contact with the lower classes in an urban environment. Three were Republicans, and none had been more
than a moderate Good Government reformer in the progressive
era. Yet all seemed to grow more radical as they grew older, and
in them progressivism does indeed become a bridge, through the
evolution of its program and in the minds of living men, to the
New Deal.

It is Norris who is probably the most puzzling figure among
those whose reform impulse and personality was strong and consistent. There seems little in his youth to have made him a reformer, unless plain honesty was enough; there seemed little in
his progressive career to point toward the depth and persistence
his liberalism was to take on.[33] He came late to reform, and did
not push for the more advanced social justice measures of the
progressive period. He lived almost isolated in his Washington
apartment, and in provincial McCook, Nebraska, and cannot
have intimately known of America's industrial and urban casualties. Yet when new and radical measures were called for in the
second reform period of his life, Norris could be counted upon to
support them.

Liberalism, as the New Dealers practiced it, required adventures in Federal regulation and planning, adventures in class politics and novel economics, that postdated progressivism and
found most progressives reluctant to go along. For those reformers
who went beyond the early policies, there were usually certain

---

33. Norris's autobiography, *Fighting Liberal*, offers little insight into the
sources of his liberalism, beyond the suggestion that a rural judge in Nebraska in the 1890's must have seen some severe examples of what weather
and depression could do to men. But he did not become a reformer at that
time. Richard Lowitt's *George W. Norris: The Making of a Progressive,
1861-1912* (Syracuse: Syracuse University Press, 1963) is the best biography
to date, but even Lowitt fails to describe Norris's political motivation satisfactorily. He did not get any closer to the enigma in his article, "The Making
of an Insurgent," *Mid-America*, XLII (April 1960), 105-15, although he was
able to pinpoint Norris's conversion as taking place during the Cannon
controversy (1908-10).

visible reasons, such as a deep commitment to the combat with wealth, an unusual flexibility of mind, political ambition, or party and personal loyalties. But the very presence among the advanced liberals in the 1930's of George Norris of Nebraska— and a few others, such as Costigan and Daniels—for whom almost all the signs pointed the other way, is enough to reaffirm the mystery of political belief, and the irreducible diversity of reform membership.

I V

I should like to mention, finally, a pair of essentially conservative men who wound up with the New Deal for what I take to be an absence of reasonable alternatives—a circumstance which must have affected all of the others to some degree, but which seems particularly apparent with the academic thinkers John Rogers Commons and Frank William Taussig.

Reflect that one who was not for Roosevelt could only be for Landon and the party of Hooverism unrepentant, and it is obvious that those of liberal inclination who were still interested in national politics at all had nowhere else to go but Roosevelt. By the circumstance of two-party politics and the behavior of the Republican party, some who would have preferred many and serious changes in the New Deal were forced, in the end and under the circumstances, to line up with Roosevelt. They ought to be noticed, so that the eventual progressive support for the New Deal can be recognized for what it was, part enthusiasm, part personal advantage, and part the reluctant admission of lack of decent alternatives.

This sort of uneasy adherence to the New Deal seems to describe especially well the reaction of Commons and Taussig. "I concede to my radical friends," Commons wrote in his autobiography, "that my trade union philosophy always made me a conservative." [34] It is easy to agree. Commons was essentially a Samuel Gompers man, full of respect for capitalists and capitalism, interested to see harmony brought to the country through labor gains won at the bargaining table, not through some alteration of the system in the direction of Federal intervention. To labor and management alike he had extolled compromise, co-operation, and gradualism, being certain that "it is not revolutions and strikes

34. *Myself* (New York: Macmillan, 1934), p. 73.

that we want, but collective bargaining on something like an organized equilibrium of equality." [35]

There was little of the radical in Commons. He disliked and feared the great cities ("New York City . . . seemed to me wholly un-American"), admired businessmen, and deplored class consciousness. Rightly regarded as an important intellectual precursor to the New Deal because of his piecemeal, pragmatic approach to industrial problems, Commons was nonetheless no friend of powerful government. Yet he had fought all his life for a more flexible approach to the problems of industrial labor than the dogmatic laissez-faire of the past, and when the New Deal came, he put aside an early suspicion of it and was on record as a supporter by 1935.[36]

What is fairly clear is that Commons saw in the New Deal enough of that pragmatism which had always been his intellectual trademark to enable him to hope for its success, even though in many ways it went far beyond what he would have wished. But for a man who had long been a friend of labor and a friend to those departures from laissez-faire (usually at the state level) sufficient to guarantee a minumum subsistence, an acceptable alternative to the New Deal was never offered. The New Deal at least (and at last) was movement, and movement aimed at helping the lower income groups. Too old to struggle for more acceptable reforms, doubtless flattered by being credited with a sort of New Deal parentage, Commons threw in with the New Deal, despite what must have appeared to him, as to William Green and all those in the Gompers tradition, as heresies.

Frank W. Taussig published, in the *Yale Review* for March 1934, a near-perfect statement of this sort of reluctant liberalism.[37] He said in essence that the end of laissez-faire was long overdue,

35. Ibid. p. 73.
36. The best example of his early coolness is his autobiography, *Myself*, published in 1934. The final acceptance was expressed in Commons, "The New Deal and the Teaching of Economics," *American Economic Review*, XXV (March 1935), 11-15, and Commons, "Communism and Collective Democracy," *American Economic Review*, XXV (June 1935), 212-23. An economist who recognized the essential conservatism of Commons is W. F. Kennedy, "John R. Commons, Conservative Reformer," *Western Economic Journal*, I (Fall 1962), 29-42; for a rebuttal, see Lafayette G. Harter, "John R. Commons: Conservative or Liberal?," *Western Economic Journal*, I (Summer 1963), 226-32.
37. Taussig, "Wanted, Consumers," *Yale Review*, XXIII (March 1934), 443-7.

and that the New Deal was to be congratulated and supported for having accomplished it. Yet he added, with considerable feeling, that the New Deal had gone far enough. "We must have a care not to drift in the direction of the German cartels. . . . Government must relax its hold." As wise as it had been to curb the excesses of business, government must not, by "dangerous talk, . . . mistakes . . . ineptitude . . . frothy talk," damage the only real hope of recovery—business confidence.[38]

This was conservative language, yet Taussig favored the New Deal in the end, overriding deep doubts about growing Federal power and the revolutionary mood in Washington.[39] When Commons and Taussig by the end of the first term came around to support the administration, the decision must be attributed in part to the absence of any alternative which would promise the more moderate reforms they had urged for so long.

V

Support the New Deal as they did, Commons and Taussig were not asked to help shape it, and it would be hard to argue that this was simply because of their age. In fact, this is true of almost all the old progressives who offered their approval and help. The New Deal not only did not carry with it the main body of the surviving progressives, but made surprisingly little use, intellectually, of those it did attract. The politicians of the progressive period who still sat in the Congress provided votes, but almost no original ideas. The writers who had armed the earlier reformers were either silenced, like Finley Peter Dunne, or, like Gus Myers, were saying the old things over again with less effect.[40] State re-

---

40. Dunne had little to say during the New Deal—indeed, after the War—and explained it by saying that life was too dull before 1929, and after that, too grim. Despite a mid-1920's dalliance with Payne Whitney and other wealthy Republicans, Dunne was back with the party of his youth by 1933. According to his son, he favored "the great bulk of Roosevelt's economic and social reforms," and praised F.D.R. for his enemies. See Philip Dunne (ed.), *Mr. Dooley Remembers* (Boston: Little, Brown, 1963), p. 111.

---

38. Ibid. p. 446.
39. Letter from Helen B. Taussig to the author, November 10, 1964.

formers who had battled political machines and the railroads had
finished their game, and could only lend moral support; and here
one thinks of John R. Haynes, Francis Heney, Francis McGovern,
Rudolph Spreckels, and John Burke. City reformers like Witt,
Howe, Fosdick, Hunt, and Bigelow, even where still militant and
ready to help, brought Roosevelt few suggestions he could use.[41]

---

41. Howe's situation is instructive. Hired to protect the consumer from inside the AAA (he was Consumer's Counsel), his
every effort handicapped an agency established to raise farm
prices. Such absurditites did not embarrass the New Deal, but
this one indicated how the best impulses and the finest veterans of progressivism might find themselves of no help to the
new order.

There was little more for the settlement house people to com-
municate, beyond the testimony that people suffered. Ministers
like Bishop McConnell and Stephen Wise could only urge more
compassion expressed through public intervention. Norman
Hapgood could only carry to Roosevelt the admonitions of Justice Brandeis, and that influence was, under the circumstances,
almost entirely negative.

In fact, nothing was more revealing of the tremendous gulf between the goals of many of the old progressives and the real world
of the 1930's than the thrust of the Brandeisian philosophy during the New Deal. The radicalism of Brandeis had always been at
bottom the fierce localism of Jefferson, humanized (as it was not
in "Jeffersonians" like James A. Reed or Albert Jay Nock*) by
deep sympathies with the unfortunate. Only that sympathy, along
with a friendship with Roosevelt and other close personal connections inside the administration, kept his dislike of centralization
and his sense of human limitations from setting him solidly
against the New Deal. As it was, Brandeis disliked more of it than
is generally acknowledged.[42] Part ascetic and part Enlightenment

---

42. Chapter 39 of Alpheus T. Mason's *Brandeis: A Free Man's
Life* (New York: Viking, 1946) presents a balance sheet on
Brandeis and the New Deal. "Measured statistically," Mason
writes, "Justice Brandeis was a New Dealer." (Mason, *Brandeis*, p. 621) But Mason makes it clear that measured less
coldly, the Justice had deep and frequent reservations.
    Alfred Lief has preserved a comment by Brandeis which re-
cent history has converted into a bitter demonstration of the

rapid obsolescence of reform ideas: "The United States is too
big to be a force for good; whatever we do is bound to be
harmful. . . . The United States should go back to the federation idea, letting each state evolve a policy and develop itself.
There are enough good men in Alabama, for example, to make
Alabama a good state." (Quoted in Lief, *The Brandeis Guide
to the Modern World*, Boston; Little, Brown, 1941, p. 70.)

philosopher, Brandeis stood for principles which, while they assisted in the construction of New Deal antitrust, tax, and securities regulation laws, were out of tune with the spirit of the New
Deal. The life of the New Deal depended upon the decision of
the Richard Neubergers, Tommy Corcorans and Felix Frank-
furters to *ignore* the Brandeisian advice to go home to the prov-
inces and seek their ends through a combination of state action
and the spread of a sense of social responsibility. For all those
progressives who were Brandeisians, and there were many, their
advice to Roosevelt could only be destructive: dismantle, decen-
tralize, localize.

None of this is intended to disparage the struggles and achievements of their earlier days, but only to recognize that the New
Deal had different problems, as others have pointed out, and that
this meant that it would require different solutions. Since this
was the case, the old reformers were generally able to offer only
encouragement, leaving those new solutions to other minds.

There were important exceptions, of course, such as Senators
Norris and Costigan, who were fertile of ideas regarding relief,
a more liberal labor policy, and so on. Another exception would
be those in social work whose efforts were promotional and
whose social work was of the preventive cast: New York's Homer
Folks, John B. Andrews and the American Association for Labor
Legislation,[43] or the editor of *Survey*, Paul Kellogg.[44] National so-

43. The contribution of this organization is surveyed in Lloyd F. Pierce,
"The Activities of the American Association for Labor Legislation in Behalf
of Social Security and Protective Labor Legislation," unpublished Ph.D.
dissertation, University of Wisconsin, 1953. In view of the obstacles and
Andrews's resources, the effect of the AALL was prodigious.

44. Kellogg's journals, *Survey* and *Survey Graphic*, with the "Survey Associates" who supported them, seem to have been a recognized source of
pressure on Roosevelt and the Congress. Roosevelt told David Lilienthal, half
humorously, that he couldn't just fire Arthur E. Morgan because "the *Survey
Graphic* group will feel that they have been let down." (Quoted in Lilienthal,
The Journals of David E. Lilienthal: The TVA Years, 1939-45, New York:
Harper and Row, 1965, p. 62.)

cial insurance owes as much to these social work progressives, and others like them who started work in the progressive period, as it does to the European example or to the New Dealers who discovered the need for it in the 1930's. Another area of liberal concern, civil liberties, benefited from the unwavering support of such progressives as Harold Ickes, E. A. Ross, and Charles Edward Russell.

But when the exceptions are granted, the pattern is fairly clear. The chief contributions of surviving progressives to the political life of the 1930's took the form of objections to reform, and even among those who approved of the New Deal there were few who found any way to make the intellectual product of the progressive years come to bear fruitfully upon the problems which defined the New Deal.

In large part, of course, this was because nothing in their education and experience had prepared them for the years after 1929. But it was also in part a result of a stubborn Protestant streak in their mental make-up, which inclined them to turn from public or mass action to an emphasis upon private solutions through the bracing of character. Despite the fact that it is now generally recognized that the historic mission of progressivism was to advance collective solutions to social problems, many of the old progressives in the 1930's fell back upon individual salvation—generally through spiritual regeneration (as with John Mandt Nelson or Carl Vrooman) or thrift and hard work. Ida Tarbell, at the end of her life, reflected as follows on ways to make the world better: "I see no more promising path than each person sticking to the work which comes his way. . . . If the need at the moment is digging a ditch or washing the dishes, that is the greatest thing in the world for the moment. . . . It is by following this natural path that new and broader roads open to us." [45]

Occasionally an old progressive would confess his intellectual helplessness. George Norris, who kept up the fight where he had begun it, in the Congress, never claimed to know what would bring the national recovery everyone sought. When asked, on February 12, 1936, what Lincoln would do, he replied: "Lincoln would be just like me. He wouldn't know what the hell to do." [46] But a large number could not endure those years of crisis without some conviction as to what ought to be done. Often, like Miss

45. Ida Tarbell, *All In the Day's Work,* pp. 404-5.
46. Richard L. Neuberger and Stephen B. Kahn, *Integrity: The Life of George W. Norris* (New York: Vanguard, 1937), p. 359.

Tarbell, they returned to familiar remedies. Herbert Seely Bigelow was an ardent New Deal Congressman during four of the most important years of the Roosevelt-led effort to reform and revive America, yet he was ultimately to decide that none of it had done any good, and he reverted to a faith in the Single Tax, which was just about where he had started in the 1890's in Ohio.[47] Charles Stelzle's organizing and promotional talents were briefly used through the Good Neighbor League to drum up support for Roosevelt's re-election in 1936 and later for his post-election program, but the poverty of much progressive thought is nowhere more evident than in the "message" this old social gospel veteran brought to his favorite audience—the laboring man—during the late 1930's. He wrote a labor column under the auspices of the Good Neighbor League from 1937 to 1940, and it appeared in the labor press as well as in a few daily newspapers. The advice he gave came down, in the end, to a series of affirmations of striking uselessness. They are all found in the statement of his social philosophy which makes up Chapter VI of his autobiography: "I believe in my job," "I believe in the home," learn a word a day, say hello to fellow workers, don't worry about being over forty, and so forth.[48] Stelzle, perhaps, represents the extreme in moral fortification combined with intellectual bankruptcy, but he was still able to make some contribution to the electoral strength of the New Deal. He and all the other progressives who adhered to the New Deal provided living evidence that the administration had assumed the moral burden of improvement and compassion that had been the heart of the earlier reform movement. But when it came to the business cycle, to the theory and practice of Federal policies sufficient to secure full employment and a rising standard of living, which was the real business of the New Deal, there was little that they could do to help.[49]

---

49. In at least one instance, the best virtues of the progressive character did not help the New Deal, and may have damaged it. In Harold Ickes, Roosevelt had all the unflinching honesty

47. U.S., *Congressional Record*, 75th Cong., 1st Sees., 1937, LXXXI, Part 10, pp. 2300-2301.

48. These remarks appear in Chapter VI of Stelzle's unpublished draft of his revised autobiography, entitled "Seven Times Ten" and written sometime in the 1930's. It may be found in the Stelzle MSS, Columbia University, along with a complete file of the labor column, "I Speak To Labor." See also Stelzle, *A Son of the Bowery: The Life Story of an East Side American* (New York: George Doran, 1926).

and dedication to efficiency in public service which were characteristic of the best of progressive politics. Yet when it was given to Ickes to direct a major part of Federal spending through PWA, the very virtues he brought to disbursing and planning so slowed the flow of Federal money that they helped ruin the possibility of recovery through Keynesian policies.

One is struck by many things common to this group of progressives, despite their heterogeneity of background and interest—common factors of education and reform experience, of temperament, of the circumstance in which their fading political hopes were set. I have tried to discuss the bearing of these factors, common or unique, that impelled them to adopt the New Deal as their own, in spite of features alien to the progressive experience. The New Deal went forward buoyantly, for the most part, full of the confidence appropriate to young men and new beginnings, a confidence which was the core of Roosevelt's personality and the key to the successes he enjoyed. Oddly enough, despite the usual exceptions, the old progressives seem to have been the most pessimistic, the saddest of the liberals.

Some of this was a residue of the disappointments of the later Wilson years, and much was due to the uncertainty of both ends and means in the 1930's—an uncertainty they had not known in the great days of prewar reform. Norris was gloomy to the end, Commons was confused, Joe Robinson doubting in secret, Peter Dunne was unable to write. Even Ickes, who rarely looked back, reflected sadly in 1937 during the Court fight that all the old progressives had gone but himself and Charles Merriam*.

"Whew! Poor me!," John R. Commons summarized for a goodly number of them, "I am not in it"—and in these words reported that less of him was a part of the New Deal, less of any of them, than has been claimed by admirers of both periods of reform.[50] Yet for those, like Commons, who finally decided to be for the New Deal, it was enough that the fight was against the old antagonists—wealth without social responsibility, hardship, unequal opportunity. Accepting this last chance at reform, they joined in slightly uneasy alliance with the new liberalism.

50. Commons, *Myself,* p. 74.

IV

The Culmination of Progressivism:
III   Liberalism Is Not Enough

> We stand in the presence of a revolution . . . whereby
> America will insist upon recovering in practice those ideals
> which she has always professed. . . . Some radical changes
> we must make in our law and practice. Some reconstructions
> we must push forward, for which a new age and new circum-
> stances impose upon us.
>
> WOODROW WILSON

The range of progressive political opinion was always rather
broad, and while this is generally admitted by commentators on
progressivism before they begin to speak of the average or typical
attitude, the effect is to obscure the edges. One could generalize
that the average progressive was a conservative reformer, anxious
to hurry certain reforms—broader exercise of the franchise, governmental regulation of business, and so on—before unchecked
forces altered the system in unacceptable ways. But this persuasion shaded, to the Right, into "reforms" of the gentlest kind,
amounting to little more than conspicious rectitude—and bringing conservative men like Bainbridge Colby or Carter Glass or
James A. Reed into the progressive penumbra.

There were also those who were deeply radical. While historians have sometimes given the impression that the radicals within
the progressive movement were greater in number and influence
than they really were, progressivism did have what Theodore
Roosevelt once called the "lunatic fringe." [1] These were men and
women who, despite their middle class origins and generally favorable personal prospects, advocated a shift of wealth and power
in the direction of the lower classes. Whatever the reasons, be
they rooted in religion or secular ethics or personal psychology,

1. An example of the other extreme, that of ignoring the truly radical reformers completely, is Gabriel Kolko, *The Triumph of Conservatism: A Reinterpretation of American History, 1900-16* (Glencoe: The Free Press, 1963).

these reformers did not identify with the interests, at least the material ones, of their own class. Inevitably, some of these men and women became interested in alternative social systems, and because of them the progressive movement spilled over, on its Left edge, into socialism.

Contemporaneous, progressivism and socialism both were dissatisfied with things as they were, and it has always been quite difficult to define the boundary between them. Classically, progressivism was middle class and capitalistic, and socialism, with its working class base and its anti-capitalistic ideology, would seem to have been another thing entirely. But socialist leadership was predominantly middle class in origin if not in outlook, and many men and women moved back and forth between the two movements.[2] A recent study estimated that 25 per cent of the reformers mentioned in W. D. P. Bliss's *Encyclopedia of Social Reforms* (considering Americans only) were socialists, and it is clear that Bliss, himself a Christian Socialist, thought of turn-of-the-century reform as being deeply involved with socialist programs and sympathies.[3]

Even if Bliss's selection exaggerated the number of socialists among reformers (the word "progressive" was not then popular), a good many men of middle class circumstances and background became interested in socialism, although their reform energies were generally channeled into typical progressive activities rather than Socialist party politics. In the present sample of 168 progressive survivors, at least 19 had been interested in socialism, most of them sufficiently interested to join some local club, study group, or even the party.[4] When the New Deal arrived, with its refusal to make fundamental economic and social changes and its occasional foot-dragging in the areas of adequate relief, banking re-

2. For a class study of Socialist leadership, see David Shannon, "The Socialist Party Before World War I: An Analysis," *Mississippi Valley Historical Review*, XXXVIII (December 1951), 279-88.
3. Henry Silverman, "American Social Reformers in the Late Nineteenth and Early Twentieth Centuries," unpublished Ph.D. dissertation, University of Pennsylvania, 1963.
4. There may, of course, have been more, but I am sure of the following: Jane Addams, Ray Stannard Baker, George Creel, John Dewey, Finley Peter Dunne, Max Eastman, Richard T. Ely, William James Ghent, John Haynes Holmes, Robert Hunter, Walter Lippmann, Scott Nearing, Joseph Medill Patterson, Ernest Poole, Charles Edward Russell, Upton Sinclair, Mark Sullivan, John Spargo, and William English Walling.

form, and the like, there were some old progressives who criticized it for not going far enough.

Among those who were on the Left edge of reform in the 1920's, who demanded greater welfare and regulatory measures within a capitalistic framework, are some of the familiar names of the progressive generation. Oswald Garrison Villard was critical of the early New Deal because it did less than enough for society's downtrodden, and he used the pages of the *Nation* to urge greater generosity to the poor and greater animosity toward the irresponsible rich.[5] The Cincinnati reformer Herbert Seely Bige-

5. Villard was increasingly conservative after 1936, winding up after the war somewhere between Taft and Dewey. He, along with several others, was in intellectual transit during those years, and can hardly be categorized. Max Eastman and Robert Hunter entered the decade as socialists, but both were over on the Right by 1940; as with Villard, the process remains obscure. Another socialist, John Spargo, became a conservative Republican in the early 1920's, and his behavior in the 1930's was consistent with that affiliation (See Ronald Radosh, "John Spargo and Wilson's Russian Policy, 1920," *Journal of American History*, LII (December 1965), 548-65, and a perceptive Ph.D. dissertation by Gerald Friedberg, "John Spargo and the American Socialist Party," Harvard, 1964). Yet another, Ernest Poole, had retreated to the White Mountains and pretty much given up on politics. He was still sufficiently interested in the urban lower classes to live briefly in the Bowery during the Depression, blamed "the system" as of old, and found that "much of the New Deal made a strong appeal to me." But at the same time he worried about the debt, the concentration of power, bureaucracy, and the sit-downs. See his autobiography, *The Bridge: My Own Story* (New York: Macmillan, 1940), which no one interested in the reform impulse should miss.

low was a no-holds-barred liberal in Congress, resembling very much the better known Maury Maverick. Bishop Francis J. McConnell was somewhere on the radical end of the social gospel spectrum, although his deep dislike of competition never quite became socialism, and he appears to have been generally content with Roosevelt.[6] Senator Edward P. Costigan had undergone a

6. In his *Christianity and Coercion* (New York: Cokesbury, 1933) McConnell predicted that "the control of industry will more and more pass to society as a whole," went on to demand old age and unemployment insurance, and hinted that dictatorship and democracy were not necessarily antithetical.

gradual evolution to the Left in the 1920's and early 1930's, had switched to the Democratic party by 1930, and was a leading advocate of government spending and planning in social welfare areas.[7] John Haynes Holmes, pastor of the Community Church in

7. Costigan is a perfect example of the progressive as bridge to the New Deal, but only a select few accomplished it. He began as a model Good Government progressive as a young lawyer (and Republican) in Denver, fighting the saloons and a corrupt city council. He bolted to Roosevelt in 1912, but liked Wilson, and was appointed to the Tariff Commission in 1917. Elected to the Senate as a Democrat in 1930, he was, with Wagner and Norris, one of the steadiest congressional advocates of welfare legislation until a stroke cut short his career in 1936. See Fred Greenbaum, "Edward P. Costigan: Study of a Progressive," unpublished Ph.D. dissertation, University of Colorado, 1962.

New York, was for half a century a "letterhead liberal." He helped to found the NAACP and the ACLU, opposed the first World War, joined the Committee of Forty-Eight in 1919, supported La Follette in 1924, defended Sacco and Vanzetti, fought Jimmy Walker in 1929-30, and admired Gandhi above all men.[8] Holmes could be counted on to side with the poor and the criminal, and to vent his active social conscience from the pulpit or, as in the case of the Passaic strike, in the streets. Yet Holmes, like the others I have mentioned, preferred to mix praise with criticism in taking his stance toward the New Deal, and was never driven to demand a solution beyond its pragmatic limits.[9]

9. A letter from Holmes to Charles Stelzle, May 12, 1936, found in the Good Neighbor League file at Hyde Park (PPF 3435), suggests otherwise: "I think the net result of whatever he [F.D.R.] may be doing is to bolster up the old capitalistic system," Holmes wrote, and added, "I am moving more and more to the Left on these social questions." Nevertheless, I do not

He was a strong and early supporter of social security (see his *By the Way: An Autobiography*, New York: Abingdon-Cokesbury, 1952), and urged a greater concern for the poor (see his debate with Arthur Hyde, *Forum*, XCIV (November 1935), 267-71).
8. See Holmes, *I Speak for Myself: The Autobiography of John Haynes Holmes* (New York: Harper, 1959), and Carl Hermann Voss, *Rabbi and Minister: The Friendship of Stephen S. Wise and John Haynes Holmes* (Cleveland: World, 1964), as well as the newspaper reports of Holmes's sermons during the period (*The New York Times*, Mondays, 1933-38).

believe that Holmes ever became convinced that socialism was the answer. In fact the large collection of Holmes letters in the Villard MSS at Harvard indicate that Holmes did not know what the answer to depression and war might be—only that he hated both, and was almost sick with anxiety after 1938. He opposed the Court Plan in 1937, but many old progressives did, and the real break with Roosevelt in Holmes's case came, interestingly enough, over collective security, not over domestic policy.

Villard, Bigelow, McConnell, Costigan, Holmes, these were some of the old progressives who tried to push Roosevelt further in the direction of social justice. The most reliable roster of those for whom the New Deal—or at least the early New Deal—was too conservative, is those who signed the joint statement presented by the "Committee of '76" to the President in April of 1934. The statement, read by Edward T. Devine after opening remarks by Villard, called for "a more ideal economic order . . . in which the private profit motive will be subordinated to the general welfare so that the few privileged shall cease to enrich themselves at the expense of the many," and for greater consumer and labor protection under NRA. The statement was signed by 153 persons, among them Costigan, Devine, Dewey, Holmes, Paul Kellogg, Owen R. Lovejoy, McConnell, E. A. Ross, Villard, Merle D. Vincent, and Stephen S. Wise.[10] These progressives of the older movement, along with Jane Addams (who died in 1935). Fred Howe, and one or two others, constitute that group of surviving reformers whose occasional unhappiness with the New Deal derived from its unwillingness, in places, to be radical enough.

I I

Five progressives, at least, repudiated the entire New Deal and hoped for an overthrow of capitalism. They were John Dewey, Scott Nearing, Charles Edward Russell, Upton Sinclair and Lincoln Steffens; four were socialists, and Steffens was, in sympathy if not in party membership, a communist.

John Dewey became a reformer before the beginning of the century, and he was one of those—Charles Beard, Richard Ely, E. A. Ross, Thorstein Veblen, Lester Frank Ward—who served as tutors to their generation. Dewey's emphasis upon the concrete,

10. The statement may be found in the Villard MSS, Harvard University.

his refusal to be content with previously accepted truths, his belief in rational control of society's affairs—these, added to a basic humanitarianism, made Dewey one of the primary mentors of reformers from the 1890's forward. Such attitudes of mind, variously labeled pragmatism or instrumentalism, found favor with many who were in a reformist mood, and came to seem the essence of the progressive attitude. But by 1929 this prototype reformer and philosopher of progressivism had made a turning, and now translated liberal reform to mean democratic socialism.

In the year of the Crash, Dewey published *Individualism Old and New,* and founded the League for Independent Political Action with Paul Douglas. In both instances, Dewey was expressing the matured belief that further progress must come through conversion to a new economic system. When he published *Liberalism and Social Action* in 1935, it was clear—as it had been to those who followed his thought in occasional articles for *The People's Lobby Bulletin* or *Common Sense* or *Nation*—that his conversion to socialism was no temporary thing. He supported in 1936 the man he had supported before Franklin Roosevelt offered an attractive liberal alternative—Norman Thomas.

What theoretical reasoning predicted, experience had confirmed: Capitalism, whether of Hooverian or New Deal design, would not work. Liberal ends, Dewey wrote in 1935, "can now be achieved *only* by reversal of the means to which early liberalism was committed. Organized social planning . . . is now the sole method of social action." [11] He did not mean the half-hearted planning of the New Deal, which he stigmatized as "coercion, intimidation, suppression and organized ballyhoo." [12] Dewey was capable of a preliminary kind word for the New Deal, but soon settled into a conviction that it would not accomplish what its admirers hoped:

"For the gulf between what the actual situation makes possible and the actual state itself is so great that it cannot be bridged by piecemeal policies undertaken *ad hoc.* The process of producing the changes will be, in any case, a gradual one. But 'reforms' that deal now with this abuse and now with that without having a

11. Dewey, *Liberalism and Social Action* (New York: G. P. Putnam's Sons, 1935), p. 55.
12. Dewey, "Imperative Need: A New Radical Party," in Alfred M. Bingham and Selden Rodman (eds.), *Challenge to the New Deal* (New York: Falcon Press, 1934), p. 273.

social goal based upon an inclusive plan, differ entirely from effort at re-forming, in its literal sense, the institutional scheme of things. . . . Today any liberalism which is not also radicalism is irrelevant and doomed." [13]

Arthur Schlesinger, Jr., has argued that Dewey as socialist was false to that pragmatic, experimental and un-dogmatic cast of mind which he more than anyone else had made so widely effective. Dewey was impatient with such criticism, which assumed that the New Deal was truly experimental, and that the experimental method was hostile to any firm ideas—for example to the solid conviction Dewey now held that liberty could be advanced only by public ownership of the means of production. The New Deal, Deweyian in its irreverence and its taste for action, was for him insufficiently rational, and he argued in the 1930's for social action guided by some sort of coherent social hypothesis.[14] Here again, from the hand of an old progressive, an indictment of the New Deal as insufficiently clarified in the minds of its authors.

Dewey operated still as the great pragmatist. He would not spell out the steps by which the new "social control of economic forces" was to be implemented or sustained, insisting that "it is no part of my task to outline in detail a program for renascent liberalism." [15] And even as he insisted upon a social alteration which sounded like old European dogma to many, he prepared the way, as he had always done, by asking men to give up an old social value (individualism as individual striving) for a new one (true individualism through collective effort).[16] In Dewey the old progressivism had come around at last to an understanding that the sort of America it wished could not be built under capitalism. "In short," he summed up the history of one wing of American reform, "liberalism must now become radical." [17]

13. *Liberalism and Social Action*, p. 62.
14. For a good brief statement of this idea, see the remarks by Dewey quoted by his daughters in the biographical sketch found in Paul A. Schilpp (ed.), *The Philosophy of John Dewey* (New York: Tudor, 1939).
15. *Liberalism and Social Action*, p. 91.
16. This was the argument of his *Individualism Old and New* (New York: Minton, Balch, 1930).
17. *Liberalism and Social Action*, p. 62. Dewey's political thought in the 1930's may also be followed in *The People's Lobby Bulletin* during these years. For a convenient guide to Dewey's work, see M. H. Thomas, *John Dewey: A Centennial Bibliography* (Chicago: University of Chicago Press, 1962). Despite Dewey's political position in the 1930's, the pragmatism associated with his name might occasionally lead to other political conclusions.

Far from being drab and monolithic, the socialist persuasion has harbored a wonderful array of deviationists. Scott Nearing's brand of socialism began at the common point, rejection of the capitalist order, but immersed itself at once in certain preferences which Dewey would have found unthinkable. Dewey began by assuming industrialization and centralization; Nearing began by rejecting them. His socialism thus concealed beneath the rhetoric of the coming class struggle and resultant worker's society a core of reaction that stamped him as a spiritual kinsman of Ralph Borsodi and the Southern Agrarians.

Born near Philadelphia and educated at Temple University and the University of Pennsylvania (Ph.D., 1909), Nearing was an influential teacher at the Wharton School and later at the Rand School in New York. His early interest in social reform led him to join the Pennsylvania Child Labor Committee, where gradualism naturally prevailed. In 1915, under the pressures of the war, he joined the Socialist party. For fifty years he has kept up a steady but little heeded criticism of American capitalism.

In many respects Nearing is an "average" socialist. In a century of war he has been always a pacifist. For the "preservation and restoration of popular government" he has always demanded "the socialization of the means of production." [18] Although not much interested in the New Deal, he described it as "ill-considered, unco-ordinated, conflicting policies and projects." [19] After World War II, seeing the United States government as "leading the anti-progressive forces of the planet," he expressed pride in the accomplishments of socialist Eastern Europe.[20] He continues to call for universal justice through the abolition of capitalism.

But the future Nearing has always hoped for resembles much less the proletarianized world of Marx and Engels—or Stalin or Debs or even Norman Thomas—than it does the village culture of Robert Dale Owen. "Economic and political decentralization

---

John R. Commons eventually endorsed the New Deal as a workable reform of the system at the same time that Dewey was rejecting capitalism, and Commons thought of himself as a Deweyian pragmatist. See John R. Commons, *Institutional Economics* (New York: Macmillan, 1934), pp. 90-91, 102.
18. *Democracy Is Not Enough* (New York: Island Workshop Press, 1945), p. 149.
19. Ibid. p. 46.
20. *Man's Search for the Good Life* (Harborside, Maine: Social Science Institute, 1954), p 134. See also *Socialism in Practice: Transformation in Eastern Europe* (New York: New Century, 1962).

and a high degree of local autonomy," he wrote in 1945, "offer the only ultimate guarantee of freedom." [21] He would reduce bureaucracy and government expense by dispersing both the industrial plant and the apparatus of public control. His quarrel is not merely with size, but with the machine itself. To reduce man's dependence on the factory, Nearing has called for a willingness to spade the garden instead of tractoring it, to perform as many tasks as possible with one's hands in order to "establish and maintain quality and simplicity as life goals." [22]

Thus while Franklin Roosevelt centralized to preserve capitalism, and Dewey hoped to centralize to supplant it, Nearing and his wife, in the Depression, practiced the radical alternative that Nearing had preached. They took a farmhouse far back in a Vermont valley, lived by subsistence gardening, shunning cigarettes, lipstick, all the expensive fads of what Nearing knew was a dying order. Progressivism had only been a way station for him on the road to a social vision that owed more to Ruskin's *Unto This Last* than to Keynes or Marx, and which illustrates in extreme but instructive fashion the curious blend of past and future, Left and Right, that characterized so much progressive thought and marked it as a movement which straddled two centuries.

Charles Edward Russell first went into revolt at the "smug religious formalism" of St. Johnsbury, Vermont, where he was in prep school, and he continued through Free Trade, the Single Tax, and muckraking to socialism. The trip from the Iowa Free Trade League to socialism took Russell about twenty-five years, a period spent as a journalist on New York's East Side and as an editor of several Minneapolis, Detroit, and New York newspapers. By 1908, an independent journalist and a leading muckraker, he was ready to join the Socialist party. Unlike Ernest Poole, William James Ghent, Max Eastman, John Spargo, Walter Lippmann and others, Russell never wavered. Reform was now to mean total reform, the substitution of the service for the profit incentive.

He remained a socialist even during the postwar years when his interest in national politics flagged and he had turned to historical studies—some articles on the Founders, a study of the early American navy, and a Pulitzer-Prize-winning biography of Theodore

21. *Democracy Is Not Enough*, p. 150.
22. *Economics for the Power Age* (New York: John Day, 1952), pp. 117-18.

Thomas (1927). Russell's autobiography of 1933, *Bare Hands and Stone Walls,* recorded the same dedication to a democratic society that had guided him from the first. In 1933, as always, this meant socialism, gradually reached. It was a steady, nonviolent faith, expressing itself through membership in groups standing for racial harmony and international amity, clemency for the criminal, and all forms of social welfare. It rested on an optimism so deep that in the dark year of 1933 Russell could be sure the world was growing better.[23]

Although a gradualist, he seemed not greatly interested in the New Deal, but busied himself with a dozen good causes, preferring to comfort the casualties of a capitalistic Western world while others tended to the revolution. He held membership in the Public Ownership League, the International Committee for Political Prisoners, the Inter-Racial Commission of the District of Columbia, the American League to Abolish Capital Punishment; his letters reveal his concern for Ireland, China, and the Philippines; they reveal that he kept his union card, and paid his dues, to the New York Typographical Union. In his seventies Russell was not tired: "Tired! Greed never tires, nor exploitation, nor graft. Next to petty quarreling among reformers and next to their tendency to put personal ambition above the goal, the greatest asset of exploitation is the weariness of those who assault it. Keep on, hold fast, seize every opportunity, despise not the small skirmish. . . . You will have the satisfaction of remembering that you have never compromised with the slave whips." [24]

Another old socialist who never wavered, and a more famous one, was Upton Sinclair. They were very much alike, Russell and Sinclair, sensitive souls in a continual state of moral outrage which they believed demanded the end of the present social system. "I don't know whether anyone will care to examine my heart," Sinclair wrote in his autobiography, "but if they do they will find two words there—social justice." [25] Sinclair narrowly missed the only opportunity offered any of the real radicals to put his socialism, such as it was, into practice, when he and EPIC

23. Russell, "An Old Reporter Looks at the Mad-House World," *Scribner's* XCIV (October 1933), pp. 225-30.
24. Typescript, Box 42, Russell MSS, Library of Congress.
25. *The Autobiography of Upton Sinclair* (New York: Harcourt, Brace, 1962), p. 329.

almost became the government of California in 1934. And if EPIC sounded more like the New Deal than Marx, Sinclair was nonetheless not watering down his socialism, but making a modest start on the immediate problem of hunger.

His socialism, contracted in 1902 through a combination of reading and the influence of George D. Herron, persisted through the New Deal as it persists still, and it prevented him from making the sort of compromise with the existing system that the New Deal represented. "End Poverty in California" actually marked the closest thing to accommodation between Sinclair and Roosevelt, and after that narrow defeat in the autumn of 1934, Sinclair moved back to his demand for a collectivist national solution (and back into the Socialist party from the Democratic party).[26] He was really no more interested than Russell or Dewey or Steffens or Nearing in the realities of power, and when the governorship slipped from him, he turned with relief back to writing and lecturing. His best years, as a writer at least, were still ahead.[27]

Lincoln Steffens left progressivism further behind, and, rare among progressives, documented his thought processes elaborately. The lengthy conversion of this wealthy, essentially unthinking young American to a sort of death-bed communism was told in his celebrated autobiography of 1931, and Steffens, if not the first then at least the most famous muckraker, has sometimes been taken as a typical progressive reformer whom World War and Depression were to drive leftward. Actually, Steffens was unique.

Fresh from the study of ethics in German universities, the young Steffens joined the staff of the New York *Evening Post* in 1892, unaware of the social tensions around him. The depression of the 1890's, as well as his exposure to New York, soon changed that, and in 1902, a member of S. S. McClure's staff, Steffens wrote

26. Roosevelt seemed cordial to the nominee of the Democratic party of California, but the administration did not intervene to help Sinclair. The literature on EPIC is extensive; one might start with Sinclair's *The Way Out* (New York: Farrar and Rinehart, 1933), Clarence F. McIntosh, "Upton Sinclair and EPIC," unpublished Ph.D. dissertation, University of Michigan, 1955, and Charles E. Larsen, "The EPIC Campaign of 1934," *Pacific Historical Review* XXVII (1958), 127-47.

27. See J. D. Koerner, "The Last of the Muckrake Men," *Atlantic Quarterly*, LX (April 1956), 221-33. Sinclair published the first of the popular "Lanny Budd" series in 1940.

the first "Shame of the Cities" article on St. Louis. It was not long before he questioned the efficacy of progressive exposure-and-reform methods, and he passed, by stages, from sympathy to socialism (about 1908) to a despair of the essential humanity of the American people (the McNamara case, 1911) to an acceptance of the need for revolution (Russia, 1917-19).[28]

Progressives, he criticized, had thought that morality would be enough, and that reform consisted in putting honest men in office. "The political problem," he concluded in his autobiography, "is an economic, an engineering—it is not a moral problem." [29] The engineering he spoke of must reconstruct the economic order as Lenin had done—not piecemeal, but all at once. "It was useless," he wrote, "to fight for the right under our system; pettty reforms in politics, wars without victories, were . . . heroic but immoral. Either . . . [we should] labor to change the foundations of society, as the Russians were doing, or go along with the resultant civilization we were part of." [30] "Liberalism," he summed up, "had been tried and found wanting." [31]

This was Steffens in 1931, the muckraker who had come from progressive moralism to the acceptance of a revolutionary path to a society purged of private property. For a time, in the 1920's, he had been sure of the need for revolution but unsure whether the way of Mussolini or Lenin was best. By the 1930's he had embraced the Russian way. "Hearst's class will not do," he wrote from California: "I don't know much about the workers, but I am for the lower class way, not the upper class way." [32]

As he shifted toward communism, Steffens dropped the earlier reliance on intelligence and engineering, which he had shared for

28. The best account of the various stages in his political attitudes, barring the autobiography itself, is probably Granville Hicks, "Lincoln Steffens: He Covered the Future," *Commentary*, XIII (February 1952), 147-57. See also Irving Cheslaw, "An Intellectual Biography of Lincoln Steffens," unpublished Ph.D. dissertation, Columbia University, 1952, and Christopher Lasch, *The New Radicalism in America* (New York: Alfred A. Knopf, 1965).

29. *The Autobiography of Lincoln Steffens* (New York: Harcourt, Brace, 1931), II, p. 567. Steffens was certainly not alone in his eventual disdain for the "replace bad men with good" methods of most reformers; Fred Howe and Brand Whitlock, to mention only two, preceded him in this. What made him unique was the post-progressive direction of his thought.

30. Ibid. p. 802.

31. Ibid. p. 831.

32. Lincoln Steffens, *Lincoln Steffens Speaking* (New York: Harcourt, Brace, 1936), pp. 174-5.

a time with Dewey, and called simply for action. "Now is not the time for the open mind," he wrote from Carmel in the 1930's; "Now is the age of decision." [33] And when action supplanted indecision, it would not come from the "nice people" nor from the old-time liberals (like himself), but from "the workers" and "the young."

Putting aside, then, the useless good intentions of middle-class reformers and the faith, out of Dewey and Veblen, in classless social engineers, Steffens happily prophesied, and stepped aside for, the "wave of the future." He never officially joined the Communist party, and refused to run for the Senate in California as a communist, pleading that as an ex-liberal he could never adjust to the new age. The job was for the young (his son Peter, he hoped) and the proletarian. Of course, he was getting old, was in financial difficulties, and suffered a stroke in 1934. But, even had his health been good, Steffens had dealt himself out, and the fruit of a lifetime of study of American life had led him to a triumphant, passive vigil for the destruction of the old America and the coming of the new order. In what amounted to his final commentary upon the liberal reform effort, of which Franklin Roosevelt was, for him, only a meek and "amusing" extension, Steffens recalled that Jane Addams led "a beautiful life . . . that failed, because it can't be done that way." [34]

Progressivism, in Steffens, admitted defeat and pretended to like it. Yet to the end he was capable of the old indignation— over Tom Mooney's jail term, for example—and the moralist in him was not quite exorcised by all the talk about the inevitable, all-correcting cataclysm to come. At the arrest of Caroline Decker in 1934, after she had organized the migrant workers in the San Joaquin Valley, Steffens wrote to Louis O'Neal: "I wish I could call on you some day in your office, close the door, and not say a word; just laugh, and laugh and laugh—and cry. Yours solemnly, Lincoln Steffens." [35]

These five men had in common that passion for social justice sufficiently strong, when sufficiently frustrated, to drive them all to the advocacy of a new social system. All favored broad state

33. Ibid. p. 302.
34. Ibid. p. 227.
35. Lincoln Steffens to Louis O'Neal, July 27, 1934, Steffens MSS, Columbia University.

action on behalf of—and in Steffens' case, by—the lower economic orders, and all believed that nothing really satisfactory could be done without the overthrow, gradual or otherwise, of the existing profit system. They were all committed to anti-capitalistic alternatives before the Great Depression: Dewey by late 1928, Nearing at the onset of World War I, Russell by 1908, Sinclair as early as 1902, and Steffens by about 1919. None would be wooed from a revolutionary ideology by the liberal program of Franklin Roosevelt. Finally, four of the five were signers of the "Call" which led to the foundation of the NAACP in 1909. The protest, then as later, was for those on the bottom.[36]

III

Why did these men follow the spirit of reform until it culminated in such deep radicalism that capitalism itself must be replaced, and New Deal liberalism seemed hypocritically niggardly? What explains their radicalism while the great majority of progressive reformers, accepting the profit system, either favored Roosevelt's efforts to heal the profit system or—in greater numbers—wished the system left substantially alone? The answer, if the historical record provides any at all, must lie in some combination of personality with life circumstances—family background, education, economic situation, daily experience.

They derived from a variety of class backgrounds: Dewey and Russell came of the comfortable middle class, Sinclair of ruined gentility, Nearing was born to a minor Pennsylvania lumber magnate and Steffens to a prosperous Sacramento merchant. Each home was traditional: pious, hard-working, encouraging the offspring to ambition and education. In no case did the home life present, as it did for example in the case of Edgar Lee Masters, the disruptive influence of a radical or eccentric parent.[37] In three cases, the upbringing was rural; Nearing was raised in both Morris Run and Philadelphia, and Sinclair entirely in cities (Baltimore and New York). It is hard to discern in the family or rearing circumstances of these men any common element that accounts for the difficult and uncomfortable political course each was to adopt.

36. The signers were Dewey, Russell, Sinclair, and Steffens.
37. Sinclair had an alcoholic father, but his mother, who raised him, seems to have been thoroughly average in behavior and values.

They varied widely in age, in sectional origin, and in educational background.[38] In religion, all were born to Protestant par- ✓

---

38. Dewey was born in 1859; Nearing in 1883; Russell in 1860; Sinclair in 1878; Steffens in 1866. Dewey was a New Englander, Nearing a Pennsylvanian, Russell an Iowan, Sinclair an Eastern seaboard product, Steffens a Californian. Dewey studied philosophy, Nearing economics, Russell law, Steffens political economy and ethics, and Sinclair literature. Four of the five did graduate work and received graduate degrees. None of them, however, was propelled into the progressive movement by graduate study, at least not directly; all became progressives after student years, and this reduces (although it does not eliminate) the importance of formal study as a reform catalyst. As Nearing put it in a letter to the author (March 15, 1966), "I took a major in economics and a Ph.D. in the subject without even having heard the names of Marx and Engels pronounced in a class room." At any rate, for the entire sample, graduate study was undertaken as often by those later to be quite conservative as by the radicals, and does not appear in itself to have had any predictable bearing upon the formation of political attitude.

---

ents, all but Steffens to parents of conspicious piety. None persisted in the Christian faith beyond early manhood, but the principles of Jesus seem to have played some part in the reform orientation of at least two of them. Still, other progressives were driven by morality derived from Christian upbringing or mature faith, and these ethical imperatives rarely required the degree of radicalism they came to. It does not appear that in rearing, religion, education or economic class, taken alone, we shall discover a principle source of their radicalism.

Yet in the circumstances of their early manhood there are certain common and suggestive features. In occupation, all were writers and intellectuals, with no real connection with business life or the conservative influences of legal-business ties. All, by force of career, thought deeply and introspectively about their own values and the society that surrounded them. Of course, this is true of most academicians and writers, and we have already seen that the muckrakers tended to be more conservative as the years went by than many other groups. Still, the importance of a standing opportunity, enforced by career, to observe society, and the professional requirement to pass occasional judgment on it, is undeniable for this group of radicals.[39]

39. For Dewey, writing and thinking could easily have taken the form of an escape into metaphysics, and since his professional concerns were unexpectedly mundane in their locus, we shall need more in his case than the effect of a career in academic philosophy.

There remains one common circumstance that helps to account for why these men were so implacable. It was not necessary to come into contact with urban areas in order to become a progressive, since men like Arthur Capper and William Allen White did it from a small-town base. But it is abundantly clear that the city, containing as it did the most graphic evidence of the loss of security and dignity among those forced to live under urban conditions by the old individualistic philosophy, had a hand in driving some progressives to the more radical forms of social reconstruction and collective protest.

It was not enough merely to live and work in the city, of course. Lawyers like Henry Stimson, Amos Pinchot, and Charles Evans Hughes had downtown (New York) offices. The factor most likely to disrupt Good Government reformism was contact with the soiled mass. That contact came to social workers and settlement people; it came to reporters, or many of them; it came to social gospel ministers who refused to move their churches out with the fleeing middle class. And such contact was patent in the early careers and continuing interests of Dewey (at Hull House, and in Chicago generally), of Nearing (who plunged into social work in Philadelphia before he was out of his teens), of Russell (on New York's East Side, and later in Minneapolis and Detroit), of Sinclair (from Chicago packing house workers to the migrant pickers of California), and of Steffens (who worked the wards of the big cities as a young reporter, who watched a part of the Russian Revolution, and whose friends in his old age were the radicals involved in the Mooney case and the San Francisco strike). New York City, Chicago, Philadelphia, Boston, Denver, Milwaukee, these were the breeding grounds of those remorseless forms of radicalism which would allow no separate peace until the unseen poor were included in the substance of the American dream.

A sample of five is poor material for these hesitant generalizations, and I have checked them by drawing up a list of those

surviving progressives who seemed to take up a consistently radical position in the 1930's (as they had, in all cases, since the beginning of their reform participation). Such a list includes many
who settled for the New Deal, but who pushed Roosevelt to do
more in the areas of social welfare and redistribution of power.
The list includes the five radicals above, plus Herbert Seely Bigelow, Senator Costigan, Max Eastman, John Haynes Holmes,
Frederic Howe, Paul Kellogg, Bishop McConnell, Mary Simkhovitch, Oswald Garrison Villard, Lillian Wald, Stephen S. Wise,
and one who died in 1935 and has been excluded before, Jane
Addams.[40] It is a group of seventeen. They were both well and

40. Others might be added, but either the information on
them was inadequate or I simply decided that, in any group of
Left radicals, they were borderline: John B. Andrews and Irene
Osgood Andrews of the American Association of Labor Legislation, George Norris, Homer Folks, Owen Lovejoy, and one or
two others. I think the list above, if not perfectly inclusive, is at
least defensible as it stands.

badly off economically, rural as well as urban in origin, religious
and agnostic, poorly and well educated. But the common features, suggested by the five most radical, are there for the larger
group: city slums encountered early, work in urban areas begun
early and continued, and, in most cases, a conspicuous dedication
to the ethical if not the theological teachings of Christianity. A
strong ethical orientation acquired as a child, fanned to deep indignation by steady exposure to New York, Chicago, Philadelphia, Denver—these seem to be the principal ingredients in the
formation of Left-progressivism.[41]

41. Presumably, to the sociology of individual life there must
be added the appropriate cast of personality before a radical is
made. The materials for such a study exist in too few cases, and
for this reason, as well as lack of training, I have made no
attempt to work into this area. The two most obvious characteristics involved would seem to be sensitivity (a sort of empa-
thy quotient) and a tendency to gravitate to an extreme position in search of the security afforded by a social viewpoint
which answered all questions. Evidence of the first is abundant
among reformers, although we cannot explain how it came to
be implanted in some people rather than in others. Evidence
of the second exists in the cases of men like Max Eastman,
Joseph M. Patterson, Spargo, and Steffens, who were sure to be

on one extreme or the other of the political spectrum, but who apparently could not bear the Center. Granville Hicks tried to explain Steffens's career in terms of this requirement for certainty; naturally, he does not explain or attempt to explain why Steffens was cursed with that need. See Hicks, "Lincoln Steffens: He Covered the Future," *Commentary*, XIII (February 1952), 147-57.

The combination of contact with urban poverty and strong Christian or other ethical orientation shows up in fifteen of the seventeen cases.[42] Of the entire sample of 168, I would estimate

42. Neither Edward Costigan nor Oswald Garrison Villard had an early or very extensive contact with urban poverty. Villard's sentiments, of course, did not remain on the Left after about 1937. Costigan's development into a strong liberal is, at least for me, enigmatic.

that only twelve more instances of this combination exist, and this group leans to the Left. Of them, five were favorably disposed to the New Deal (John R. Commons, Raymond Fosdick, Ben Lindsey, Charles Stelzle, and Peter Witt), only Robert Hunter was opposed, and the others (Raymond Robins, Lee Beattie, William Adams Brown, Harris Cooley, Edward Devine, and William English Walling) could not be categorized with any certainty. Admittedly, this combination did not always result in New Deal or Left-of-New Deal sympathies, nor were such sympathies limited to those whose backgrounds show these features. All I am arguing here is that this cluster of factors, based on this sample of progressives, is more prominently associated with strong Left-of-Center political sentiment than any other factor or factors that have come to my attention.

I V

These radicals wrote almost nothing, and apparently thought as little, about Roosevelt's New Deal. Unlike most other old progressives, the five on the Left who entirely rejected the New Deal did not laboriously indict it on progressive principles, but dismissed it along with the entire liberal outlook (unless they redefined "liberal," as Dewey did) as a hopeless attempt to save the going system. All five had come to this view before the years of F.D.R., and it followed that they paid little attention as the New

Deal engaged in strenuous and sometimes contradictory efforts to hold the profit system together.

Committed as they were to radical change, it might seem that they would have resented the New Deal as an objectionable delay, a futile (perhaps even Fascist) holding action. This was not the case. There is nowhere in their writing the sort of angry attack upon the President and his work so frequently heard on the Right, or among those in transit to the Right.[43] They did not

---

43. Men like George Creel, Hiram Johnson, and Burton K. Wheeler* were by 1937 midway between a noisy progressivism and a noisy reaction, and abused Roosevelt as being a potential dictator so effectively that F.D.R. must have longed for the criticism of standpat conservatives.

---

take the New Deal seriously, either as promising improvement or as delaying it. Dewey thought it "half-hearted," Sidney Hook reports, and Steffens was "amused" at the picture of a President trying to save capitalism while the capitalists themselves fought him off; but none of them spent much mental or verbal energy on the New Deal.[44]

When they attacked, they attacked the profit system; when they analyzed American society, it was in quite general terms; when they spoke up, it was to make the clear, high call for social justice, and almost never to make a close inspection of a New Deal agency or law. Finally, they no longer spoke as progressives, but as radicals who had started as progressives and followed mind and conscience until they were no longer friends to the American system.

V

There thus turned up far to the Left of the New Deal a handful of old progressives on every issue more radical than the administration. As much as these five differed from all the others, in one important respect their attitude toward the New Deal reflects a desire for intellectual clarity shared by the great majority of progressives of Right or Left. Many progressives on the Right had criticized the New Deal for confusion, for inconsistency passing for a principle, for carelessness with the Constitution and the incentive system—in other words, for the pragmatic attitude that

44. Sidney Hook, *John Dewey: An Intellectual Portrait* (New York: John Day, 1959), p 165; Steffens, *Lincoln Steffens Speaking,* p. 961.

many have seen as the overriding virtue of the New Deal. But most progressives were deeply attached to ideas, and they wished always for a clear and logical understanding between government and citizen of the political aims and specific courses of action of public authority. The New Deal went forward on trust in a charismatic leader, making little effort to conceal its confusion and changes of mind. It was a sort of intellectual log-rolling contest, and, in its novel and opportunistic course, it spun too fast for those who held and cherished fixed opinions.

As it spun too fast for some progressives and rolled them to the Right, so its opportunism and intellectual inconclusiveness drove a few to the far Left. But those on the two political extremes shared a devotion to doctrine, to some sort of firm position arrived at by hard, disciplined thought. The five radical progressives watched the New Deal avoid clear choices, and they knew that courses not clarified and never long persisted in would not take America far from her current arrangements.

They were flexible, of course, in many things. Charles Edward Russell's irreverent remarks on the Constitution are a good example: "How would it be possible for the Blessed and Revered Fathers of 1789 to have hit upon the last word in government and political institutions when they missed out on everything else? Why should their ideas about government be any more sacred than their ideas about anaesthetics or artificial light and heat? . . . They just groped and stumbled." [45] Steffens, even as his outlook hardened into Marxism, wrote,

> "I teach my child . . .
> That nothing is done, finally and right,
> That nothing is known, positively and completely." [46]

As for Sinclair, his open-mindedness where radicalism was concerned rivaled that of Horace Greeley; his taste in schemes was eclectic, so long as the schemes were radical. Sinclair may have been a socialist, but his socialism was of the gradualist variety, tactically unstructured. He found time to establish a communist society at Helicon Hall in New Jersey, to go on diet fads, and to live in the Single Tax community at Fairhope, Alabama. EPIC itself, so narrowly defeated and so spectacularly feared, involved

45. From a draft of an article in *Real America,* dated February, 1936 (p. 20), Russell MSS.
46. *Lincoln Steffens Speaking,* p. 147.

only the grafting of a few "production for use" facilities upon a capitalistic trunk which Sinclair proposed to leave, at least for the moment, untouched. He even filed for governor as a Democrat, since the Socialists had no chance.

Yet while they were impatient of inherited truth and pragmatists in small things, they were ideologues in political attitude, ready to oppose the New Deal patchwork with the demands of inflexible theory. In this resides the kinship between Dewey and George Record, between Steffens and James A. Reed; when the core of things was reached, abstractions mattered most. For these radicals, the showy experiments of Franklin Roosevelt were not pragmatism at all, but fatal carelessness with ideas. Members of the progressive generation despite their longevity and the intellectual migrations of later years, they found the only guide for political action to be clear thinking: first the selection of goals, and then the means appropriate for realizing them. First one sorts out matters intellectually, and then one goes ahead.

But the New Deal followed the Napoleonic directive, *"on s'engage et puis on voit,"* reversing the priorities. And whatever such a method might be called, it was not, in the eyes of Dewey himself, pragmatism as he used that term: "Experimental method is not just messing around nor doing a little of this and a little of that in the hope that things will improve. Just as in the physical sciences, it implies a coherent body of ideas, a theory, that gives direction to effort." [47] Thus Dewey, and the others who favored more thorough measures, rejected the New Deal for some of the same reasons as those who voted for Landon: there was little to hope for, and perhaps much to fear, in a political whirlwind without fixed and stated aims and methods. The old progressives, fond of logical thought, wanted their ideas clear and any necessary action impeccably in line with those ideas.

Villard spoke for both the Right and the Left, in a way, when he told Steffens that Roosevelt asked the Cabinet if they could see "where we are going," and when none could answer, said: "No, no, you are too busy, but I, who have time and the duty to look around and see ahead—I don't see either."[48] And whether it ever

47. John Dewey, "The Future of Liberalism," *School and Society,* XLI (January 19, 1935), 75.
48. Reported by Steffens in a letter to Frederic Howe, May 11, 1934; found in Ella Winter and Granville Hicks (eds.), *The Letters of Lincoln Steffens, 1920-36* (New York: Harcourt, Brace, 1938), vol. II, p. 985.

happened or not, Villard ruefully cited it as the flaw of New Deal liberalism which sent so many old reformers off to the Right and the Left in search of a more predictable vehicle of salvation in America's most risky decade.

V

Farewell to Reform: The Transfiguration of the Progressive Impulse

> The truth is, we are all caught in a great economic system which is heartless.
>
> WOODROW WILSON

Progressivism played out sometime between the three-way election of 1912 and the onset of World War I, for reasons that are not entirely clear. But we now know that progressive groups had a substantial if harrassed survival throughout the 1920's, that at least some of the reformers retained a faith in progress through politics. The 1930's, of course, provided a climate that excited the interests of reformers old and new and made politics again the art of the possible. Whether the old progressive hailed or hated the New Deal, it was at least true that he was again absorbed in politics and national affairs, and it was natural that he should be. Progressives believed that political effort and active citizenship mattered—both to society at large, and to the keeping of one's own conscience. But in the 1930's a significant number of these progressives had resigned from reform entirely—they no longer cared about events outside a narrowly personal orbit.

Most progressives, of course, did not return to reform after World War I, but this as often as not was less a deliberate disavowal of the old goals than the sad recognition that no one was interested. By 1933, most of those who survived were glad that reform was in the air again, were ready to pay close attention to public affairs and to sympathize, if not to act, in the old causes. But there was a small group that had given up long ago, and there was to be no luring them back.[1] When we know why they

---

1. Of 168 survivors, 105 were interested enough in the New Deal to declare themselves for or against, some many times. Many of those in the "No (or Insufficient) Data" category were interested and even active, but I could not be sure of their

position. Owen R. Lovejoy, for example, was active on the National Child Labor Committee, and Irene Osgood Andrews was almost certainly as active as her husband in the fight for welfare legislation. All ten of those in the category "Other"—Ashurst, Baker, Brandeis, Eastman, Owen, Poole, Robins, Tarbell, Tumulty, and Villard—were interested, often deeply, in the political issues of the hour. Illness excluded, it was a rare progressive who was not; the exceptions were as conspicuous as sleepers in an audience. They were Samuel Hopkins Adams, Winston Churchill, Charles R. Crane, William J. Ghent, William H. Hatton, Hutchins Hapgood, Henry French Hollis, Samuel Merwin, Walter Sachs, and Marie Van Vorst. Others who expressed preferences but were nearly as withdrawn were Burton Hendrick, Wallace Irwin, Reginald Wright Kauffman, Edgar Lee Masters, and Carl Vrooman. I shall occasionally refer to them in this chapter, and to Brand Whitlock and Fremont Older*, men who are not a part of the 168 but who were well-known progressives.

----

dropped out, and what sort of people they were, we learn a great deal about the points of strain, the sectors of greatest disillusionment, within progressivism. Since they said nothing about the New Deal they enlighten us in only one way about it; not even that great opportunity for social change was able to draw all the old reformers back from their private pursuits to even a *pro forma* support or enmity.

I I

For the ten progressives who seem most clearly to have kept strictly to private concerns, the point of disillusionment arrived at varying times.[2] We have from men like Frederic Howe (in *Confessions of a Reformer*) and Charles Edward Russell (in *Bare Hands and Stone Walls*) recapitulations of the burdens on those who yearned, and worked, to improve America. But most progressives gave very little explanation for the decision to quit. From the pattern of those private activities that lured them away, it is

----

2. For Samuel Hopkins Adams, the mid-1920's; for Churchill, about 1916; for Crane, sometime after 1912; for Ghent, about 1926; for Hatton, 1916; for Hutchins Hapgood, between 1914 and the end of the war; for Hollis, it coincided with a move to France sometime in the 1920's; for Merwin, during or just after the war; for Walter Sachs, before the war; for Marie Van Vorst, the emigration to Rome in 1916 seems to mark the break.

possible to get a good idea of what sort of people they were, and what the costs of progressivism had been.

William H. Hatton, in his littered office in an upper Wisconsin town, represents an extreme example of what was to claim the energies of many progressives when they were through with reform. Hatton turned abruptly from progressive political activities in Wisconsin to the amassing of wealth in the lumber business, and the contrast between his years as a state senator and the miserly years in his New London (Wisconsin) office marks him off in degree, but not in kind, from many who turned entirely to private careers.[3] Walter Sachs, who had served briefly as Treasurer of the NAACP (he was one of five founders), followed the same track back into the full-time making of money. Neither made public explanation, and of course there was no need to explain. The impulse that sent them out into the reform orbit had simply played out, and they went back to private life, opting, as someone said of Donald Richberg's return to law practice in the 1920's "for the flesh pots after a life with the crack pots." The return to personal career of Hatton and Sachs, and others like Newton Baker and A. Mitchell Palmer, constitutes a primary reason for the termination of the cycle of progressive reform.

We know even less about why they left reform than about their original decisions to become reformers, in most cases. We only know that sometime after 1912 the falling away began, with reformers returning to career and wealth and family, appearing at no meetings, writing no exposés, adding their names to few if any letterheads during the years that followed the war. For a few, the attractions of private gratifications must have been matched by a sudden and strong disillusionment, for not even the revival of reform under F.D.R. could draw so much as a public statement or a letter to an editor. Progressivism, when it infected the businessman or the lawyer who had the potential for a lucrative career, tended to have a short life.

Perhaps the second most-traveled exit from reform was into writing. The muckrakers, especially, went from jobs with *McClure's* and *Collier's* into free-lance writing, or jobs with the *Saturday Evening Post* or the *Reader's Digest*. As public tastes changed, ex-muckrakers turned without complaint to the produc-

3. For Hatton's career, see the obituary, *Milwaukee Journal*, April 22 and 24, 1940.

tion of innocuous romances. Hutchins Hapgood, whose early articles revealing the unenviable lot of the American laborer demonstrated his own deep sympathies with the underdog, withdrew
after the war into writing, acting, travel, and a grimly successful
debauchery.[4] Samuel Merwin left journalism in order to have
time for the Player's Club on Gramercy Park, his playhouse at
Concord, and some light writing for the *Saturday Evening Post*.[5]
Samuel Hopkins Adams, whose exposures of patent medicine had
done so much toward the passage of the Pure Food and Drug law
of 1906, turned out novels, short stories on crabbing and conquering old age (again, for the *Saturday Evening Post*), and biographies of Alexander Woolcott, Daniel Webster, and Warren Hard-
ing.

Adams's interests bridged the fiction that served some and the
historical investigation that engaged others. He wrote steadily
until his death in 1958, and his novel *Revelry* (1926) was really
the last to utilize a current social theme. Adams was through with
exposure, and combined fiction with history in an effective double retreat from present concerns. Many of his novels have an
historical setting, often the Erie Canal country of his early life,
and this, combined with the two forays into biography, constituted insulation from the siren call of public service through reporting that had attached him and so many others to reform
journalism.

History, without the fiction, occupied several others. William
James Ghent gave up on reform about 1926, and devoted himself
to the history of the American West. He became something of an
expert, preparing some 175 sketches on Westerners and others for
the *Dictionary of American Biography*. "I have pretty well been
squeezed out of the field of social politics by the turn which
affairs have taken," he wrote to an old colleague in the Public
Ownership League in 1930, "and have become so absorbed in the
history of past time (particularly of the frontier) that I can give
little attention to what is going on."[6] He must have expressed a

4. See Hutchins Hapgood, *A Victorian in the Modern World* (New York:
Harcourt, Brace, 1939). Hutchins, who thought the years 1924-39 largely
"a blank," hints in his autobiography that his sympathies—when he could
raise them—were still with the labor movement. See also Mabel Dodge
Luhan, *Intimate Memories* (New York: Harcourt, Brace, 1936), pp. 45-57.
5. See obituary, *The New York Times*, October 18, 1936.
6. William J. Ghent to Carl D. Thompson, September 11, 1930, Container 7,

similar sentiment to Gustavus Myers six years later, for Myers's reply came back: "Do not think that a waning interest in various things is peculiar to you: many of us experience it; but is it not because we no longer look upon certain matters with the great and exciting importance we once attached to them? We see that it is no longer worth while getting stirred up, and if there is any stirring up necessary, let the young generation (which has the necessary energy and shall I say illusions?) work itself up into agitation." [7]

Ghent, writing his sketches of nineteenth- and early twentieth-century reformers; Samuel Hopkins Adams writing his biographies of Woolcott or Webster; Edgar Lee Masters writing a biography of Lincoln[8]; Burton J. Hendrick doing his study of the Confederacy and a biography of Lee; Brand Whitlook attempting a biography of Jefferson; these were tasks repeated many times as old reformers turned resolutely away from the intractable present. That so many of them selected American historical themes interprets itself: the old reformer, disillusioned with the projects and goals of earlier days, feeling the American future to be a thing somewhat out of control, turns in search of reorientation to the usable past.[9]

The choice of biographical writing can hardly be construed any other way. Edgar Lee Masters on Stephen Douglas, Will Irwin on Hoover, Ray Stannard Baker on Wilson, Ida Tarbell on Lincoln, to mention only a few, resurrected political figures whose principles were both undoubted and currently appealing; whose conservatism was unquestioned, yet whose basic humanity was never in doubt; and who lived and died in times of crisis when the American system was threatened.[10] Ida Tarbell ex-

---

Ghent MSS, Library of Congress. On Ghent, see Harold S. Smith, "William James Ghent: Reformer and Historian," unpublished Ph.D. dissertation, University of Wisconsin, 1957.

7. Gustavus Myers to Ghent, January 22, 1936, Container 5, Ghent MSS.

8. Masters's turn to history, biography, and poetry, almost all of them reminiscent of the southern Illinois country where he was raised, is perceptively examined in Lois T. Hartley, "Edgar Lee Masters—Biographer and Historian," *Journal of the Illinois State Historical Society*, LIV (Winter 1961), 1-56.

9. The "wave of remembrance" that set in during the 1930's had a wide effect, and is discussed in Alfred Kazin, *On Native Grounds* (New York: Harcourt, Brace, 1942), chap. 15.

10. Or, like Oswald Garrison Villard, they wrote a life of a steady reformer like Wendell Phillips, who somehow found his way through the difficulties of a turbulent period when new circumstances made the old approaches inapplicable. "I am deliberately beginning a *Life of Wendell Phillips* to go along with my *John Brown,* to seek escape from what is happening and to refresh my soul with another study of the finest and most successful group of Americans who ever lived." (Villard to John Haynes Holmes, June 27, 1940; Villard MSS, Harvard University.)

pressed as well as anyone the function of the biographical subject when she wrote, "My chief consolation in what I looked on as the manhandling of democratic ideals and processes in all ranks of society, public and private, was Abraham Lincoln. . . . He had won the biggest battle for freedom we have yet had to fight. He had done it by . . . squaring his conduct always with what he believed to be just, moral principles. . . . Feeling as I did and do about him, I have kept him always on my workbench. . . . The result has been five books, . . . and a continuous stream of articles, long and short."[11]

Others, unaware of the irony, chose to write laudatory biographies of the very businessmen whose antagonists they had been in the great days of revolt. Judson C. Welliver worked on a biography of George Pullman. Ida Tarbell wrote biographies of Judge Gary and Owen D. Young, and a little book (*New Ideals in Business,* 1916) hailing the arrival of the socially responsible "new employer." Burton Hendrick wrote a biography of Carnegie, and his indulgent *The Age of Big Business* in two volumes (1919-21) was finished before Wilson left office. Whatever the form, whether it be fiction, history, biography, drama, poetry, or some combination of them, writing occupied many of those who did not return to social concerns even under the stimulus of the New Deal.

Other areas invited the tired progressive. Winston Churchill and Carl Vrooman turned to religion—the novelist to a mysticism engendered and encouraged by sickness, the agriculturalist to a last wistful faith in the Oxford Movement.[12] A few found sufficient

11. *All In the Day's Work,* p. 385.
12. A pair of good doctoral dissertations provide us insight into these lesser known progressives. See Warren I. Titus, "Winston Churchill: American—a

escape in travel—even, in some cases, in expatriation. Henry French Hollis left the Senate in 1919, where he had been a staunch Wilson man, and lived until his death in Paris. Marie Van Vorst, who wrote *The Woman Who Toils* in 1903, retired from the study of the ills of industrial society, removed to Italy, and eventually completed forty novels in her Florence home. Charles R. Crane had always spent much time abroad, and the 1930's found him either occupied with European travel, or engrossed in date farming at Palm Springs. "It looked like valuable work," he wrote to his son in 1933, describing his days of reform activity, "but nothing really has been accomplished. . . . The gist of the thing is this—where there is money to be made or power to be acquired, a little amateur organization, with a short life . . . cannot hold out against the persistent drive of more vitally interested forces. This all leads me to say that you must not spend too much of your life and strength trying to save the world because it is in the first place pretty far gone and in the next place it is not at all interested in being saved." [13] And to McAdoo, in 1936, "I have definitely retired from any ideas about politics. . . . There are many things going on which, to us old-fashioned people, are troublesome and not understandable. . . . However, I myself am only really interested in date growing"—a pursuit Crane recommended "when you are looking around for something peaceful and stable and want to get out of a world which is apparently so meaningless and for which we have no systems of weights and measures to go by, all the old ones having been thrown on the scrap heap." [14]

Brand Whitlock rested at Cannes, writing a little. Scott Nearing shut himself away, the Vermont hills offering retreat enough. Whatever the form of escape, whether into the struggle for economic security or a life of pleasure, fiction or history, Europe or the American hinterland, old progressives in surprising numbers could not be lured from them by the return of reform hopes under Franklin Roosevelt. [15]

Critical Biography," unpublished Ph.D. dissertation, New York University, 1957, and Ross Paulson, "The Vrooman Brothers and the American Reform Tradition," unpublished Ph.D. dissertation, Harvard University, 1962.
13. Charles R. Crane to John O. Crane, December 15, 1933, Crane MSS, Institute of Current World Affairs, New York.
14. Crane to William G. McAdoo, February 25, 1936, Crane MSS.
15. Lincoln Steffens chided Ray Stannard Baker for escaping to the woods

I I I

The decision of many individuals, taken at about the same time, to limit or stop their efforts at social improvement, is perhaps the most interesting problem associated with progressivism. Along with the problem of the origin of the movement, the question of the nature and timing of its termination goes to the heart of the inner aspirations and working experience of the progressive effort. We have a number of theories about the decline of progressivism, all of them familiar by now. Arthur Schlesinger and Charles Forcey see cycles in American reform, and argue that progressivism simply played out when it had run its chronological course. Other historians, more interested in what impels the pendulum than in measuring its arc, have pointed to World War I especially, with its double effect of disillusionment and the siphoning off of moral energies. Richard Hofstadter, among others, has argued that the progressive impulse was redirected toward immigration restriction, prohibition, and similar defensive mechanisms after the war, thus in a way disguising and eventually transforming itself. Arthur Link, in an article on the end of progressivism, arranged a number of these views in a persuasive synthesis, pointing especially to problems of leadership, cohesion among reform-minded groups, and the inadequacies of the original progressive program.[16]

---

to write the David Grayson book, *Adventures In Contentment;* Baker then chided Steffens for escaping into dogma! An exchange of remarks reported by Baker in his Notebook, entry for December 18, 1939; Notebook 54, Baker MSS.

16. See A. M. Schlesinger, in *Paths to the Present* (New York: Macmillan, 1949), pp. 77-92; Charles B. Forcey, *Crossroads of Liberalism* (New York: Oxford University Press, 1961); Richard Hofstadter, *The Age of Reform* (New York: Alfred A. Knopf, 1955); Arthur Link, "What Happened to the Progressive Movement in the 1920's?", *American Historical Review,* LXIV (July 1959), 833-51. Other studies bearing upon the problem of the survival of reform in the postwar years are Paul U. Carter, *Decline and Revival of the Social Gospel: Social and Political Liberalism in American Protestant Churches, 1920-40* (Ithaca: Cornell University Press, 1954); Clarke Chambers, *Seedtime of Reform;* Robert M. Miller, *American Protestantism and Social Issues, 1919-39* (Chapel Hill: University of North Carolina Press, 1958), esp. pp. 44-48; George Mowry, *The California Progressives* (Berkeley: University of California Press, 1951), chap. 11; Herbert F. Margulies, "Recent Opinion on the Decline of the Progressive Movement," *Mid-America,* XLV (October 1963), 250-60.

But we have primary evidence bearing on the problem. The great majority of progressives dropped out between 1912 and 1919, the degree of residual involvement ranging from a nostalgic support for La Follette in 1924 or a continued subscription to the *Survey,* to the complete severance shown by those ex-reformers who have been the subject of this chapter. Presumably they know why they did so, and they are an indispensable source of information about the end of the movement.[17]

17. Sigmund Diamond has very correctly pointed out to me that the decision of the old progressives to quit, even if we understood it, would not entirely explain the decline of reform in the 1920's. An equally important question is, why did new recruits not *enter* the movement during those years?

Those who deliberately absented themselves from public life, who abruptly de-commissioned themselves as reformers, predictably refused to publish a word of explanation. Still, they can be identified, and starting with that it should be possible to get some idea of the cause of their retreat. I have gathered the names of twenty of those who wished no more involvement in uplift or social correction, and over against them, an Honor Roll of twenty reformers who stayed in the thick of the fight long after the public—and most of their old companions in revolt—had turned their backs on it. The briefest comparison of the two lists suggests at least one conspicuous element in the formula for deconversion.[18]

18. Those completely quitting reform were Samuel Hopkins Adams, Norris Brown, Winston Churchill, Charles Crane, William Hatton, Hutchins Hapgood, Henry Hollis, Burton Hendrick, Will and Wallace Irwin, Reginald Kauffman, Edgar Lee Masters, Sam Merwin, Ernest Poole, William Ghent, Walter Sachs, George Sheldon, Joe Tumulty, George Rublee, and Marie Van Vorst. Others may have escaped as decisively from reform in my sample of those surviving, but we know so little about them that their silence may simply be due to poor sources. A good example would be Jersey City's Mark Fagan.

The most unflinching reformers seem to have been Edward Costigan, John Dewey, Homer Folks, John Haynes Holmes, Harold Ickes, Paul Kellogg, S. McCune Lindsay, Ben Lindsey, Owen Lovejoy, Francis McConnell, George Norris, Amos Pinchot, Charles Edward Russell, Mary Simkhovitch, Upton Sinclair, Graham Taylor, Oswald Garrison Villard, Lillian Wald, Stephen S. Wise, and Mary Woolley.

It is clear that those progressives most likely to become disillusioned with reform and to become permanently estranged from "causes" were those who contributed to the cause by writing about it, especially those journalists who were muckrakers. The next occupational groups most prone to return to exclusively private concerns were lawyers and politicians—and many progressives were both. Among the staunch reformers were many occupational types: politicians, clergymen, lawyers, one reporter and one editor. The predominant group, not surprisingly, were the social workers.[19]

19. Of the twenty who so thoroughly renounced reform, ten were journalists, four were lawyers, four were politicians, and one (Ghent) hard to categorize. Of those on the other list, six were involved in social and/or settlement work, and there were no other important concentrations.

These concentrations, while unsurprising in themselves, suggest that a controlling factor was a change in the temper of the constituency for which a man served. Reform enlisted some men because of, and only after, the general outcry against public evils. These were the men who dropped out first, and most irrevocably, when the public changed its tastes. They were often the sort of people one is surprised to find among the reform element in the first place, and for them the sensational critical effort of progressive campaigns was not only in the long run distasteful, but had never been exactly what they had wished to do. Louis Filler notes that only Upton Sinclair and Ray Stannard Baker among the muckrakers were interested in social causes in the 1920's, and locates the principal reason in the loss of public interest in the sort of work these writer-progressives had done.[20] This loss of audience, for men whose preference had always been for fiction and whose normal style was nonpolitical, was enough to riddle the ranks of progressive journalists.

The termination of progressivism was a complex thing, and one does not explain it, much less the abrupt and total reversal of interests among a few individual men, solely through reference to public mood. But those who escaped most totally gave no explanation, and we can make a beginning at understanding them by this sort of occupational comparison. Apparently it was chiefly

20. Louis Filler, *Crusaders for American Liberalism* (New York: Harcourt, Brace, 1939), 344-6.

those whose reformism had both intellectual and occupational roots—clergymen, academics, or social workers whose agitation sprang from a combination of ideas and a steady association with those whom laissez-faire had condemned to poverty—only these, with few exceptions, did not retreat from reform. And of all progressives it was the writer, especially the writer whose tastes ran to fiction and drama, who had the weakest attachment to the task of social reform.

When exposure proved unavailing aginst social evil, when reform became a matter of pitting class against class and employing a coercive state, the writers and the lawyers whose practice centered in industry and finance were the men who would often return to legal practice, or fiction, or history. They had enlisted late and under subtle pressures, often enough, and they left the service of reform at the first sign that it was not to be a six-week, but a trench campaign. Burton Hendrick, typical of this type of reformer, tossed off his brief fling as a critic of things as they were with the following comment: "I got mixed up in all this initiative and referendum business. . . . I was a supporter of the progressive movement. . . . . I approved of all this popular work. The ideas of most of it I think I have outgrown." [21]

With the hope of an easy victory now untenable, with political and social issues confused and the real world a grimmer place, several old progressives—most of them journalists—beat a permanent retreat to the comforts of book and typewriter in the years after World War I.

IV

The death throes of the movement and the lean years that followed in the 1920's reveal much about progressivism that could not be learned from its days of power and promise. One need only read Arthur Link's provocative article on progressivism in the 1920's to see how adversity laid bare the inner structure of the movement.[22] These quite naturally turned to introspection when their expectations were shattered, but, fortunately, not all of those who left reform after the war disengaged themselves so

21. "Reminiscences of Burton J. Hendrick," Columbia University Oral History Collection, 1949, pp. 28-9.
22. Link. "What Happened to the Progressive Movement in the 1920's?," *American Historical Review*, LXIV (July 1959), 833-51.

completely that they were unwilling to re-examine the old issues.
Now that no one seemed any longer interested in reform, a few
were prepared to raise important questions that they had for-
merly been too busy to ask: Why had we become reformers in the
first place? What were our goals and assumptions? Where had we
made our political and intellectual errors?

After the publication of Frederic C. Howe's autobiography in
1925, *Survey* magazine conveniently brought together the post-
mortems of several old reformers who were willing to commit to
paper the reasons for their own defections.[23] The essays rather
thoroughly explore the decline of progressivism, even if they do
not agree about what should be done to ignite the movement
again.

Newton Baker thought progressivism had completed its work
when it had reorganized municipal and state governments, and
he saw little need for further exertions. Norman Hapgood, too,
thought there was little left for reformers to do: "The greatest
American problem I cannot pick out, because there does not seem
to be any, unless it might be the problem of protecting world
peace," Hapgood wrote.

Others found plenty to be done, but thought that the progressive creed was deficient and had nothing else to offer. William
Allen White and Fremont Older* had lost faith in the people,
especially the laboring people and the poor, who seemed not to
respond properly to middle class altruism. Ray Stannard Baker
reported that he had lost all confidence in changes in laws and
constitutions, and thought that improvement might come through
glacially slow alterations in men's ideas. In any event, he thought
progressivism, with its legal tinkering, inadequate to the task of
human rejuvenation, if the task could be done at all.

One, Charlotte Perkins Gilman, agreed that progressivism supplied no effective remedies, and advocated socialism. Suspecting
that progressive reformers had been headed in that direction all
along, Ida Tarbell and William Hard angrily took their names
off the reform masthead. Miss Tarbell denied having been a reformer at all, and Hard predicted that "those who lay hold of
government excessively to serve their purposes will ultimately
perish excessively by government."

23. "Where Are the Pre-War Radicals: A Symposium," *Survey*, LV (February
1, 1926), 556-64.

They were disagreeing only about the best path to take when leaving the progressive camp; all were agreed that one need not, could not, or should not be a progressive any more. In the 1930's, some of those who had written for the *Survey* symposium changed their minds and gave reform one more try—although many did not. Still, ten short years after Wilson's triumphant re-election, Stuart Chase could conclude those essays with: "Shall we lay a wreath on the Uplift Movement in America? I suppose we might as well." [24]

The movement was badly riven in those interwar years, and the symposium only formally brought in the open what every reformer knew. Even admitting Link's observations about the continued presence of a liberal bloc in the Congress in the 1920's, and admitting the existence of that hardy band of social work progressives that Clarke Chambers has so well described in *Seedtime of Reform,* progressivism was close to extinction. Most of the old leaders were dead—Roosevelt, Wilson, Tom Johnson, and, one year after the 1924 campaign, Bob La Follette. For those who survived there had arisen a swarm of problems both internal and external, in their sum fatal to any hope of a unified and revived progressivism.

The *Survey* respondents spoke of some of these, and most of the autobiographies published by old reformers in the 1920's—Frederic Howe, Charles Edward Russell, Charles Stelzle, and others—have filled out our picture of the outside pressures and loss of inner certainty that joined to drive reformers into retirement. They had been disheartened by the war and then again by the peace; by seeing their prewar struggles for a new mayor or a regulatory commission or an extension of the suffrage nullified and undone by public apathy or the relentless maneuvering of special interests; by the high personal cost of attention to public affairs, costs both financial and professional; by the minimal effect upon the visible ills of America—industrial strife, urban crowding, changing morals—of any and all progressive remedies. The "People" seemed unable to perceive the common good—had in fact almost never turned out when issues came to a vote. And compounding these ills and others there was that persistent leadership crisis, as Norris pointed out ruefully in his autobiography,

24. Ibid. pp. 556-63.

Fighting Liberal. If a leader arose, they could not unite behind him; if unity seemed close at hand, jealousies among the leadership opened to the view of the rank-and-file the deep character deficiencies of the great, and the movement was fragmented again.

In the light of their complaints, we are hardly surprised at the number of those who ignored during the 1930's, as they had for years, all sights and sounds of American political life. And this seems to be the real importance of those vacant places in the ranks during the New Deal years. Those who escaped from reform call attention to something not sufficiently realized, the tremendous strains and difficulties—financial, psychological, intellectual—inherent in the practice of reform. No reveille would bring them out of the hills, no promises of success would cajole them again. When George Norris lingered for months, in the 1920's, over the decision whether or not to resign from the Senate and give up, he reflected a general feeling among the older progressives; that there might be no way to make America what they wanted her to be.

Edgar Lee Masters put it well in a passage from his autobiography, *Across Spoon River:* "All these reverses [the failure of all liberal programs in Chicago, such as municipal ownership of the streetcar lines, etc.], my own included, gave me a revaluation of life, and filled me with a skepticism about a new day of justice in American politics; and many other things caused me to look forward to a career for myself in which I would accept the country as it was, and interpret it as I saw it. At the same time I meant now to make some money." It was then 1917: "The United States had just declared war on Germany, and the Chicago of 1914, and just before, and the America of that period, were saying their last lines of a happy day which had promised to be happier . . . and I decided to buy a country place and to have apple trees and bees, flowers and vegetables, and to work in the open air and to have tranquillity for writing. If there was forever to be war, first the Spanish-American War, which changed the form of our government, and now war upon Germany, which would solidify that change, I wanted to get to the hills." [25]

Thus a major part of the story of the progressive impulse cannot be told in the familiar terms at all, but tells itself through the

25. Edgar Lee Masters, *Across Spoon River: An Autobiography* (New York: Farrar and Rinehart, 1936), 316, 381.

retreats that claimed some of them completely and attracted many more: writing, travels, the making of money, religious consolations, homes in the country—like Ray Robins's Chinsegutt—where New York and her modern insoluble miseries could not intrude.

VI

Dispersion and Disagreement:
The Progressive Heritage

> When we have freed our government, when we have restored freedom of enterprise, when we have broken up the partnerships between money and power which now block us at every turn, then we shall see our way to accomplish all the handsome things which platforms promise in vain if they do not start at the point where stand the gates of liberty.
>
> WOODROW WILSON

"They have been mad, confusing, discouraging years," said William E. Borah of the years 1912-37.[1] He spoke for most of those who, thinking of themselves as associated with the reform hopes of the Roosevelt–Wilson era, survived to ponder the effects of their uprising and the prospects of the hopes they shared as young men. It had been their aim to arouse the People, to employ public indignation, the vengeance of the ballot, and wherever necessary the coercive power of a responsible government, all in an effort to set America back on the old paths. Could they take satisfaction in the condition of affairs at the end of the reforms of yet another Roosevelt? Was the promise of American life closer than when they began, or drifting farther out of reach?

The progressive remnant gave no single answer to these questions. Whatever our hopes for finding an uncomplicated relationship between progressivism and the New Deal, we must be very careful in tracing the ideas and people bridging the two eras. Progressivism flowed in several channels after the war put an end to the exhilarating days when all reformers felt a part of a common effort. Each branch, each cause, had a different development in the interwar period, some gaining strength, some dying, all undergoing change. The sense of unity, joining them for one last brief time in the spring and summer of 1933, was never to be fully recovered. We have seen that most progressives who survived de-

1. Speech of September 16, 1937, Box 12, Borah MSS, Library of Congress.

cided, after that initial enthusiasm, that the New Deal was destructive of their political and social hopes for America; that a smaller but still considerable number professed to see in it the culmination of a lifetime of effort; and that, for a very few, it was not nearly radical enough.[2] By an uncanny coincidence, Ohio's

2. In order to get an idea of the probable inclination of those progressives who could not be categorized "for" or "against" or "Left," I took whatever evidence there was and made a decision wherever possible as to how the uncategorized reformers probably leaned in the 1930's. The results may be totaled as follows: *Probably Against:* Norris Brown, William Adams Brown, Everett Colby, Austen G. Fox, Royal Meeker, Victor Murdock, John M. Parker, Miles Poindexter, E. R. A. Seligman, Francis Louis Slade, Judson C. Welliver, Henry Fountain Ashurst, Max Eastman, Robert L. Owen, Ray Robins, Ida Tarbell, Joe Tumulty (total—seventeen). *Probably For:* Irene Osgood Andrews, Harris Cooley, Edward T. Devine, Frances Kellor, S. McCune Lindsay, Owen R. Lovejoy, Shailer Mathews, Mary Ovington, George Rublee, William E. Walling, Ray Stannard Baker, Louis Brandeis, O. G. Villard (total—thirteen). If there is any value in these guesses, it is simply that the proportion derived from those about whom we are more certain—roughly 60-40 against the New Deal—seems to hold for those for whom we cannot be sure.

three "Boy Mayors" who launched reform movements simultaneously in Cleveland, Cincinnati and Toledo at the height of Ohio progressivism wound up in the 1930's at three of the major terminals of the progressive experience. The better known of them, Newton Baker of Cleveland, opposed the New Deal; Henry T. Hunt of Cincinnati worked for the NRA, and Brand Whitlock of Toledo secluded himself at Cannes with his books, his memories, and his disillusionment. Whitlock, who had given up on reform early in the war years, disliked the New Deal intensely, when he allowed himself to think about politics at all.

I I

The New Deal drew strength from several sectors of the original movement. Chief among them was the profession of social work, particularly those among the early social and settlement workers who shared an interest in the preventive possibilities of social action. Their aid to the New Deal has been noted earlier. Joanna Colcord has detailed the contributions of individual social workers and voluntary associations in the field of social service to the early stages of the adventures in Federal relief.[3] The role of those whom Brandeis tartly called "the social work–progressive crowd" in the drafting and legislative support of the Social Security Act of 1935 and the Wages and Hours Act of 1938 may be followed in Robert Bremner's *From the Depths,* or in the recently published account of the writing of the Social Security Act by Edwin E. Witte.[4] The pressure they brought to bear on the New Deal had its clear beginnings in the stirrings of the middle class conscience, i.e. among progressives, in the early years of this century.

The study of survivors has indicated other groups and areas of pronounced affinity for the New Deal. Many members of the academic community, men like E. A. Ross or Dean William Draper Lewis of Pennsylvania or John R. Commons, men Joseph Dorfman called the "Elders," thought Roosevelt's use of government was closely in line with ideas they had advanced for years.[5] The

---

5. Not all the "Elders," of course, agreed that the New Deal was what they had been teaching in the universities. Dorfman discusses only four—Commons, Ely, Seligman and Taussig—and of them, only Commons showed much enthusiasm for the New Deal, with Taussig apparently inclined to prefer it to plausible alternatives, Seligman maintaining what seemed to be a disapproving silence, and Ely actually hostile. See Dorfman, *The Economic Mind In American Civilization* (New York: Viking, 1946-59, 5 vols.), vol. 5.

---

3. Joanna Colcord, "Social Work and the First Federal Relief Programs," in National Conference of Social Work *Proceedings* (New York: Columbia University Press, 1943), pp. 382-94.
4. Edwin E. Witte, *The Development of the Social Security Act* (Madison: University of Wisconsin Press, 1964). Witte's account is sprinkled with the names of old progressives—John B. Andrews, Paul Kellogg, Grace Abbott *—who helped shape the Social Security Act. Harry Malisoff's story of the beginnings of unemployment compensation, however, makes it clear that in that area the New Dealers had literally no American precedent to build on but the Commons-inspired plan adopted by Wisconsin in 1932, a voluntary employer reserve plan that was rejected by the Committee on Economic Security. See Malisoff, *Political Science Quarterly,* LV (June 1939), LV (September 1939), and LV (December 1939).

clergy were conspicuous among those hailing the Roosevelt years; notably, Charles Stelzle, Stephen S. Wise, Herbert Seely Bigelow, Bishop McConnell, and, always seeking more for the poor, John Haynes Holmes. And if a small sample gives any ground for generalizing, women progressives almost invariably followed their progressivism straight into the arms of the New Deal—notably Lillian Wald, Mary Simkhovitch, Mary Woolley, and probably Frances Kellor, Irene Osgood Andrews and Mary White Ovington.[6] One can then say of the new Deal progressive that he or she

6. No women in the sample opposed the New Deal. All these women, however, were from the field of social work except Mary Woolley (who was President of Mount Holyoke), and this, rather than their sex, was probably the controlling factor. Other women progressives outside the sample, such as the New York civic reform leader Mrs. Francis Louis Slade*, were prominent in the Landon campaign.

Concerning the decisiveness of the social work connection, it is interesting to notice what happens to the Bull Moose group in the 1930's if the social workers are removed. The group then becomes very strongly anti–New Deal, and those who signed the "Bull Moosers for Landon" letter in *The New York Times* (October 18, 1936) appear to faithfully represent the Bull Moose majority.

was likely to be a person who lived in one of the larger cities and whose work was of the social work, social settlement, religious, or voluntary association variety, rather than a part-time involvement in political or moral "clean-ups" undertaken from a professional base such as law or politics (and, by the 1930's, long since over). An astonishing number of friends of the New Deal, progressive and otherwise, were recruited in New York City.[7]

Because the New Deal found strong support among progressives associated with urban social problems, it was natural that a part of its program and of its characteristic spirit reflected their

7. For insight into the role of the city as a center of the production of reformers, see the symposium, "Pioneers and Professionals: Chicago's Contribution to Social Service," *Social Service Review*, XXVII (March 1954), 1-64. Among those associated with Chicago progressivism were Jane Addams, Graham Taylor, Mary McDowell, Edith and Grace Abbott, Sophonisba Breckinridge, Julia Lathrop, and Florence Kelley. On New York's importance in sustaining reform leadership, see Clarke Chambers, *Seedtime of Reform,* pp. 260-61.

own approach to American issues. When the administration secured Federal programs in old age and job security, Federal underpinnings to relief of poverty, Federal limitations on hour and wage standards and the employment of children, it was but implementing programs that had been largely the custody of one group of progressives, the professional altruists of the social work fraternity. The expansion of government into these areas had never seemed to them unwise or unconstitutional. "If we turn to government with confidence, and act with vigor," Homer Folks said in his seventieth year, "we will not be disappointed." [8] And they shared with the New Dealers, those men and women of the social service field and their allies from clerical and academic professions, an urgent concern for the pragmatic result, without deliberation about the possible violation of constitutional or other metaphysical limits. The social worker, Folks said in 1923, "looks only to results; he is not made afraid by any labels or precedents, or any device or plan which, to the satisfaction of all reasonable tests, contributes to human well-being." [9]

---

9. Quoted in Walter Trattner, "Social Statesman: Homer Folks, 1867-1947," unpublished Ph.D. dissertation, University of Wisconsin, 1964, p. 431.

I have been arguing that the social work, social settlement, academic, and clerical sector of progressivism made the strongest connection to the New Deal, and this includes the leadership if not the membership of those voluntary associations formed to advance social justice. Since these organizations were almost all active on the Left in the 1930's the argument seems the more persuasive. Actually, even here we encounter the extent of the transformation that was necessary to make a progressive into a liberal. The existence in the 1930's of such organizations as the American Association for Labor Legislation, the National Consumer's League, the National Child Labor Committee, and Survey Associates, all generally sympathetic to the New Deal, are not the solid evidence of progressive–New Deal continuity that they might appear to be. These organizations were the same in name only (the exception being the AALL, which was never more or less than John B. Andrews), having undergone considerable alteration in personnel and po-

8. From "Some Recollections on a Seventieth Birthday," speech delivered February 18, 1937; typescript in file "Addresses, 1937," Folks MSS, New York School of Social Work.

litical outlook. A good example of this shift is the Tenement House Committee of the COS of New York, which under Lawrence Veiler in the progressive period had been hostile to the idea of public housing and placed reliance on restrictive legislation. The lineal descendant of that organization welcomed the New Deal entry into the public housing field, but it had changed its name (in 1938 to the Committee on Housing of COS, and in 1939 to the Committee on Housing of the Community Service Society, successor to COS) and, more to the point, undergone "reluctantly" a change of heart with regard to public housing in the late 1920's. Veiler, who lived through the New Deal, was generally unhappy with it. See John G. Hill, "Fifty Years of Social Action on the Housing Front," *Social Service Review,* XXII (June 1948), 160-79. Another progressive organization, the National Consumer's League, had so changed its political attitudes that Newton Baker, a former president, felt compelled to resign in the middle 1930's rather than be associated with policies which increasingly veered leftward. (See C. H. Cramer, *Newton D. Baker,* Cleveland: World, 1961, p. 193.) And the People's Lobby, another progressive group appearing in the ranks of reform in the 1930's, was a different organization entirely, having been revived by John Dewey in 1929 and staffed with new people, among them that steady friend of radical causes, Benjamin Marsh.

Along with specific and time-ripened proposals in the field of social welfare, and an attitude hostile to abstractions which might impede the immediate realization of relief and support for society's lesser members, they brought that irreducible optimism which is the *sine qua non* of any social experimentation. Florence Kelley, Felix Frankfurter remembered, always referred to herself as "the most unwearied hoper"; that same untiring optimism sustained Jane Addams, Homer Folks, Lillian Wald, Graham Taylor, and others, long after events seemed to some to have made their persistence ridiculous.[10] The New Deal borrowed heavily

10. Ben Reitman, a Chicago anarchist, was sufficiently annoyed by Graham Taylor's hopeful gradualism to write: "On the whole your book [Taylor's autobiography, *Pioneering on Social Frontiers*] left me disconsolate. Your optimism if sincere is impossible. . . . You know perfectly well that there is more unemployment, delinquency, perversion . . . than when you, Jane Addams and Mary McDowell started." Reitman to Tay-

lor, June 16, 1931, quoted in Louise C. Wade, *Graham Taylor: Pioneer for Social Justice, 1851-1938* (Chicago: University of Chicago Press, 1964), p. 218.

from that same "anything can be done" spirit.

III

Because of these close affinities between the two reform eras, reducible always to the use of government to achieve both economic and humanitarian ends not served by the processes of the market place, a good many old progressives found it possible to participate in or support popular movements in both periods. They should be regarded, however, as the exception to the rule, outnumbered by those who saw in Roosevelt's work those same fatal tendencies they had long contested against. Even some of those who finally voted for Roosevelt in 1936 were less than enthusiastic. When Harlan Fiske Stone said "I suppose no intelligent person likes very well the way the New Deal does things," he alluded to that combination of haphazard methods, contradictory and pyramiding agencies, and collective solutions to hitherto individual problems, which seemed almost more than some old reformers, basically inclined to wish the New Deal well, could take.[11] Ray Stannard Baker was a loyal Democrat, as behooved the biographer and admirer of Wilson, and was a humane and open-minded man with a long and honorable record in the service of reform. He finally voted for Roosevelt in 1936, but his support was grudging: "I am going up soon to vote for FDR, not because I think him a Savior, . . . but because that between the two the country will be safer with Roosevelt. But it will not be safe. . . . Our government has ceased to be a duty, to be sacrificed for, and become a privilege somehow to be used for ministering to our needs and our greeds." [12]

Even Herbert Seely Bigelow, who voted and talked as a New Deal enthusiast during his two terms in Congress (1934-38), admitted at the end that "I did not [when I voted for the New Deal measures] believe in regimentation . . . . I believed that with a

11. Quoted in A. T. Mason, *The Supreme Court from Taft to Warren* (New York: W. W. Norton, 1964), p. 92.
12. Entry of November 3, 1936, Notebook 53, Baker MSS.

new money system and a more rational tax system we could raise wages naturally and restore prosperity and get away from all this government planning of private industry and go back to Jeffersonian democracy." [13] He repeated these complaints on the floor of the Congress a year later: "We are getting all bogged down with political machinery. . . . Is it possible that with different treatment we might dispense with this mushroom growth of bureaus and political managers and return to the Jeffersonian idea that the government is best which governs least? As a member of the Seventy-fifth Congress I have voted for this New Deal legislation, but never with complete confidence. It does seem to me that there is a better way." [14]

I V

If even these friends had doubts and objections about the New Deal, it was no surprise that more progressives could see no progress in it at all, and stood over against it in such numbers as to constitute a sort of progressive referendum against the reforms of the 1930's.

As with the others, they generally came from predictable areas within the broad spectrum of progressivism. The reformer who became a politician, and especially one who adjusted easily to political life and held elective office for many years, usually found the New Deal indulging in too many constitutional innovations and trying to apply Federal solutions with alarming frequency. If he had been a journalist, the odds were heavy that he would sympathize more with the leaders of business than with the young professors and idea men of the new era, and that he would pen some mild or not so mild condemnation of the New Deal—or, failing to penetrate its mysteries as readily as he had the mayoral campaigns or stock swindles of an earlier day, he might retreat to a condemnatory silence. Politicians and writers, along with many lawyers and businessmen who had devoted part of their time to citizens' better government groups, produced most of the progressive criticism of the reformer in the White House after 1933.

13. U. S., *Congressional Record,* 75th Cong., 1st Sess., 1937, LXXXI, Part 10, 2300-2301.
14. U. S., *Congressional Record,* 75th Cong., 2nd Sess., 1938, LXXXIII, Part 2, 3074.

Herbert Croly had very early dismissed most of progressivism as "a species of higher conservatism," and without accepting all that he meant by that judgment, we can agree that, more often than not, those progressives who survived until the New Deal era were basically conservative. They should have recognized that the part of the progressive legacy they drew upon to oppose the New Deal closely resembled the arguments used against progressivism itself by their old enemies, the corporation counsels and standpat politicians of the days of George Baer. Class unity, progress through public education rather than extensive institutional alteration, a Jeffersonian distrust of the state, a deep-set fear of collective action involving (as it nearly always did) some reduction of individual liberty, and the determination to put to any proposed change the requirement that it leave America as little changed as possible—these principles were not new to progressivism, but were moved to the foreground by the actions of Franklin Roosevelt.

When the New Deal recognized and dealt with particular classes and social groups, it undid the work of years of progressive effort, for it divided rather than united the American people. The original progressive intention had been to fight the growing gap between those with something and those with nothing to lose. This could be done by filling that gap with one's physical self, as the settlement people had done (Graham Taylor liked to call it "standing in the breach"), or by exhorting all within range to talk, not of the material issues that divided, but of higher (meaning "spiritual") matters that united us.[15]

---

15. While they placed chief reliance, in this matter of the prevention of class animosities, upon the avoidance of the wrong sort of talk, a good number believed to greater or less extent in the sort of actual redistribution of wealth which they provided for in the Sixteenth Amendment, and which they advocated and occasionally secured through higher inheritance taxes.

They detected the New Deal's redistributionist tone and intent even if they overestimated its success, and they complained that Roosevelt could not seem to resist the political power produced by the agitation of material issues. In this he did not adhere to the progressive design. "What a sordid decade is passing," William Allen White wrote in 1940. "The spirit of our democracy has turned away from the things of the spirit. . . . What a joy it would be to get out and raise the flaming banner of righteousness." [16]

Righteousness, here, should be read "non-economic issues," and White was expressing the same preference for a healing national self-denying fervor that caused Carl Vrooman to remember the war-bond drives of the World War I as the high point of the progressive movement.[17] Arthur Koestler once wrote that political

---

17. See Vrooman, *The Present Republican Opportunity*, pp. 67-90. It seems to me that Vrooman came as close to defining the progressive impulse as can be hoped when he wrote: "For many years I sought eagerly not only in America but throughout Europe for a political party, a reform movement, a labor union, a church or any other organization that was able to make good men and women get up as early, stay up as late, work or fight as hard and get as much kick out of life as do . . . the fanatical apostles of Communism, or the no less fanatical soldiers of fortune in the world of high finance." (p. 67.) Vrooman found his movement in the Oxford Group, but it was his search, not its culmination, which was typical of numbers of progressives.

---

and social change, in symbolic terms, must come by way either of the Yogi or the Commissar. The Yogi places his hope in internal change, in the gradual elevation of the mind and spirit of individuals, while the Commissar, impatient, turns to radical and even violent changes in institutions. The progressives, by an overwhelming margin, preferred the way of the Yogi, which is to say that they relied upon education rather than coercion whenever possible. When the New Dealers seemed to be abandoning the ideal of educating the electorate as a whole, they had provided; as Rush Welter writes, "the bridge by which former progressives might cross over to the conservative position." Welter adds: "So many made the journey that at times they seemed to be the leading figures in the opposition." [18]

A final vital principle with them, an individualism so stubborn that very few forms of collective action were really acceptable, had once been a revolutionary principle, in the days of the young Republic. This individualism had been the heart of nineteenth-century liberalism, the faith of their Mugwump fathers, and they

16. From White's introduction to Halford E. Luccock, *American Mirror* (New York: Macmillan, 1940), p. 49.
18. *Popular Education and Democratic Thought*, p. 316.

had not rejected it as decisively as their resort to government might lead us to believe. Their advocacy of increased governmental activity was closely hedged about by the requirements that the right man be entrusted with power, that reformers display the right spirit of deliberation and caution, that they move according to a clear plan. Only under these conditions, progressives were willing to enlarge the state.

Still they were individualists at heart—the word "individualism" appears hundreds of times in their literature—and they typically practiced an individualistic politics. The early progressives in the Congress were dubbed "Insurgents" to denote that ungovernable, kick-over-the-traces attitude that made it so difficult for them to unite in substantial numbers behind any one leader, subscribe to any one program toward any one end. William E. Borah exemplifies this innate maverick quality to a well-publicized perfection, but many progressives, especially those who were visible in politics or muckraking, were similarly unsuited by temperament to enduring the very collective controls the progressive movement is historically credited with advancing.

Some would submit to the yoke of party (they were usually Southerners), but little else could bind most progressives to a belief or policy determined by remote authority. Hutchins Hapgood, although an extreme case of this unruly individualism, confessed to it in the following words: "I attack the powerful and prevailing thing in art, industry, in all fields, just because it is prevailing, irrespective of the merits of the case." [19] Few of Hapgood's contemporaries in the reform era were as irreverent as he, but they were perhaps more amply endowed than the average American of that era with a stiff-backed individualism that resisted most forms of coercion. They had revolted in the first place when they discovered that the trusts were plotting to fasten control over them. At that, their revolt was characterized more by energy than by co-ordination, for the average progressive did not take easily to direction or to the subordination of his own pet theories to some organizational doctrine. Without that individu-

19. Quoted in Mabel Dodge Luhan, *Movers and Shakers* (New York: Harcourt, Brace, 1936), p. 52. Hapgood insisted that his lifelong intention, expressed in such ritualistic revolts, had been to take America back "to the old, deep ideals and lofty hopes of the race," and he called himself an "Insurgent-Conservative" (Luhan, p. 53).

alistic temperament, of course, there would have been no citizens'
uprising at all, and the progressive movement offered many out-
lets for a man who was ready to fight to give the individual more
responsibility and more freedom from restraint. But it could have
been predicted that men of that temperamemt would probably
not approve of the reform cause in this country if it shifted its
primary goals from freedom to security, and if it came to rely
more on compulsion than on exposure and enlightenment. They
wanted to do good, but they wanted to do it at the demand of
their own conscience—else there would be no pleasure or credit
in doing it at all. They were less than enthusiastic over doing the
right thing as part of some obedient mass and at the demand of
some bureaucrat. Understandably, many of them found the "conservative" side, the side of individualism and liberty, congenial
in the 1930's.

Felix Frankfurter was perhaps too harsh on one of them, Ellery
Sedgwick, when he said of him that "he wanted to be on the side
of the angels. He wanted to be for decency, he wanted to be for
'liberalism'—provided it didn't cost him too much with what he
regarded as the 'right people.' " [20] But when progressives battled
against Franklin Roosevelt, a fellow progressive from the group
that supported him could be even harsher. In the constitutional
crisis of 1937, with Roosevelt's Court Plan being defeated by a
widespread defection among "liberals," the progressive Madison
(Wisconsin) newspaper editor William T. Evjue* wrote to Oswald Garrison Villard: "The President is licked because some of
the so-called liberals who have been deprecating the trend toward
a judicial oligarchy failed to stand back of him. It is the same old
story—the President didn't do it the right way. Mr. Villard wants
it done this way. Mr. Shipstead wants it done another way . . .
and other weak-kneed progressives who talked about these issues
abstractly were afraid to meet the issue when the actual test
came." [21]

20. Harlan B. Philips (ed.), *Felix Frankfurter Reminisces* (New York: Reynal,
1960), p. 214.
21. Evjue to Villard, no date (1937), File 3311, Villard MSS. With his usual
pungency, Ezra Pound rendered his own verdict upon progressivism in a
letter to Amos Pinchot: "You are an old man, but you have not been a
coward. . . . But I suspect the WHOLE of your generation in the USA was
fed on second rate English slop." Pound to Pinchot, December (no date),
1936; Box 58, Pinchot MSS.

To find this preponderance of progressive sentiment against the New Deal is to become conscious of considerable differences between the two reform movements of the first half of this century. This does not mean that the New Deal was as revolutionary as so many progressives feared; on the contrary, they misread its intentions and exaggerated its extent as badly as did the business classes. But the strong dissimilarities are there, and we may speak of them without forgetting that the New Deal nonetheless little merited the fears of its progressive opponents and the uneasiness of so many of its progressive friends. The response of surviving progressives reminds us that important intellectual sources of the New Deal were more recent than progressivism. One of the preoccupations of the progressives who were unhappy with the New Deal was to cite new figures with new ideas, men who had come from nowhere and who were going too far. They overworked the names of Tugwell and Berle and Corcoran, perhaps, but some of them were aware of Stuart Chase, John A. Ryan, Foster and Catchings, Eccles and Keynes, Lewis Mumford and Frederic Delano—and, of course, Coughlin, Townsend, and Long.

But a part of the responsibility for the generation of such ideas, for the sudden importance of such men, and for the incorporation of their schemes in Federal legislation, rested with the progressives themselves. There is, of course, the delicate question of the culpability of the progressives for the breakdown of a system they had so recently improved. We may, however, seek a less speculative level. Walter Lippmann, in an article in 1934, pointed out that there was no body of progressive economic thought which could be made available to an administration in desperate need of an understanding of the business cycle and anti-depression economics.[22] The work of a few well-known progressives, such as that of Taussig in international trade and tariffs, or of Edwin Seligman in taxation and public finance, was of little importance in the present emergency. Most progressives either accepted the impassioned economics of Henry George, or resigned themselves to knowing little about that opaque subject. As George Record told Amos Pinchot, a few months before he died, "we have got to

22. "Recovery by Trial and Error," *Yale Review*, XXIV (September 1934), 1-13. A student of the period tells us that the Depression of 1929 caused Irving Fisher "to study, for the first time, specifically the problem of booms and depressions." See Joseph Reeve, *Monetary Reform Movements,* p. 171.

learn more about this money question. We are not up to date." [23]

In line with that advice, Pinchot joined the Sound Money League and began to study monetary theory, but he was never sure of himself in economic matters. In that he was typical, for a great many of the old reformers found the Depression baffling. A few were willing to admit the irrelevance of their own experience and accumulated expertise to the crisis of the early and middle 1930's. Ray Stannard Baker wrote in his Notebook toward the end of 1936: "Of this I am sure. I cannot settle . . . the tremendous problems now plaguing the world. Most often I cannot fully understand. The factors are too complex." [24] Ernest Poole, an associate in the muckraker movement in New York, complained in his autobiography that he found it hard in the 1930's to write as he had written earlier, about reformers and the urban poor, because he found at the center of things the "brilliant young men" of the New Deal who offered only "plans and figures that gave no chance whatever to my humble writer's pen. I've always liked more human stuff." Poole added: "As the New Deal rushed on its way, it grew more complicated and bewildering all the time." [25]

---

25. *The Bridge: My Own Story* (New York: Macmillan, 1940), p. 384. Writers, far from the center of government, might be excused this confusion. But it was found everywhere, even among those at the center of action. Hiram Johnson wrote to his son: "I am extremely troubled about his demand for Four Billion Dollars un-earmarked. I may accept this because I don't know what to do myself in curing our country's ills, and inasmuch as I am unable to present a plan, I may be justified in giving him the purse strings of the nation." Hiram Johnson to Hiram Johnson, Jr., January 26, 1935, Johnson MSS.

Another old muckraker, Wallace Irwin, was even more candid: "It is difficult for an old man, who has gone through three wars and had so little to do in any of them, to confess anything more

---

23. From an unpublished essay on Record by Amos Pinchot, File 100, Pinchot MSS. Newton Baker left his library, over 400 books, to Cleveland College, and a shelf list is re-printed in Willis Thornton, *Newton D. Baker and His Books* (Cleveland: Press of Western Reserve University, 1954). I counted eleven books on economics; the bulk concerned politics, history, military affairs, or biography. We are fortunate to have this knowledge of Baker's library, and I suspect his tastes were rather typical.
24. Notebook 53, Baker MSS.

than the philosophy of Confusion. I call this book "I Look at Me," yet today whenever I gaze into my shaving mirror, I see no more than the baffled face of a worn human who in youth took sides ardently, cheerfully, and in age finds himself a-straddle of the fence." [26]

---

26. Wallace Irwin, "I Look at Me," unpublished autobiography, p. 431, Irwin MSS, Bancroft Library.

It was easy enough for Baker, Poole, or Irwin, all of them writers, to confess economic ignorance, or for a senator to confide self-doubts to his son. But the ignorance was widespread, and was shared by some who found it hard, especially if they were academic people (or bankers), not to pretend that they understood both the Depression and the way out. It was an era when a little carefully placed bluster often covered a great deal of bewilderment. Richard T. Ely wrote: "Unemployment is the result of faulty distribution of the working forces or of some maladjustment of relations which prevents the ready exchange of products and services. . . . We need more production of goods and services . . . but they must be properly distributed so as to give us balance and proportionality. To bring about this balance and proportionality is a problem to which we should direct all our efforts." Ely to editors of the *National City Bank Bulletin* (September 1933), copy in Albert Shaw MSS, Box 2.

It was precisely at this point, where the New Deal became so heavily engaged in economic matters, that New Deal liberalism began to disengage itself from the earlier reform tradition. While it resumed certain old progressive tasks—conservation, the regulation of sectors of the business community, and toward the end some trust-busting—the New Deal ignored most of the agenda the progressives had been working on when they were interrupted. Clarke Chambers has remarked how the New Deal actually collided head-on with at least two important progressive aspirations and the organizations formed to realize them—the "dry" forces and the many groups, usually composed of women, formed to advance world peace. Progressivism, in its larger aspect individualistic and oriented toward freedom from both the conditions and the sensation of restraint, was not to be fulfilled in a movement that increased the power of the meddling state. Focusing always on what was morally right, and finding that invariably in a state of mind that looked beyond self and class, the progressives felt defeated by any "reform" that accepted special claims and honored them. Aimed at unifying the American people, progressivism would produce few men who, even after the social education acquired during lenthy careers in public affairs, could accept frank class legislation.

With such goals as they had, in fact, they could hardly have met with any substantial success. Centralization was the forecast for America, in industry, in government, in demography. Only those progressives who limited their hopes to a more humane treatment of the poor were able to find satisfaction in the achievement of Roosevelt's general welfare state. A short time before he died in 1933, George Record, speaking for those progressives whose original and sustaining impulse had been to restore the small-town synthesis their fathers had presumably enjoyed, was able to sum up their efforts in a sentence: "I think if you are going to write the history of that movement you ought to write it from the standpoint that it was a failure." [27]

V

The student of history sees in a longer perspective what any American observes in his lifetime, the inexorable democratization of our common life—the enlargement of political rights, material security, meaningful freedom. Liberalism is the name of the movement that, through ideas and political action, has sought to hasten this process. In an era when institutions and social patterns are transformed every generation, it is not just the ordinary, conservative citizen who finds himself and his standards outmoded by the arrival of the next generation with its new problems and its inevitable irreverence. Such is the pace of change that the greatest losses of liberalism are by defection. There are men whose function it is at one phase of history to announce new

27. Quoted in R. E. Noble, "Henry George and the Progressive Movement," *American Journal of Economics and Sociology*, VIII (September 1949), 269; see also Noble, "George L. Record's Struggle for Economic Democracy," *AJES*, X (October 1950), 71-83. John B. Andrews, speaking for another type of progressive, disagreed. In looking back over 100 years of agitation, he wrote, "gradually, through persistent agitation one step after another was taken in shortening the hours of labor until, in 1938, the Congress of the United States crowned all these century-long efforts with the adoption of the Fair Labor Standards Act." (Andrews quoted in "In Memoriam: John B. Andrews, 1880-1943," *Social Service Review*, XVII (March 1943), 97-8.

social imperatives to a reluctant community and to demolish the resisting barriers of habit and self-interest; but who, lingering too long, cannot find it in themselves to abandon the issues and techniques of their great campaigns, and all too often become gradually identified with views and social classes which are either irrelevant or reactionary. This was in fact the fate of a great number of the progressives.

Innumerable careers illustrate this mismatch between human flexibility and the pace of change. William E. Borah remained in the Senate until 1940, keeping alive and undiluted a widely shared brand of progressivism. Many were disappointed that his career was so unproductive, that he squandered the last decades of his life in windy senatorial speeches which were invariably negative. In the forefront of reform in Wilson's day, Borah was to take almost no constructive part in any social advance for the rest of his career. During two decades when some men grieved for lynched Negroes, German Jews, or the peddlers of Dedham, Borah grieved for the Constitution. He was never again near the front lines of liberal reform.[28]

The explanation is uncomplicated; it rests in the consistency of his life and outlook. When as a young man he had asserted that government might not be used by selfish interests, he was a reformer; it came out only later that he, and many progressives with him, took their Jefferson undiluted, without Croly's Hamiltonian admixture. Borah's constitutional views were those of Justice Stephen J. Field, but Borah was consistent. Freedom was threatened by collective power, economic or political. The plutocracy at the turn of the century had captured both kinds, and reform meant not recapturing that power but shrinking the institutions through which it operated. Progressivism meant that no one was to be allowed special advantages through combination. Left alone, the citizens would resume as individuals the national march toward greatness.

It was pure Jefferson, and while these views were suited to the disestablishment of the special interests that were reaching for unlimited power as the twentieth century began, they prevented

28. It fell to the Southern liberal, Charles Ervin, to say that Borah reminded him of the MGM lion—nothing there but the growl. See Ervin, *Homegrown Liberal: The Autobiography of Charles W. Ervin* (New York: Dodd, Mead, 1954), p. 171.

any national solutions to a host of national problems when anti-trust failed to set the nation right. Borah, like most progressives, would never become a tory. Throughout the interwar years he spoke for the "rights" of labor, criticized the standpatters in his own party, and quietly voted for more New Deal measures than his oratory seemed to allow. But that powerful, famous voice was to be raised time after time against the New Deal. Borah, and progressives of his ideology like Edgar Lee Masters, William Randolp Hearst, Albert S. Burleson, A. Mitchell Palmer, James A. Reed, and all of those who stood in the Jeffersonian tradition, held to their distrust of the state with the tenacity of men who were not sufficiently adroit intellectually to admit how varied were the prerequisites of true freedom, and who could not learn to balance their distrust of power against the necessary use of it. But if Borah could not see his way to a new conception of freedom, he could at least follow with stubborn courage and unflinching consistency the only political economy he knew.[29]

The same difficulties with Federal power eventually brought a more intelligent and resourceful reformer, Oswald Garrison Villard, to the same unproductive end. Heir to a magnificent reform tradition reaching back to abolitionism and the revolution of 1848 in Prussia, it was natural that Villard would be prominent in the progressive era agitation. No one could question his radicalism; although a reformer of average zeal during the Wilson reforms, he foreshadowed his capacity for growth by taking up the cause of the Negro as one of the founders of the NAACP. He took over as editor of *The Nation* in 1918, and that sedate journal, mired for decades in the now conservative mugwump attitudes of Godkin and Schurz, became in the postwar years a lead-

29. Both of Borah's biographers, Claudius O. Johnson and Marian C. McKenna, found Borah a somewhat inaccessible personality, and his personal papers (in the Library of Congress) are the main reason why; they are voluminous but largely unrevealing. See Johnson, *Borah of Idaho* (New York: Longmans, Green, 1936), and McKenna, *Borah* (Ann Arbor: University of Michigan, 1961). A brilliant biographical essay by William E. Leuchtenburg appears in the *Dictionary of American Biography*, sup. 2. Many of Borah's speeches are available in the public record. For an interesting exchange of views, see John M. Cooper, "William E. Borah: Political Thespian," *Pacific Northwest Quarterly*, LVI (October 1965), 145-58, and the following criticism by Claudius Johnson. I also learned from Edwin Kemmler, *The Deflation of American Ideals* (Washington: Public Affairs Press, 1941), pp. 104-8.

ing advocate of social reform and civil liberties. Villard's *Nation* was always to the Left of the winning presidential candidate, and when the New Deal came, Villard in its early years spoke in a clear voice for "planning" and a "new era."

Yet when Villard saw what Roosevelt's New Era was like, he could not endorse it. At times he wrote as if Roosevelt had not done enough for the poor, and while he could never bring himself to embrace socialism, he voted for Norman Thomas in 1936. But the close observer could tell that what Villard wanted was all of the goals of the New Deal *without a welfare state*. The more he saw of the state, with its military potential and its inclination to trample the rights of dissenters, the less he could feel at ease with domestic advances reached through government. Granted, as Michael Wreszin argues, his pacifism soured him on Roosevelt, but it is also true that he came out against the Court Plan, criticized the labor militancy of 1937, and even regretted the "tremendous power" the NAACP had become by the end of the war and registered his continuing faith in the Booker T. Washington philosophy. He relinquished the editorship of *The Nation* in 1933, and after the election of 1936 felt that the journal was becoming too radical. In 1940, the year he voted for Willkie (he had not backed a winner since 1912, and approved of no President after Grover Cleveland), he gave up his column amid a gathering flurry of critical letters. "I feel that I have been left high and dry by a backwash," he wrote John Haynes Holmes, "and I wonder if you and I, and other steadfast liberals, are not merely back numbers left stranded because of the alarming clash between radical and fascist forces." [30] And to William Allen White in 1939: "I feel as though I had lived too long. I had hoped for another kind of world which I hoped we would reach through another corridor. . . ." [31]

Of course it was war that most depressed him, war in the main that had set him against two Democratic reformers, Wilson and Roosevelt. But pacifism does not explain his uneasiness with the New Deal, whether he appeared to criticize from Left or Right. He shared with Borah that final inability to expect progress from collective solutions, from the raw power of majorities who were unwilling to wait for the awakening of individual virtue. He sent this poem to his son, one month before Pearl Harbor:

30. Villard to Holmes, March 25, 1937, File 1739, Villard MSS.
31. Villard to William Allen White, January 28, 1939, File 4161, Villard MSS.

He grew old in an age he condemned,
Felt the dissolving throes
Of a social order he loved
And like the Theban Seer
Died in his enemies' day.[32]

Most progressives fell somewhere between Borah's moderate progressivism, with antimonopoly its main hope, and Villard's more headlong indignation at social injustice. And just as were Borah and Villard, most of them were troubled by the interventionist state of the 1930's, and went reluctantly, often unwillingly, into a future where the state took on such powers, where the individual counted for so little. It may seem odd that they proved in the end to have such a distrust for a democratic government, since their generation is remembered chiefly for its use of national power. But only a gifted few progressives understood that they were helping to create a new political philosophy. It is easy for us now to see that their era was the crucible where, by the classic Hegelian process, a new political philosophy was in the making. From the time of the Founders there had been two attitudes toward the state: the Jeffersonian, relying upon a minimal state, decentralized institutions and the good sense of the local yeomanry; and the Hamiltonian, at home with vigorous government and a national outlook, but interested before all else in the welfare of the managers and owners of the commercial, banking, and industrial enterprises of the country. By the beginning of this century there was emerging a third, the liberal-collectivist, sharing with the first its democratic sympathies and with the second its national and statist focus.

The progressives may have played an important part in this intellectual transition, but they did not do so consciously in most instances. They had not moved as far from the Founders' fear of

32. Quoted in Michael Wreszin, *Oswald Garrison Villard: Pacifist at War* (Indianapolis, Bloomington: Indiana, 1965), p. 271. Villard's papers are at the Houghton Library, Harvard. See also his "Issues and Men" in *The Nation*, 1933-40; and his autobiography, *Fighting Years: Memoirs of a Liberal Editor* (New York: Harcourt, Brace, 1939); see also D. Joy Humes, *Oswald Garrison Villard: Liberal of the 1920's* (Syracuse: Syracuse Press, 1960). Two short pieces which are very perceptive about Villard are Max Lerner, "The Liberalism of Oswald Garrison Villard," *New Republic*, XCVIII (April 26, 1939), 342-4, and Stephan Thernstrom, "Oswald Garrison Villard and the Politics of Pacifism," *Harvard Library Bulletin*, XIV (Winter 1960), 126-52.

political power as their practice suggested. With the example of Italy and Germany before them in the 1930's, they were not convinced that the confident democratic planners of the new school could avoid falling, along with their enlarged state, into the hands of the Hamiltonian plutocrats who knew a few tricks of their own about governing. The progressives were fated to live and act in the age when the tactics and political philosophy of democrats were being altered to take into account the fantastic private governments being erected all around them. They shared in that alteration, but they did not find it intellectually or emotionally easy. The New Deal in part actually mirrored their confusions, and the unreconciled state of American political ideas, but it was less concerned with polity than politics, afraid not of rash action but of not acting at all. It, therefore, despite its apparent good intentions (in which only a minority of them consistently believed), threatened rashly to deliver the hopes of liberalism into the hands of those who wished nothing more than to be handed the instruments of tyranny.

With the American future as the stakes, their crippling apprehensions and confusions are more readily forgivable. To accept what Roosevelt and the New Dealers had done and wished to do demanded more openness to experiment with political institutions, more trust in the tractability of the state to democratic purposes, more willingness to turn the cumulated rancor of the lower third against the upper, than most progressives could produce, although these had been the very qualities that had marked them as reformers, sometimes as radicals, in their own day.

The space that separated reform periods was less than twenty years. Yet, as Rex Tugwell once remarked, the 1920's were the longest decade in history, a time of vast and accelerating changes in morality, technology, and human density. Measured by mental and physical changes, the progressive era was thus farther back than the calendar admits, and to sense this is to bring into focus at once the dynamics of history and the revolutionary nature of our material life. The pace of that change in the twentieth century made it a near impossibility for men who had been born of fathers who fought for Lincoln, who lived from the world of the barge and the wagon to the world of the *Enola Gay* and through all the social revolution her cargo symbolized, to claim, at the end, a lifetime of reform.

Appendix I
The Derivation of the Sample

Before anything else is said about progressivism, one must admit its persistent variety. There was great divergence in the focus of the various reform efforts, in geographical origins, in goals and programs, in degree of success. The movement encompassed so many aims and extended itself over such a long period that its outlines are not and probably cannot be clear. While we may say with confidence that Senator Aldrich was *not* a progressive and that Senator Norris *was*, there are men such as James C. McReynolds who inhabit the Right limit of progressivism's vague territory, and men such as the wealthy socialist Joseph Medill Patterson who inhabit the Left. To differentiate between surviving Populists, socialists and trade unionists, who were all reformers, and the reformer who was a progressive, we utilize (as did contemporaries) such tests as "middle class" origin and interest in a set of familiar reforms of the political system and in the areas of morals, urban, and industrial problems. Thus men like McReynolds and Patterson, like the ex-Populist Peter Witt of Cleveland or the socialist Charles Edward Russell, were sufficiently engaged in activities on the progressive order to edge into the penumbra of the movement. Most men like La Follette and Amos Pinchot and hundreds of others, give us no trouble. But since we cannot define what the word "progressive" means with precision, there must always be some causes and individuals whose claim to the label is moot.

I have determined, in recruiting a sample of progressives, to list those social reformers from the turn of the century to World War I who have been called progressives by historians or contemporaries, and who were engaged in one or more of the varied causes which progressives initiated. The sample was taken from progressive organizational lists and from reliable historical studies, and I searched in seven areas: national politics, state politics, municipal reform movements, voluntary associations formed to advance social justice or democracy, thought and publicity (muckrakers, writers, professors), social gospel representatives, and consumer organizations. In addition to securing a number of reformers from each of these areas, I culled the name of every progressive from three major studies of the movement—those of Arthur S. Link, George Mowry, and Russel B. Nye.[1]

Progressivism, when it finally arrived at the national political level, had energetic, colorful leaders and a widely publicized program. It is at this level that the movement is most fully documented, and this is especially true of the apogee of reform pressure upon national politics, the campaign of 1912. Wilsonian or "New Freedom" progressives were gathered by searching Link's multi-volume biography of Wilson (33 names) and by including the members of Wilson's cabinet (19 names).[2] Roosevelt Progressives, the "New Nationalism" progressives of the Bull Moose effort, were secured by culling Amos Pinchot's history of the Progressive party (28 names).[3] A list of senatorial insurgents of the Taft period was obtained from Howard W. Allen's close study of voting on reform issues in the 1911-16 period (15 names).[4] Finally, I took the names of the 50 progressives who joined themselves in the National Progressive Republican League in 1911 to advance the presidential candidacy of Robert M. La Follette.[5]

Progressivism operated through political reforms at the state level before it moved into presidential politics. What occurred in Wisconsin later occurred in lesser degree in almost every state, with the New Jersey movement producing a President. George

1. Arthur S. Link, *Woodrow Wilson and the Progressive Era* (New York: Harper, 1954); George Mowry, *The Era of Theodore Roosevelt* (New York: Harper, 1958); Russell B. Nye, *Midwestern Progressive Politics* (East Lansing: Michigan State University Press, 1959).

2. Arthur S. Link, *Wilson: Road to the White House* (Princeton: Princeton University Press, 1947), chaps. 14-15, and Link, *Wilson: The New Freedom* (Princeton: Princeton University Press, 1956), chaps. 1-8 and 12-14. All the members of the cabinet, it might be objected, were not progressives. But there is no need to inquire deeply into the credentials of any but those surviving through 1936, for only those could affect the study. Surviving were Burleson, Colby, Daniels, Glass, Houston, McAdoo, McReynolds, and Palmer. Some case for progressivism could be made for all but Houston, and he was dropped.

3. Amos Pinchot, *A History of the Progressive Party, 1912-16*, edited by Helen M. Hooker (New York: New York University Press, 1958).

4. "Geography and Politics: Voting on Reform Issues in the United States Senate, 1911-16," *Journal of Southern History*, XXVII (May 1961), 216-26. The senators qualifying as reformers were those Allen found voting on the reform side of 134 selected issues at least 75 per cent of the time.

5. *La Follette's Weekly Magazine*, III (February 4, 1911).

Mowry's fine study of California progressives includes a lengthy roster of reformers; I took 15 names, those Mowry reported as having left substantial collections of papers.[6]

The explosive and unplanned growth of the American city after the Civil War produced far-ranging social problems; by the turn of the century, the city was the center of a wide variety of reform efforts directed toward their solution. These municipal reformers typically sought improvement through "citizens' " movements to oust an unsavory mayor or city council, or to change the city charter. In New York, fifteen citizens formed the Committee of Fifteen to combat prostitution, and published the influential report *The Social Evil* (1902). To follow up that report and to make such a committee permanent, a new group designated themselves the Committee of Fourteen in 1905. There was no overlap in membership, and the combined committees produced 29 names.[7] The officers of the National Municipal League for the year 1904 were a group of eight reformers.[8]

Voluntary associations grew up to combat a variety of evils— child labor, the growing separation of classes in urban slums, the situation of the Negro or the working woman. Much of their attention was centered on urban problems, but they concentrated on aiding injured groups rather than on honesty in urban government. Further, these associations generally developed a nationwide organization. The National Child Labor Committee in 1905 listed 15 officers and trustees.[9] A middle class organization formed to advance the position of the laborer was the American Association for Labor Legislation. Its letterhead in 1916 listed, as general officers and members of the Executive Committee, 26 prominent progressives.[10] Five white reformers met in 1909 to take the first steps toward founding the National Association for the

6. *The California Progressives* (Berkeley: University of California Press, 1951). See his Bibliographical Note.
7. The Committee of Fifteen, *The Social Evil* (New York: G. P. Putnam's Sons, 1902). The Committee of Fourteen, *The Social Evil in New York: A Study of Law Enforcement* (New York: G. P. Putnam's Sons, 1910).
8. A list of the officers of the League, formed in Philadelphia in 1894, is in Frank M. Stewart, *A Half-Century of Municipal Reform: The History of the National Municipal League* (Berkeley: University of California Press, 1950).
9. *Proceedings* of the First Annual Meeting of the National Child Labor Committee (1905).
10. AALL to Library of Congress, June 1, 1916; AALL Collection, Library of Congress.

Advancement of Colored People.[11] In all, these three groups yielded a total of 46 names. An important component of voluntary activity of this sort was the settlement house movement, but there seemed no need to make special efforts to recruit a sample of settlement workers, since they were so well represented in the three general studies I used.

The progressive movement received its publicity and much of its impetus from the reporters and writers involved in the muckraker movement. Louis Filler's book, *Crusaders for American Liberalism*, is a classic study of their exposure of graft, monopoly, and the gamut of progressive concerns.[12] For social critics of a less sensational sort, I turned to David Noble's study of some of the intellectual leaders of progressive reform (eleven names).[13]

Two familiar studies of the social gospel movement during the progressive period, those of Charles H. Hopkins and Henry May, yielded 33 names.[14] Consumer groups were spontaneous products of this era of heightened awareness of the need to organize the unorganized, and from the National Consumers' League (general officers and vice-presidents, 1911) and the People's Lobby (First Governing Board, 1906), I derived 29 names.[15]

The total, after eliminating names appearing more than once, was a group of 402 men and women who took part in the far-flung enterprises of progressive reform. Further study revealed that even the broadly lenient standards used to identify a "progressive" disqualified two men, and their names were dropped.[16] The sample of reformers stood finally at 400.

11. Mary White Ovington, *The Walls Came Tumbling Down* (New York: Harcourt, Brace, 1947).
12. (New York: Harcourt, Brace, 1939).
13. *The Paradox of Progressive Thought* (Minneapolis: University of Minnesota Press, 1958).
14. Hopkins, *The Rise of the Social Gospel in American Protestantism: 1865-1915* (New Haven: Yale University Press, 1940), 16 names. May, *Protestant Churches and Industrial America* (New York: Harper and Brothers, 1949); chapters 2 and 4 of Part IV yielded 17 names. In the Hopkins book there were over a hundred social gospel ministers and writers mentioned; I selected the sixteen who were most prominent.
15. *Work of the National Consumers' League* (American Academy of Political and Social Sciences, 1911), II; thirteen names. Samuel Merwin, "The People's Lobby," *Success Magazine*, IX (November 1906), 25-6; sixteen names.
16. James Carsen Needham appeared in Mowry's bibliographical note, since his papers (at Stanford) contain frequent references to California politics in the progressive period. But Needham was no progressive, but a staunch

II

Of the 400 selected, 204 died before 1933. An additional 22 died before the first four years of the New Deal were completed, and I have not considered them.[17] For another six I could not locate satisfactory data about their subsequent careers and death dates. Dropping those who died before 1936, and those for whom no data at all could be discovered, I ended by examining a group of survivors totaling 168.[18]

I have arranged these progressives in the following categories of political attitude: the category "Consistently More Radical than the New Deal" for those of a critical stance who assumed that only a radical change in the profit system offered real improvement; "Supported the New Deal" for those who generally applauded what was done, although they may have objected to certain laws or policies; "Opposed to the New Deal" for those who disliked most or all of it, the principal sign being a vote for Landon; "Other" the evasion I adopted for those whose response was so complex or shifting as to make categorization impossible, as they mixed distaste for the New Deal with hopes for true reform in a way that constituted neither approval or rejection; "Retreated from Political Concern" for those ten progressives who

---

opponent of the reformers of the Lincoln-Roosevelt Republican League and kindred disturbances. David F. Houston, Wilson's Secretary of Agriculture, was never a reformer, either before national prominence or after.

17. They were Jane Addams (d. 1935); Joshua W. Alexander (d. February 1936); James Mark Baldwin (d. 1934); Elmer J. Burkett (d. 1935); William J. Cary (d. 1934); Christopher P. Connolly (d. 1933); Joseph M. Dixon (d. 1934); Henry W. Farnam (d. 1933); Walter L. Fisher (d. 1935); Gilson Gardner (d. 1935); Charlotte Perkins Gilman (d. 1935); Gilbert N. Haugen (d. 1933); William Travers Jerome (d. 1934); William S. Kenyon (d. 1933); Henry C. King (d. 1934); William L. La Follette (d. 1934); Edward J. McGuire (d. 1934); Walter Owen (d. 1934); John B. Payne (d. 1935); George L. Record (d. 1933); Brand Whitlock (d. 1934); William B. Wilson (d. 1934).

All saw Roosevelt elected and witnessed a part of the New Deal, but only a part, and I have not used their responses in tabulating results. In cases where the response was rather well articulated, as for Jane Addams or George Record for example, I have worked that attitude into the study at the appropriate place.

18. For the following no death dates could be found, nor very little other information: Harry W. Cadman, Hugh T. Halbert, Paul Latzke, Georgine Milmine, John B. Moran, Andrew J. Smith.

An alphabetical list of the full sample may be found in Appendix III.

clearly decided to have nothing more to do with politics, reform, or social causes. Forty-two others had to be put in the category "No (or Insufficient) Data."

CONSISTENTLY MORE RADICAL THAN THE NEW DEAL:
John Dewey, Scott Nearing, Charles Edward Russell, Upton Sinclair, Lincoln Steffens.

TOTAL: 5

SUPPORTED THE NEW DEAL:
John B. Andrews, Herbert Seely Bigelow, John Burke, John R. Commons, Edward P. Costigan, Josephus Daniels, J. Lionberger Davis, Finley Peter Dunne, Joseph Eagle, Homer Folks, Raymond B. Fosdick, Norman Hapgood, John R. Haynes, Francis J. Heney, John Haynes Holmes, Frederic C. Howe, Henry T. Hunt, Harold L. Ickes, Paul U. Kellogg, William Draper Lewis, Benjamin B. Lindsey, William G. McAdoo, Francis J. McConnell, Francis E. McGovern, Gustavus Myers, George W. Norris, Joseph Medill Patterson, George Foster Peabody, Joseph T. Robinson, E. A. Ross, Mary Kingsbury Simkhovitch, Rudolph Spreckles, Charles Stelzle, Frank W. Taussig, Graham Taylor, Merle D. Vincent, Lillian D. Wald, Stephen S. Wise, Peter Witt, Mary E. Woolley.

TOTAL: 40

OPPOSED TO THE NEW DEAL:
Henry J. Allen, Newton D. Baker, Robert P. Bass, William S. Bennet, William E. Borah, Jonathan Bourne, Joseph L. Bristow, John Graham Brooks, Albert S. Burleson, Arthur Capper, Irwin S. Cobb, Bainbridge Colby, Coe Crawford, George Creel, Frederick Morgan Davenport, E. A. Dickson, Richard T. Ely, Irving Fisher, James R. Garfield, Carter Glass, William Hard, William Randolph Hearst, Burton J. Hendrick, Charles Evans Hughes, Cordell Hull, Morton D. Hull, Robert Hunter, Wallace Irwin, Will Irwin, Hiram Johnson, Reginald W. Kauffman, James H. Kirkland, Irvine L. Lenroot, Walter Lippmann, Samuel S. McClure, Vance C. McCormick, James C. McReynolds, Edgar Lee Masters, John M. Nelson, Chase S. Osborn, A. Mitchell Palmer, George Cooper Pardee, Arthur J. Pillsbury, Amos Pinchot, Gifford Pinchot, Atlee Pomerene, James A. Reed, Chester H. Rowell, Ellery Sedgwick, Albert Shaw, Charles M. Sheldon, George Shel-

don, John Spargo, Henry L. Stimson, Marshall Stimson, Mark Sullivan, William S. U'Ren, Carl S. Vrooman, Felix M. Warburg, William Allen White.

TOTAL: 60

OTHER:

Henry Fountain Ashurst, Ray Stannard Baker, Louis D. Brandeis, Max Eastman, Robert L. Owen, Ernest Poole, Raymond Robins, Ida Tarbell, Joseph P. Tumulty, Oswald Garrison Villard.

TOTAL: 10

RETREATED FROM POLITICAL CONCERN:

Samuel Hopkins Adams, Winston Churchill, Charles R. Crane, William J. Ghent, William H. Hatton, Hutchins Hapgood, Henry F. Hollis, Samuel Merwin, Walter E. Sachs, Marie Van Vorst.

TOTAL: 10

NO (OR INSUFFICIENT) DATA:

Robert McDowell Allen, Irene Osgood Andrews, Lee Beattie, Norris Brown, William Adams Brown, Everett Colby, Harris Cooley, Edward T. Devine, Rhetta Childe Dorr, Mark M. Fagan, Frank H. Fayant, Austen G. Fox, Franklin Hichborn, Frederick Ludwig Hoffman, Frances A. Kellor, Adolph Lewisohn, S. McCune Lindsay, Lucius N. Littauer, Owen R. Lovejoy, Henry L. McCune, Theodore Marburg, Shailer Mathews, Royal Meeker, H. Pereira Mendes, Elmer A. Morse, Victor Murdock, Charles P. Neill, Mary White Ovington, John M. Parker, Miles Poindexter, Erman J. Ridgway, George Rublee, Theodore A. Schroeder, Edwin R. A. Seligman, Francis Louis Slade, Edgar C. Snyder, Ethelbert Stewart, George Kibbe Turner, William English Walling, Judson C. Welliver, John Wilson Wood, Clinton Rogers Woodruff, Charles R. Zahniser.

TOTAL: 43

As has been said many times, progressives were intensely individualistic. The categories above were therefore not designed to contain them neatly, but in order to make some general view possible. Many progressives changed their minds about the New Deal, and had to be categorized by their principal, usually their final, response. There was some monolithic approval or rejection, but just as frequently some parts of the New Deal were welcomed, other parts regretted, and even others never passed upon.

An idea of the complexity of the effort to order individual responses may be gained by comparing some of those within a given category. For example, James A. Reed and William Allen White are both set down as opposed to the New Deal, although the nature of their criticism varied greatly. Reed vocally despised it all, while White was decidedly uncomfortable with Landon in 1936, and made most of his criticism in a rueful, apologetic tone. Cordell Hull, another in that category, was able to act as Roosevelt's Secretary of State and bear in silence his disapproval of the President's domestic policies. Chase Osborn was a Landon man and a critic of the New Deal in the middle years, but in 1933, and again in 1937, he was found praising the President and his efforts. Such are the diversities of political opposition.

Among New Deal sympathizers there is little more neatness or consistency. The list of the administration's friends and well-wishers includes the affable and loyal Josephus Daniels, the taciturn Gustavus Myers, who continued to muckrake the American rich but who apparently had no real interest in politics, and a man with spectacular changes of mind, Joseph Medill Patterson, who left his strong New Deal stance about 1940 to become a vitriolic critic.

But these men and women are at least susceptible to some grouping. There were those, like Oswald Garrison Villard or Raymond Robins, who followed a torturous course beyond category. Robins might stand as the most baffling member of that segment of reformers who, governed both by their individualism and their humanity, simply could not decide what to do or think. The consequence was generally a political course of great ambiguity, and even when that course could be described as for or against the New Deal, it spoke clearly only of confusion and conflicting impulses. Men like Borah, Chase Osborn, Richard Ely, Albert Shaw, Marshall Stimson, William Allen White, Henry Fountain Ashurst, Ray Stannard Baker, or Edward T. Devine were most representative of this sort of vacillating political loyalty, but Ray Robins was surely the most confused.[19] I claim little

---

19. Robins, ex-cowhand, minister, lawyer, and social worker, was rusticated in Florida during the 1930's. Yet he found time

for political sympathies. A Republican and friend of Herbert Hoover, he visited the Soviet Union in 1933 and praised her extravagantly; he criticized the New Deal, remained a Republican (favoring Borah) through 1936, and then switched to Roosevelt to the extent that he lauded the Court plan, and seems to have voted for him subsequently. Robins—charismatic, messianic, and not a little neurotic—was never able to decide what to do with himself. A letter to William Hard in 1938 mirrors these confusions: "I certainly agree with you that normalcy is not enough. We have to restore a democratic ["democratic" marked out and "dynamic" penned in] economic system in America. . . . We have to accommodate a growing and moving society to the just human needs of the relatively inefficient and unfortunate. . . . How to accommodate change to security? How to produce a system that moves and at the same time has normalcy ["normalcy" penned out and "mercy" penned in] . . . that is the basic problem, as I look at it." Robins to Hard, letter of no date (1938), Box 28, Robins MSS, Wisconsin State Historical Society.

more for the groupings above than that they provide a method for presenting with reasonable accuracy the *general* pattern of progressive thought and opinion in the New Deal years.

III

What follows is an analysis of the biographical data gathered on the surviving reformers, considered first as a whole (168 of them), and then in two sub-groups, the opponents (60) and the supporters (40) of the New Deal. The data include age, type of reform activity, geographical origin (based on place of rearing rather than place of birth), party affiliation, education, social class (early or family class standing, and then class at maturity), and religion.

The patterns emerging from these data in some cases suggest obvious theories of causation. Because I have not used multivariate analysis, and because the actual mechanism of causation is usually obscure, I have been cautious in its interpretation. As the tobacco industry says of cigarettes and cancer, a high correlation between, let us say, political radicalism and graduate study in Germany is "a mere statistical regularity," and no proof of anything. Nevertheless, this sort of information, both where it shows apparent correlation between political ideas and sociological situation, and where it does not, brings us closer to an understanding of recent American reform.[20]

TABLE 1   YEAR OF BIRTH

	All Survivors (168)	Anti–New Deal (60)	Pro–New Deal (40)
Mean	1868	1868	1867
Median	1867	1867	1867
Mode (12)	1868		

Those opposing the New Deal were, on the average, only one year older than those supporting it. This is an insignificant gap, and indicates that political conservatism had no direct relation to age, at least within this group. The span of years among the surviving 168 progressives was considerable; the oldest was born in 1846, the youngest in 1889. It might have been expected that the older progressives would have proven more conservative in the 1930's, but this was not the case. Neither was the reverse the case. Within the sample itself, age apparently had little if anything to do with acceptance or rejection of the New Deal. In the absence of a control group, we cannot be sure that advancing age did not incline them all equally in some direction—presumably a conservative one.

It should be noted that the 168 survivors were younger than the average. When the *entire* sample is surveyed (birth dates are available for 364), the mean year of birth is 1861, the median 1862, and the modal year 1859. For the entire sample the range is also greater; the oldest was born in 1819, and several were born in the 1830's. Nonetheless, most were born between 1855 and 1872. With a mean year of birth of 1861, progressives were relatively young men, as other surveys have shown. Richard Hofstadter's comment seems valid, that they were the generation that came of age in the 1890's.

Many progressives were involved in more than one type of reform activity. I have used each one's chief interest in such cases.

As may be seen, there are marked differences in the distribu-

20. On career line analysis and its limitations, see E. N. Saveth, "The American Patrician Class: A Field for Research," *American Quarterly*, XV (Summer 1963), 235-52.

TABLE 2 TYPE OF REFORM ACTIVITY

	Entire Sample	Anti–New Deal	Pro–New Deal
Politics	29% (48)	44% (26)	17% (7)
Municipal reform	9% (15)	3% (2)	20% (8)
Social Justice	12% (20)	8% (5)	8% (3)
Social gospel	8% (13)	2% (1)	13% (5)
Settlement–social work	6% (11)	0 0	20% (8)
Journalism-editing	29% (47)	37% (22)	13% (5)
Expert: economics, etc.	5% (10)	3% (2)	8% (3)
Other	(3)	(1)	(1)

tion of reform interests between groups of similar political attitude. The New Deal drew strong support from settlement house
and social workers, ministers, and municipal reformers. There
was strong opposition among politicians and the journalist-editor
group.

Of the entire sample, at least thirteen reported having done
work in settlement houses, even if this was not their central interest. Ten of these favored the New Deal. This strong association of
the settlement house–social work progressive with a continuing
reformism appears to be the strongest connection between any
area of progressive effort and the reforms of the 1930's.

TABLE 3 REGIONAL ORIGINS

	Entire Sample (Data for 140)	Anti–New Deal (Data for 57)	Pro–New Deal (Data for 40)
New England	9%	10% (6)	10% (4)
Middle-Atlantic	31%	25% (14)	28% (11)
Middle West	38%	44% (25)	37% (15)
South	14%	10% (6)	17% (5)
Far West	8%	10% (6)	8% (3)

Of 168 surviving progressives, reliable data on area of rearing
could be obtained for only 148; of these, five were born in Germany, two in England, and one in Ireland, and they were
omitted from the above figures.

There seems to have been little difference in attitude toward
the New Deal from region to region. Progressives of all regions
show more opposition than support toward the New Deal. The

South (including Kentucky) offered more New Deal support than any other region, although even there we find opposition to be stronger among the old progressives. The data is too thin to be conclusive here, and it must be remembered that opposition to the New Deal in the South necessarily meant a breach in that region's historic allegiance to the Democratic party (see Appendix II).

In addition to data on region of rearing, it was possible to obtain information locating the childhood years of these reformers in either a city, small town, or rural setting. This could not be done with any great precision, not only because many families moved about in a given community or between communities, but also because "Boston" or "near Buffalo, New York" permits only a general estimate of the demographic situation in which individuals spent their formative years. Street addresses or other precise locations were rarely given. The figures that follow are therefore intended as rough estimates.

Of a group of 140 for whom data is sufficient, 30 per cent were raised in cities, 50 per cent in small towns, and 20 per cent on farms. Of those opposing the New Deal, 23 per cent were city-raised, 52 per cent in small towns, and 25 per cent on farms. It thus appears that the anti–New Deal group derived from rural origins slightly more often than average and from city origins slightly less often; the reverse was true of the group favoring the New Deal. Only the city, of the three locations, produced as many of those supporting reform in the 1930's as those who opposed it then.

TABLE 4   PARTY AFFILIATION

Party	Anti–New Deal	Pro–New Deal	No Conclusive Information
Democrats (37)	15	14	8
Republicans (55)	31	6	18
Socialists (10)	3	1	3[a]
Independents (18)	4	10	4

a Four other Socialists—John Dewey, Scott Nearing, Charles Edward Russell, and Upton Sinclair—were to the Left of the New Deal.

Of the surviving progressives, I discovered avowed party affiliations for 102. Another eighteen called themselves Independents, or consistently pursued an independent voting course. Of the rest nothing substantial could be learned about their voting records or continuing political allegiances.

The important years for this party determination were taken to be 1904-20; the Progressive party affiliations were ignored here, and will be discussed shortly. There was some shifting around among parties as the progressive period began (chiefly in the 1890's), and almost as much again during the war years and the 1920's. Still, most progressives stayed in one party for life.

The data suggest that, among those for whom party affiliation and response to the New Deal are both known, Democrats were more likely to oppose than support the New Deal (by a very slight margin), Republicans were considerably more likely to oppose, and the old Socialists divided rather evenly between a continuing radicalism and a reactionary shift over to the Right of the New Deal. Roosevelt got more support from Democratic progressives than from Republicans, but more opposition than support from both. Those progressives who had never established a party affiliation had a strong tendency to support the New Deal.

Of the thirty-two Bull Moose veterans whose response to the New Deal is known, twenty-one opposed and eleven supported it. The Bull Moose group thus appears slightly more conservative than the Democrats, but not so conservative as the group of thirty-seven Republicans whose attitudes to the New Deal are known. The Bull Moosers who argued during the campaign of 1936 that F.D.R. was *not* the heir to the Bull Moose–New Nationalism mantle had the agreement of most of the Bull Moose remnant encountered in this study.

Table 5 presents data on formal education. There was no way to assess the informal education—reading, conversation, lectures, travel—that these men and women might have undergone, and this is regrettable in view of its probable importance. But formal education repays investigation nonetheless.

The extent of formal education appears to have had little relation to political attitudes during the 1930's. Neither college degrees, graduate work, nor European study, taken alone, appear to have influenced progressives either toward a continued reformism or away from it.

If the group with graduate degrees is scrutinized as to discipline, an interesting pattern appears. Among those who *opposed*

TABLE 5   EDUCATION

	Entire Sample	Anti–New Deal	Pro–New Deal
No formal education	1	0	0
Some secondary	7	4	1
High school diploma	8	2	4
Some college	16	8	4
College degree	117 (78%)	43 (75%)	27 (75%)
TOTAL: b	149	57	36
College graduates with some post-graduate study	14	4	5
Graduate degree	61 (40%)	19 (33%)	13 (36%)
European study	20 (13%)	6 (11%)	5 (14%)

b Educational data was adequate in only these cases.

the New Deal and possessed graduate degrees, law degrees predominate; twelve, or 64 per cent, had degrees in law, and only seven, or 36 per cent, had master's or doctor's degrees. Among those who *supported* the New Deal and possessed graduate degrees, law degrees are in a minority; three or just under 25 per cent, had degrees in law, and ten, or just over 75 per cent had either master's or doctor's degrees.

Of a total of 117 college graduates, twenty-nine, or 24 per cent, were Harvard graduates. Of these, thirteen, or 45 per cent, opposed the New Deal, five, or 17 per cent, supported it, and for eleven there is no reliable information. The concentration of Harvard graduates is high among progressives, and Harvard graduates turned out to be more likely to oppose the New Deal than the sample as a whole.

It was difficult to determine the social and economic situation into which progressives were born—or which they later attained —in more than a very general sense. Information was either lacking entirely, or fragmentary. A progressive might speak, for example, of being born and raised on a farm in Iowa, which would leave to the imagination the size and productivity of the farm, the income of the family, the social origins of the parents, and so on. A fairly detailed autobiographical account such as that of Mark Sullivan in his *The Education of an American,* giving a full pic-

ture of family finances, furnishings, food, etc., was a rare exception. It proved possible, however, to arrive at a rough estimate of
social class at birth and in full career in the cases of 126 out of 168
surviving progressives. Of these, political response to the New
Deal could be determined in 83 cases.

It has often been said that the progressive was a middle class
reformer. Used in the broadest sense to indicate adherence to the
middle class values (honesty, religious observance and piety, thrift,
ambition, etc.), and implying the possession of some property,
this generalization is correct in most cases, but hardly useful.
For the purposes of this study a class spectrum of the simplest sort
was adopted, based upon a family's (or an individual's) economic
situation only, and assuming a "middle" as average. The categories were "Lower," "Lower Middle," "Middle," "Upper Middle,"
and "Wealthy."

An example of lower class origin might be that of Charles Stelzle, who was born and raised on the East Side of New York, lost
his father at nine, and was supported by a mother who took in
washing and sewed women's wrappers in their tenement room.
John Haynes Holmes might be said to have been raised in the
lower stratum of the middle class, for his father had attempted to
be a furniture merchant, failed, failed again at being a traveling
salesman, and forced the family after years of hardship to fall
back upon maternal grandparents.

The "Middle" defines a situation of regular employment for
the father, regular meals and habits, sufficient prosperity for
home ownership and a few cautious investments—the world, for
instance, of William Allen White's upbringing in Kansas. Hutchins and Norman Hapgood represent the typical "Upper Middle";
born to an Alton, Illinois plow manufacturer who "once made
and saved $100,000" and who sent his sons to Harvard, the Hap-
goods grew up in comfort but never in lavish surroundings. And,
for the youth of a progressive born to wealth, one might read Oswald Garrison Villard's autobiography *Fighting Years*, or W. A.
Swanberg's *Citizen Hearst.*

Arranged along that scale, the progressive generation demonstrates a greater diversity of class origins than is commonly al-
leged. There is some bunching in the "Middle" and "Upper
Middle" categories, but the poor and the very rich are well represented.

There is some difference, although not a striking amount, be-

TABLE 6   CLASS ORIGINS

	Entire Sample	Anti–New Deal	Pro–New Deal
Lower	15 (12%)	6 (12%)	5 (16%)
Lower Middle	20 (15%)	7 (14%)	8 (25%)
Middle	35 (28%)	16 (31%)	10 (31%)
Upper Middle	34 (27%)	16 (31%)	6 (19%)
Wealthy	22 (18%)	6 (12%)	3 (9%)

tween the class origins of progressives favoring the New Deal and those opposing it. A slightly greater proportion of those who were born lower than "Middle" ended in the 1930's by supporting Roosevelt. Among those favorable to the New Deal, about 40 per cent were born below "Middle," and only about 25 per cent above. Among those opposed, the proportions were almost exactly reversed. Still it must be remembered that men and women born to wealth supported the New Deal, and many born to poor families did not approve of the welfare and other measures of the second Roosevelt.

When the data on class are assembled for progressives in full career, it is first of all apparent that almost every one of them greatly improved in economic situation. Of a sample of 126, only eighteen might be said to have remained in "Middle" circumstances or lower. Among all progressives in this study, only Samuel S. McClure, to my knowledge, was in serious economic distress in the later years of life.

Working with such information as could be found, I have been able to arrive at the data shown in Table 7 regarding class at maturity and political attitude.

These figures indicate a slight tendency for opposition to the New Deal to increase with affluence, but the figures convey a degree of precision which the evidence would not allow.

While working with class categories, I kept a record of occupation. The relation between area of reform activity and political attitude in the 1930's has already been discussed (see Table 2), and there would be little point in presenting occupational data at the same length, since the categories and the results are quite similar. As might be expected, lawyers and politicians tended to oppose the New Deal (about three to two), while editors, publishers, and writers showed an even stronger anti–New Deal senti-

TABLE 7   CLASS AT MATURITY[c]

	Entire Sample	Anti–New Deal	Pro–New Deal
Lower	0	0	0
Lower Middle	4 (3%)	1 (2%)	2 (7%)
Middle	14 (11%)	3 (6%)	5 (16%)
Upper Middle	79 (63%)	35 (66%)	20 (64%)
Wealthy	29 (23%)	13 (25%)	4 (13%)

c Incomes fluctuated considerably due to job changes, illness, or the Crash of 1929. The base period was the decade of the 1930s, although some consideration was given to the style of life established from about 1920 forward.

ment (at least four to one). Social workers, clergymen, and teachers tended to support the New Deal quite consistently.

Some of these men and women pursued more than one career at a time, not to mention occasional career changes, so that the following occupational data contain a margin of arbitrariness. I called Carter Glass a politician, for example, when he was also a publisher. But with that in mind, the figures tell an interesting story. The occupational breakdown for surviving progressives is as follows: lawyers, 31; writers and journalists, 26; editors and publishers, 20; politicians, 19; businessmen, 15; teachers, 14; clergymen and social workers, 13 each; farmers and doctors, 2 each.

It is also instructive to look more closely at the group of lawyers who survived to observe the New Deal and whose political attitudes are recorded. Of a group of twenty-eight, eighteen opposed the New Deal and ten supported it. But the ten who favored the New Deal were an unusual group of lawyers. Two (John Burke and Ben Lindsey) were judges, and none of the others was practicing law in the 1930's. Like Harold Ickes, Henry T. Hunt, or Frederic C. Howe, they were New Dealers, or, like Raymond B. Fosdick, they had long ago gone into other lines of work. The practicing lawyer tended to oppose the New Deal, then, but a good bit more strongly than the eighteen to ten proportion would suggest.

There were no significant variances in political attitude among Catholics, Jews, Protestants, and those of no religious affiliation. No pattern could be discerned among any of the major religions (nor between those who called themselves atheists or agnostics and the believers) which would associate religious affiliation to an unusual degree with either conservatism or liberalism. It might be thought that Catholics and/or Jews would demonstrate a more favorable attitude toward the New Deal than Protestants, because of the appeal of the Democratic party traditionally, and the New Deal more immediately, to new ethnic and urban groups. For these progressives, at least, a strictly religious test does not reveal strong differences in political outlook. Protestant progressives opposed the New Deal more often than they favored it, but the proportion was almost exactly that of the group as a whole. A small group of Catholics and Jews for whom there was reliable information on political attitude in the 1930's split evenly, for the New Deal and against.

There seemed, then, to be no significant correspondence between denominational affiliation and political attitude. Yet it still might be true that religious faith encouraged certain political preferences and the lack of it encouraged others. Since it was easier to know who was religious than who was not, I gathered all those progressives of unusual piety, or a close observance, verbal and otherwise, of religious obligations, in order to test for political homogeneity. They were Bigelow, William Adams Brown, Cobb, Davenport, Garfield, Holmes, Kirkland, McConnell, McReynolds, Nelson, Osborn, Robins, Charles Sheldon, Stelzle, Marshall Stimson, Wise, Wood, and Woodruff. The fourteen whose response to the New Deal is known divided nine against and five supporting. That proportion is almost exactly the same as that of the entire sample, and seems to disallow any simple connection between deep religious feeling and any one political leaning. More important than the intensity of faith, of course, was what sort of faith it was. The moralistic protestantism of men like Justice McReynolds or James R. Garfield probably added to their distaste for the New Deal, and the social Christianity of men like Bishop McConnell or John Haynes Holmes virtually assured their warm reception for the administration that brought welfare to Washington. Observers of modern "conservatism" cannot be unaware of the persistent association of conservative political views and fundamentalist religious views, but it would be a bold investigator who would claim to know which was primary.

Appendix II
A Critical Evaluation of the Sample

The sample is open to certain objections. The progressives selected were leaders, and a possibility of error inheres in whatever differences in outlook might have existed between the leadership and the sympathizing, voting, inarticulate rank and file. That difference might make the sample a bit more radical than if it were representative of progressivism from base to leadership, but we can only speculate here, since progressives of little attainment or reputation rarely put their reflections into writing. Even the most active and articulate of the reformers, well enough known to have been selected in my canvas, failed in forty-three cases to have left sufficient published or unpublished material to enable me to discover their political views in the 1930's.

Another problem was that of proportion. It is virtually impossible to be sure of the proportion of their energies that went into the various causes of the era, trust-busting, honest government, eradication of child labor, conservation, and so on. A sample can only approximate the proportions we sense from an uneven historical literature and public record. Concerning this sample in particular, the names gathered from secondary accounts may reflect an over-representation of two types of reformer, the politician and the muckraker (not only journalists, but authors of books of social criticism in general). The sample of muckrakers from Filler's book, seventy-two in number, was scaled down considerably in the end by the subsequent obscurity of so many, and a marked decline in their interest in political affairs. Nonetheless, writers and politicians dominate contemporary reports, secondary literature, and this study, even though they certainly do not numerically dominate any substantial reform movement.

At the local level, such as the Chicago Civic Federation or the "New Idea" clubs in New Jersey, more businessmen are encountered than this sample included (about 6 per cent of the whole). Alfred Chandler's study of Bull Moosers, for example, turned up 95 businessmen out of 260, a proportion of some 40 per cent.[1]

1. "The Origins of Progressive Leadership," Appendix III of vol. VIII, *The*

Chandler was able to work with lower-echelon reformers since he needed only biographical data. Similarly, Samuel P. Hays's study of Pittsburgh reformers reported that 52 per cent of a sample of 745 were businessmen.[2] It is clear that progressivism in most of its local forms contained a greater proportion of businessmen than my sample. How many more, and what effect they would have had on the political center of gravity, we cannot be sure. Unfortunately, businessmen were for the most part part-time progressives, active at the local level principally, and such men usually fail to leave the historian the sources he needs to determine complex political attitudes.

This sample included many progressive types, some in sufficient quantity that I have confidence that further work would not alter the pattern established in this study. If the sample did not contain enough businessmen or enough "ordinary," rear rank progressives it did contain a large number of social workers, journalists, academic people, lawyers, and politicians. The clergymen in the sample, however, are probably not representative of all clergymen who were caught up in progressivism. They were predominantly big parish clergymen, undoubtedly less conservative than most who responded to the books of Charles Sheldon or Walter Rauschenbusch. There are women in the sample, but there can be no doubt that these women—Lillian Wald, Jane Addams, Mary Simkhovitch, and so on—were quite unlike the average woman who belonged to a local temperance group or the Woman's Trade Union League. A study of a large number of female progressives of all types would undoubtedly reduce the overwhelming statistical association of women with New Deal sympathies which this study discovered.

Few reformers were touched by only one reform interest, but when they were one can test that particular interest for its fate in the 1930's—at least as its old partisans saw things. This could be done to a greater extent than I have been able to do for the peace progressives, for temperance reformers, and for conservationists. In the instance of those interested largely or entirely in outlawing drink, one of course expects serious disagreements with the New

Letters of Theodore Roosevelt, edited by Elting E. Morison (Cambridge: Harvard University Press, 1954).
2. "The Politics of Reform in Municipal Government in the Progressive Era," Pacific Northwest Quarterly, LV (October 1964), 160.

Deal. This is so not only because the New Deal made America wet again, and seemed to like it so, but also because it was in a broad cultural conflict with those classes where prohibition had its strength. The relation of peace progressives to the New Deal is complicated, for although the pacifist element—John Haynes Holmes, Villard, and probably Jane Addams if she had lived— had reason to dislike Franklin Roosevelt's foreign policy, some members of the peace forces had strong internationalist convictions and one guesses that at least some of them would come to agree with Roosevelt that world peace required not only a sense of collective responsibility but the willingness to use force. Enough progressives of both these types, the drys and the peace advocates, must surely have lived through the New Deal to justify substantial research projects to extend our understanding of these idealisms into the 1930's and beyond.[3] The temptation to seek out additional groups and individuals is persistent, but the process would be endless. These two groups represent perhaps the most important reform interests to escape my canvass.

"One-interest" progressives who were conservationists provide another problem which this study has not solved. The sample included many progressives interested in conservation, such as Gifford Pinchot, James R. Garfield, George Pardee, Franklin Hichborn, John R. Haynes, E. A. Dickson, Francis J. Heney, and others. But few of them were exclusively interested in conservation or remained close to conservation work, so that their responses to the New Deal were based on a variety of things and tell us little about the relationship of Roosevelt's conservation policies to the older ideals. Conservation, of course, attracted a broad and diverse following. It was divided along "preservation" versus "use" lines, sections and regions disagreed, resource users differed in outlook according to size and nature of the use, water power development often conflicted with recreation. To get a clear idea of what type of conservationist tended to respond in what way to

3. For instance, the Anti-Saloon League's Wayne B. Wheeler died in 1928, but E. H. Cherrington and Bishop Cannon lived to see the New Deal. The two studies of the temperance crusade written since the 1930's do not touch on the New Deal (Andrew Sinclair stops in 1933, James Timberlake in 1920). There is a brief discussion of the political attitudes of temperance reformers in Joseph Gusfield, *Symbolic Crusade: Status Politics and the American Temperance Movement* (Urbana: University of Illinois, 1963), pp. 149-53, in which he tells us that Ida B. Wise Smith of the WCTU was strongly opposed to the New Deal, and suggests that her response was typical.

what New Deal policies, a much larger sample would be needed. It would be interesting to take the bureau chiefs mentioned in Donald Swain, *Federal Conservation Policy, 1921-33* (Berkeley: University of California, 1963), such as R. Y. Stuart of the Forest Service or Horace M. Albright of the National Park Service who began their careers as Pinchot and T.R. were awakening the public to the cause of conservation, and follow them into the 1930's. The same could be done with many conservationists mentioned in Elmo Richardson's *The Politics of Conservation: Crusaders and Controversies, 1897-1913* (Berkeley: University of California, 1962) or Samuel P. Hays, *Conservation and the Gospel of Efficiency: The Progressive Conservation Movement, 1890-1920* (Cambridge: Harvard University Press, 1959), gathering data on men such as H. H. Bennett, Elwood Mead, and Earle Clapp, and piecing together their relation to the New Deal. While closer study of peace progressives and prohibitionists would probably emphasize discontinuity between these sectors of reform and the New Deal, conservationists undoubtedly found much more in the New Deal to support.[4] But since conservation meant many things, one would need quite a large sample to be sure the patterns were reliable.

I have taken the opportunity in the text to lament the inadequacy of the designation "urban reformer," considering the immense variety of reform interests which churned to the surface in urban America during the progressive years. Each city was likely to have a different problem at the center of its reform pressures— taxation, political corruption, utility rates, public health, public services such as education or recreation, saloons, housing, and so on. The same city might and usually did contain at the same time a strong charities movement, a civic organization working for "clean government," housing reformers, and groups for the suppression of vice. If occasionally a political campaign (usually for mayor) brought the reformers together, this could not homogenize their differences of outlook. While some reformers entered into many of these activities, many were limited to one interest and, if they lived through the 1930's and retained that interest, may have left evidence as to the mesh of their particular crusade with New Deal policies. My own sample contained enough and

4. As, for example, did Judson King, as reported in his *The Conservation Fight, From Theodore Roosevelt to Tennessee Valley Authority* (Washington: Public Affairs Press, 1959).

sufficiently various "urban reformers" to suggest certain conclusions, i.e. that those working for honesty in government, charter reform, or moral improvement, were more likely to stand to the Right of fellow progressives and well to the Right of the New Deal; similarly, city planners and the social service group seemed to feel that they had much unfinished business at the end of progressivism and that the New Deal addressed itself to these goals with generally gratifying results.[5] But considering the magnitude and variety of the progressive movement in American cities, there is surely room for further work of the sort attempted here—as there is, of course, for all other phases of urban reform.

But the question of Southern progressives has given me most concern. It is now a commonplace that Southern progressivism was much more extensive than historians have credited it with being, although this gap in the literature is now being filled. But we have no book-length synthesis to match Russel B. Nye's book on Midwestern progressives, and to deliberately recruit Southern progressives would have led me to use Arthur Link's article, "The Progressive Movement in the South, 1870-1914," *North Carolina Historical Review*, XXII (April 1946), 172-95, or C. Vann Woodward's *Origins of the New South, 1877-1913* (Baton Rouge: Louisiana State University Press, 1951), chap. xiv. A glance at both showed that, of the progressives mentioned there, an unusually large percentage did not survive into the 1930's—men like Hoke Smith, Napoleon B. Broward, Alexander J. McKelway, Walter Hines Page, Edgar Gardner Murphy, and Walter Clark. I therefore recruited a sample of 400 progressives without special effort to include Southerners, and found that a reasonably large number found their way in: Burleson, Daniels, Eagle, Glass, Hull, Kirkland, McReynolds, Parker, and Robinson, all of whom remained in the South, and Cobb, McAdoo, Poindexter, Robins, Sinclair, and Walling, who were raised in the South but moved away.

These men provide enough evidence to enable us to see the

5. One is not surprised, for example, to learn that Richard S. Childs, founder of the Short Ballot Organization and prime mover in the campaign to advance the Council-Manager form of city government, was also a businessman, and voted against Roosevelt three times. A different view of the relation between urban progressivism and the New Deal was given by Otis Pease in his paper "Reformers and the Politics of Urban America," delivered at the Organization of American Historians convention, Cincinnati, April 28, 1966.

general pattern of Southern progressive–New Deal relations: Most did not like the New Deal (Glass, Hull, Robinson, Kirkland) as one would expect of conservative men from a conservative social class. A minority, like Daniels, remind us that there is such a thing as a Southern radical tradition.

Although I believe this to be a fairly accurate projection of the encounter between vestigial Southern progressivism and the New Deal, the subject deserves extensive treatment. Complicating the story is the paradox that those old Wilsonians I have named were often the legislative pillars of Roosevelt's program, despite the deepest sort of private objections. And although the historical literature does not generally enumerate them, there was a large contingent of Southern politicians who entered the Congress in Wilson's day and who would have to be called progressives, men who were still around in the 1930's and who were the legislative backbone of the early New Deal: John and William Bankhead, Alben Barkley, James Byrnes, Duncan Fletcher, James Garner, Pat Harrison, Sam Rayburn, Ellison Smith, Morris Sheppard, and many others. The slightest acquaintance with their voting records from 1933 to about 1936 shows that the New Deal would have been crippled without these men. Yet we know that almost without exception they developed a distaste for Rooseveltian liberalism; went along with it only because of the national and even greater sectional emergency, and because party regularity meant so much; and were, in the end, the heart of that coalition which frustrated the New Deal after 1937.[6]

But Southern progressivism produced more than a crop of Wilsonian congressmen and senators. There were many cities with reform movements, there were reform governors in most states, there was a muckrake movement, a small settlement house move-

6. Discussions of the relationship of Southern Democrats with the New Deal may be found in Frank Freidel, *F.D.R. and the South* (Baton Rouge: Louisiana State University Press, 1965), James T. Patterson, "The Failure of Party Realignment in the South, 1937-39," *Journal of Politics*, XXVII (August 1965), 602-17, and Dewey Grantham, Jr., "The South and the Reconstruction of American Politics," *Journal of American History*, LIII (September 1966), 227-46. Though most had extensive doubts about the New Deal in the early years, they supported their party's program and kept silent. Roosevelt's political mistakes in 1937-38 and a growing awareness of the New Deal's threat to Federal–state equilibrium and eventually to the bi-racial system overcame party loyalty and the desire for Federal funds, at least for most of them, and these old New Freedom Southerners helped bring the New Deal to a halt in 1938.

A CRITICAL EVALUATION OF THE SAMPLE 211

ment, a strong child labor protest, and a Southern Sociological
Congress which brought together philanthropists, public health
crusaders, and all the scattered social justice impulses of Southern
society.[7] Veterans of all these campaigns might be followed into
the 1920's and 1930's.[8] The Southern progressives in Franklin
Roosevelt's day will probably fall into three broad groups: the
moderate-conservative, caught in a crossfire between the economic
desperation of his constituents and his own fear of allowing power
to shift to the liberals and urbanites of the Northeast; the reaction-
ary-racist, whose Good Government progressivism melts away very
early in the 1930's to be replaced by a relentless obstructionism;
and the liberal, who speaks to the end for the social ideals of Jefferson, the early Tom Watson, and Woodrow Wilson. In the first
group, Florida's Duncan Fletcher, Arkansas' Joseph T. Robinson,
Virginia's Andrew Jackson Montague;[9] in the second, Carter Glass,
Theodore Bilbo, "Cotton Ed" Smith, Harry Byrd; in the third,
Josephus Daniels, Frank Graham, Alben Barkley, Hugo Black,
and younger men like Lister Hill, Will Alexander, and Claude
Pepper. And there will always be the progressive like "Boss" Ed
Crump of Memphis, who confounds all the categories by being a
machine politician who was also a reform mayor and a New Deal
congressman.

These are, of course, only educated guesses, based on the
Southern progressives in my own sample and upon what has been

7. A review of the growing literature on these aspects of Southern reform
may be found in Dewey Grantham's essay in A. S. Link and Rembert
Patrick (eds.), *Writing Southern History: Essays in Honor of Fletcher M.
Green* (Baton Rouge: Louisiana State University Press, 1966).
8. As George B. Tindall did in his article, "Business Progressivism: Southern
Politics in the 1920's," *South Atlantic Quarterly*, LXII (Winter 1963), 92-106.
E. Charles Chatfield carries his account of the Southern Sociological Con-
gress to 1920, and there is a hint that what had commenced in 1912 as an
attempt to bring the social gospel and modern science to bear upon Southern
social and racial ills was transformed by 1920 into an adjunct of the Red
Scare. "The object of the Southern Sociological Congress," said Bishop T. D.
Bratton to the convention in 1920, was to "keep America American" by
warning of the peril of reds and aliens. Chatfield, "The Southern Sociological
Congress: Organization of Uplift," *Tennessee Historical Quarterly*, XIX
(December 1960), 328-47.
9. See William Larsen, *Montague of Virginia: The Making of a Southern
Progressive* (Baton Rouge: Louisiana State University Press, 1965), and James
W. Flynt, "Duncan Upshaw Fletcher: Florida's Reluctant Progressive," un-
published Ph.D. dissertation, Florida State University, 1965, for the similarity
between their response to the New Deal and that of Robinson.

written so far touching on this problem. The several fates of Southern reform elements in the 1930's justifies a major research effort of its own, largely because a combination of circumstances deposited such tremendous political power with one type of Southern progressive, the New Freedom Democratic congressman or senator, twenty years after Wilson began his presidency. Men of that sort appear in this study, but they do not dominate it, for in the larger story of the American progressive movement they were not the movers and shakers or the heroes of that movement, but peripheral figures who came late to their mild reform sentiments and reaped for Woodrow Wilson what others had sown. But their story should be told, for the American political fates were to select them to be the reluctant agents of another transformation of American society, one which they would recognize too late as the very antithesis of the New Freedom.

Appendix III
The Sample: An Alphabetical Listing

The following is an alphabetical list of all reformers selected in the initial canvas for this study, to a total of 400. The names of those surviving through 1936 are in bold face. Death dates, where known, are listed to the right.

Francis Abbott	1903	Charles Joseph Bonaparte	1921
Ernest Hamlin Abbott	1931	**William Edgar Borah**	1940
Lawrence Fraser Abbott	1933	**Jonathan Bourne**	1940
Lyman Abbott	1922	James Henry Brady	1918
Frederick Upham Adams	1921	**Louis Dembitz Brandeis**	1941
Henry Carter Adams	1921	**Joseph L. Bristow**	1944
Samuel Hopkins Adams	1958	**John Graham Brooks**	1938
Jane Addams	1935	Charles Rufus Brown	1914
Felix Adler	1933	**Norris Brown**	1960
Joshua Willis Alexander (Feb.)	1936	Thomas Edwin Brown	1924
Chester Hardy Aldrich	1924	**William Adams Brown**	1943
Henry Justin Allen	1950	William Jennings Bryan	1925
Robert McDowell Allen	1948	Francis M. Burdick	1920
Irene Osgood Andrews	Alive	**John Burke**	1937
John Bertram Andrews	1943	Elmer Jacob Burkett	1935
Henry Fountain Ashurst	1962	**Albert Sidney Burleson**	1937
William J. Ashley	1927	George Burnham, Jr.	1924
Charles Brantley Aycock	1912	Harry W. Cadman	?
Alfred Landon Baker	1927	**Arthur Capper**	1951
Newton Diehl Baker	1937	Joseph Maull Carey	1924
Ray Stannard Baker	1946	William J. Carey	1924
James Mark Baldwin	1934	Andrew Carnegie	1919
William Henry Baldwin, Jr.	1905	William Hamlin Childs	1928
Mrs. W. H. Baldwin, Jr.	1905	**Winston Churchill**	1947
Thomas Robert Bard	1915	Moses E. Clapp	1929
John Bascom	1911	Samuel Langhorn Clemens	1910
John Foster Bass	1931	Hovey Clarke	1931
Robert Perkins Bass	1960	**Irvin Shrewsbury Cobb**	1944
James Phinney Baxter	1921	**Bainbridge Colby**	1950
Lee W. Beattie	1937	Everett Colby	1943
Edwin Webster Bemis	1930	**John Rogers Commons**	1944
William Styles Bennet	1962	Christopher Patrick Connolly	1933
Albert J. Beveridge	1927	Charles Horton Cooley	1929
William Dwight Porter Bliss	1926	Harris Cooley	1936
Herbert Seely Bigelow	1951	Henry Allen Cooper	1931
Edward Bok	1930	**Edward Prentiss Costigan**	1939

Charles Richard Crane	1939	William James Ghent	1942
Coe I. Crawford	1944	Richard Watson Gilder	1909
George Edward Creel	1954	Charlotte Perkins Gilman	1935
Herbert Croly	1930	Washington Gladden	1918
Ernest Crosby	1907	Carter Glass	1946
Albert Baird Cummins	1926	Arthur Gleason	1923
Josephus Daniels	1948	Rufus Lot Green	1932
Frederick Morgan Davenport	1956	Thomas Watt Gregory	1933
Charles R. Davis	1930	Asle J. Gronna	1922
J. Lionberger Davis	Alive	Arthur T. Hadley	1930
Jefferson Davis	1913	Herbert Spencer Hadley	1927
Oscar K. Davis	1932	Hugh T. Halbert	?
William R. Davis	1915	Edward Everett Hale	1909
Robert Weeks De Forest	1931	Matthew Hale	1925
Edward J. Dempsey	1930	Benjamin Bowles Hampton	1932
Harry H. Devereaux	1926	Hutchins Hapgood	1944
Edward Thomas Devine	1948	Norman Hapgood	1937
John Dewey	1952	William Hard	1962
Edward Augustus Dickson	1956	William Hatton	1937
Frank Lambert Dingley	1918	Gilbert N. Haugen	1933
Joseph M. Dixon	1934	John Randolph Haynes	1937
Jonathan Dolliver	1910	William Randolph Hearst	1951
Rheta Childe Dorr	1948	C. R. Henderson	1915
Finley Peter Dunne	1936	Burton Jesse Hendrick	1949
Joseph H. Eagle	1963	Francis Joseph Heney	1937
Max Eastman	Alive	Robert L. Henry	1931
Richard T. Ely	1943	George Davis Herron	1925
Joel B. Erhardt	1912	Franklin Hichborn	1963
Mark M. Fagan	1948	Dean George Hodges	1919
Henry Walcott Farnam	1933	Frederick Ludwig Hoffman	1946
Frank Fayant	?	Henry French Hollis	1949
Joseph Fels	1914	John Haynes Holmes	1964
Irving Fisher	1947	Frederic Clemson Howe	1940
Walter Lowrie Fisher	1935	William Dean Howells	1919
William Flinn	1924	Elbert H. Hubbard	1912
Benjamin Orange Flower	1918	Charles Evans Hughes	1948
Josiah Flynt	1907	William Hughes	1918
Joseph Wingate Folk	1923	Cordell Hull	1955
Homer Folks	1963	Morton Denison Hull	1937
John Franklin Fort	1920	Henry Thomas Hunt	Alive
Raymond Blaine Fosdick	Alive	(Wiles) Robert Hunter	1942
Austen G. Fox	1937	Frederick Dan Huntington	1904
Harold Frederic	1898	Paul Oscar Husting	1917
Ernest Freund	1932	John S. Huyler	1910
Issac Kahn Friedman	1931	Harold LeClair Ickes	1952
George W. Galvin	1928	Wallace Irwin	1959
Robert Jackson Gamble	1924	William Henry Irwin	1948
Gilson Gardner	1935	Fred S. Jackson	1931
James Rudolph Garfield	1950	J. W. Jenks	1929
Lindley Miller Garrison	1932	William Travers Jerome	1934

Francis Howe Johnson	1920	**Vance Criswell McCormick**	1946
Hiram Warren Johnson	1945	**Henry L. McCune**	1943
John A. Johnson	1909	**Francis Edward McGovern**	1946
Thomas Lofton Johnson	1911	Edward Joseph McGuire	1934
E. Clarence Jones	1926	Alexander Jeffrey McKelway	1918
Samuel Milton Jones	1904	**James Clark McReynolds**	1946
Wesley Livsey Jones	1932	**Theodore Marburg**	1946
David Starr Jordan	1931	Edwin Markham	1924
Reginald Wright Kauffman	1959	James Edgar Martine	1925
Florence Kelley	1932	**Edgar Lee Masters**	1950
Paul Underwood Kellogg	1958	John Lothrop Mathews	1916
Frances Alice Kellor	1952	**Shailer Mathews**	1941
George Kennan	1924	**Royal Meeker**	1953
John Stewart Kennedy	1909	**Haim Pereira Mendes**	1937
William Kent	1928	Edwin Thomas Meredith	1928
William Squire Kenyon	1933	**Samuel Merwin**	1936
Henry Churchill King	1934	Clarence Benjamin Miller	1922
James Hampton Kirkland	1939	Georgine Milmine	?
Robert Marion La Follette	1925	John Purroy Mitchell	1919
William L. La Follette	1934	Cleveland L. Moffett	1926
Franklin K. Lane	1921	Alexander Pollock Moore	1930
Harry Lane	1917	John Brown Moran	?
Robert Lansing	1928	**Elmer A. Morse**	1945
Julia Lathrop	1932	Frank Andrew Munsey	1925
Paul Latske	?	**Victor Murdock**	1945
Thomas W. Lawson	1925	Edgar Gardner Murphy	1913
Victor Fremont Lawson	1925	**Gustavus Myers**	1942
Irvine L. Lenroot	1949	**Scott Nearing**	Alive
Alfred Henry Lewis	1914	Henry Beach Needham	1915
William Draper Lewis	1941	George Arthur Neely	1919
Adolph Lewisohn	1938	**Charles Patrick Neill**	1942
Charles A. Lindbergh	1924	**John Mandt Nelson**	1955
Samuel McCune Lindsay	1959	Knute Nelson	1923
Benjamin Barr Lindsey	1943	Francis Griffith Newlands	1917
Walter Lippmann	Alive	Richard Heber Newton	1914
Meyer Lissner	1930	Frank Norris	1903
Lucius Nathan Littauer	1944	**George William Norris**	1944
Henry Demarest Lloyd	1903	William J. O'Brien	1917
George Sperry Loftus	1916	Alexander Ector Orr	1914
Jack London	1916	**Chase Salmon Osborn**	1949
Owen R. Lovejoy	1961	**Mary White Ovington**	1951
Seth Low	1916	**Robert Latham Owen**	1947
David Lubin	1919	Walter Owen	1934
Valentine Everit Macy	1930	Walter Hines Page	1918
Edmond H. Madison	1911	**Alexander Mitchell Palmer**	1936
William Gibbs McAdoo	1941	**George Cooper Pardee**	1941
Charles McCarthy	1921	**John Milliken Parker**	1939
Samuel S. McClure	1949	Frank Parsons	1908
Francis John McConnell	1953	Simon Nelson Patten	1922
Joseph Medill McCormick	1925	**Joseph Medill Patterson**	1946

216

John Barton Payne	1935
George Foster Peabody	1938
George W. Perkins	1920
John Punnett Peters	1921
Madison Clinton Peters	1918
James A. Peterson	1928
James Duval Phelan	1930
David Graham Phillips	1911
Arthur Judson Pillsbury	1937
Amos R. E. Pinchot	1944
Gifford Pinchot	1946
Hazen S. Pingree	1901
Samuel Plantz	1924
Miles Poindexter	1946
Atlee Pomerene	1937
Ernest Poole	1950
Louis Freeland Post	1928
Henry Cadman Potter	1908
Joseph Pulitzer	1911
George Haven Putnam	1930
J. Willard Ragsdale	1919
Walter Rauschenbusch	1918
George L. Record	1933
William Cox Redfield	1932
James Alexander Reed	1944
John Reed	1920
James Bronson Reynolds	1924
John Harsen Rhoades	1906
Dudley Ward Rhodes	1925
Charles Richardson	1922
Erman J. Ridgeway	1943
Jacob Riis	1914
Raymond Robins	1954
Joseph Taylor Robinson	1937
Gilbert E. Roe	1929
Theodore Roosevelt	1919
Edward Alsworth Ross	1951
Chester Harvey Rowell	1948
George Rublee	1957
Charles Edward Russell	1941
Joseph Hine Rylance	1907
Walter Edward Sachs	Alive
Jacob Schiff	1920
Theodore Schroeder	1953
Edward Syllis Scripps	1926
Henry Rogers Seager	1930
Ellery Sedgwick	1960
Edwin Robert Anderson Seligman	1939
Isaac Newton Seligman	1917

John Franklin Shafroth	1922
Anna Howard Shaw	1919
Albert Shaw	1947
Charles Monroe Sheldon	1946
George Lawson Sheldon	1960
Mary Kingsbury Simkhovitch	1951
Upton Beall Sinclair	Alive
Francis Louis Slade	1944
William Nichols Sloan	1919
Albion Small	1926
Andrew J. Smith	?
Charles Sprague Smith	1910
Charles Stewart Smith	1909
Hoke Smith	1931
Edgar Charles Snyder	1953
John Spargo	1966
Rudolph Spreckels	1958
Lincoln Steffens	1936
Charles Stelzle	1941
Ethelbert Stewart	1936
Henry Louis Stimson	1950
Marshall Stimson	1951
Oscar Solomon Strauss	1926
Josiah Strong	1916
Thomas Nelson Strong	1927
Walter Roscoe Stubbs	1929
John Henry Wilburn Stuckenberg	1903
Mark Sullivan	1952
Ida Minerva Tarbell	1944
Frank William Taussig	1940
James Albertus Tawney	1919
Graham Taylor	1938
James M. Taylor	1916
Merrill A. Teague	1914
Frederick Thompson	1906
Benjamin Ryan Tillman	1918
William Jewett Tucker	1926
Joseph Patrick Tumulty	1954
George Kibbe Turner	1952
William Simon U'Ren	1949
Charles R. Van Hise	1918
Marie Van Vorst	1936
James K. Vardaman	1930
Thorstein B. Veblen	1929
Oswald Garrison Villard	1949
Merle D. Vincent	1958
Carl Schurz Vrooman	1966
Walter Vrooman	1909
Lillian D. Wald	1940

John Brisben Walker	1931	Harvey Wiley	1930
William English Walling	1936	Mary E. Wilkins	1930
Thomas J. Walsh	1933	Charles Dwight Willard	1914
Felix Moritz Warburg	1937	Charles David Williams	1923
Paul Moritz Warburg	1932	Gaylord Wilshire	1927
Julius H. Ward	1897	William Bauchop Wilson	1934
Lester Frank Ward	1913	Thomas Woodrow Wilson	1924
John Weaver	1928	Otis T. Wingo	1930
Henry Kitchell Webster	1932	**Stephen S. Wise**	1949
Towner K. Webster	1922	**Peter Witt**	1948
Judson Churchill Welliver	1943	**John Wilson Wood**	1947
Walter Edward Weyl	1919	**Clinton Rogers Woodruff**	1949
Benjamin Ide Wheeler	1927	**Mary Emma Woolley**	1947
William Allen White	1944	John D. Works	1928
Brand Whitlock	1934	**Charles Reed Zahniser**	?

Bibliographical Essay

A conventional bibliography, listing all the published material which I have used in coming to an understanding about reform politics and personalities from T.R. to F.D.R., would be intolerably long. Since good bibliographies for these years have appeared in other places—for instance, in the "New American Nation" volumes for the period, written by George Mowry, Arthur Link, John D. Hicks, and William E. Leuchtenburg—I will not present such a listing here, although my debt to this material is great, as the notes in the text indicate.

The essay that follows will attempt two things. In the first part, the interested student or scholar will find a discussion of the literature on the relation between progressivism and the New Deal. The coverage is selective, dealing with writing which best illustrates the main points made in this running controversy. Notice that the historical problem surveyed here is not "the origins of the New Deal," which would involve much more than progressivism, but the connection between progressivism* and the New Deal. My own book, needless to say, was planned as a contribution to that controversy.

The second part constitutes an alphabetical list of the sources which were most useful to me in attempting to reconstruct the political views of the living progressives in the 1930's. Again, not everything which I consulted could be listed here, but the list will provide other scholars with the main sources upon which I based my judgments about that elusive and shifting quantity, individual political attitude.

I

There was obviously some connection between progressivism and the New Deal, and no history of the twentieth century has failed

* The usage I have adopted throughout this book requires that "progressivism" not be capitalized when the general movement is meant; when capitalized, "Progressive" or "Progressives" denotes men and women associated with Theodore Roosevelt's "Bull Moose" party.

to say something about these continuities. As in any historical problem and especially those involving the derivations of large political movements, most treatments have been careful to admit both continuity and discontinuity; in this case, emphasizing that the New Deal was both a lineal desendant of progressivism, and at the same time different in important respects. But the impression left by the standard treatments of modern reform was that New Dealers were latter-day progressives, with any alterations in style or philosophy not going down to the fundamentals.

Such a view had the advantage of giving consistency to fifty years of American politics: from the earliest stirrings of municipal reform, American political forces had been aiming at the liberal philosophy and its institutional embodiment, the Welfare State. To emphasize continuities also had the welcome effect—since most scholars are liberals—of giving the New Deal a legitimate, American ancestry, of making it seem historically inevitable, and of providing it (remember that it was always under heavy fire) with a defense against charges of "un-Americanism," socialism, and the like.

This general viewpoint may be followed in almost any text, and is sensibly and very persuasively put in Henry Steele Commager, *The American Mind* (New Haven, 1950), Eric Goldman, *Rendezvous With Destiny* (New York, 1952), Arthur Schlesinger, Jr., *The Crisis of The Old Order* (Boston, 1957) and *The Coming of the New Deal* (Boston, 1959), and Arthur S. Link, *American Epoch* (New York, 1955). The Link volume is probably the strongest statement of continuity among the general surveys. An essay devoted to pointing out the many New Deal roots in the pre–Depression period is Richard Kirkendall, "The Great Depression: Another Watershed in American History?," in John Braeman, Robert Bremner, and Everett Walters (eds.), *Change and Continuity in Twentieth Century America* (Columbus, 1964). "After the lapse of a decade and a half," Commager put it, "Franklin Roosevelt took up once more the program of the Populists and Progressives and carried it to its logical conclusion." (*The American Mind*, p. 337.)

These general arguments rest upon a base of monographic or other detailed inquiries which have found progressive ideas and individuals within the New Deal, and New Deal precursors within progressivism. The most indisputable evidence of a strong bond between the two reforms was that cadre of old progressives who enlisted with the New Deal. Sidney Fine, in his *Laissez-Faire and the General Welfare State* (Ann Arbor, 1957), listed Bull Moose Progressives who aided the New Deal—Senators Edward P. Costigan and Bronson Cutting, Harold Ickes, Hugh Johnson, Donald Richberg, and others (p. 392). Arthur Schlesinger, Jr., noticed the strong Bull Moose contingent which "played a creative role" in the 1930's: Frank Knox, Henry Stimson, Harold Ickes, John G. Winant, Charles Evans Hughes, Gifford Pinchot, and William Allen White (see his *The Vital Center*, Cambridge, 1949, p. 24; Schlesinger was careful to claim only that they "played a creative role," not that they liked the New Deal, which most of those he listed did not). And whenever an old Wilsonian showed up within the New Deal, as did Josephus Daniels, for example, his biographer was sure to point out how the reform line had carried true from one Democratic reform President to another (see E. David Cronon, "A Southern Progressive Looks at the New Deal," *Journal of Southern History*, XXIV (May 1958), 151-76). Also, the strong contingent of progressive social workers who swung to the New Deal has often been noted as evidence of connecting personnel. For a typical example, see James M. Patterson, "Mary Dewson and the American Minimum Wage Movement," *Labor History*, V (Spring 1964), 134-44.

In no area of New Deal action was the debt to certain progressives more obvious than in the area of social insurance—social security, unemployment compensation, wages and hours standards. The contribution of La Follette's Wisconsin to these programs is documented in Arthur J. Altmeyer, "The Wisconsin Idea and Social Security," *Wisconsin Magazine of History*, XLII (Autumn 1958), 19-25. Clarke Chambers has convincingly described how much these aspects of the New Deal owed to the untiring efforts of social work progressives, in "Creative Effort in an Age of Normalcy, 1918-33," *Social Welfare Forum* (1961), 252-71; "Social Service and Social Reform: A Historical Essay," *Social Service Review*, XXXVII (March 1963), 76-90; *Seedtime of Reform: American Social Service and Social Action, 1918-33* (Minneapolis, 1963). Similar credit is given to this group of progressives in Robert Bremner, *From The Depths: The Discovery of Poverty in the United States* (New York, 1956) and Joanna C. Colcord, "Social Work and the First Federal Relief Programs," *Proceedings* of the National Conference of Social Work (1943), 382-94. The old progressive as lobbyist for the Social Security Act

and other welfare measures of the New Deal may be observed in
Lloyd F. Pierce's unpublished doctoral dissertation, "The Activities of the American Association for Labor Legislation in Behalf
of Social Security and Protective Labor Legislation," University
of Wisconsin, 1953.

The New Deal borrowed from both the New Freedom and the
New Nationalism (see my "The Historian and the Two New
Deals: 1944-60," *Social Studies,* LIV (April 1963), 133-40; see also
William H. Wilson, "The Two New Deals: A Valid Concept?,"
Historian, XXVIII (February, 1966), 268-88), but it has become a
commonplace that the spirit and letter of the New Nationalism
were more congenial to New Dealers. That influence would have
been greater if Rexford Tugwell's influence had not diminished;
Tugwell discusses the Croly–Van Hise component of the New
Nationalism philosophy in his "The Sources of New Deal Reformism," *Ethics,* LXIV (July 1954), 249-74. The importance of
the Bull Moose Platform of 1912 as a seedbed of New Deal policy
is the burden of A. M. Scott's article, "The Progressive Era in
Retrospect," *Journal of Politics,* XXI (November 1959), 685-701.
Scott, to my mind, has confused Progressivism, and only a campaign document of that, for progressivism in the large, an elemental error which caused this attack upon the *Age of Reform* to
miscarry. A good statement of the view that the New Nationalism
school of progressive thought made extensive connections with
the New Deal may be found in Sidney Fine, *Laissez-Faire and the
General Welfare State,* chapter xi.

George Norris' biographer, Richard Lowitt, has recently argued that the origins of the concept that became TVA, one of the
New Deal's most daring innovations, go back to the Wilsonian
period; see Lowitt, "A Neglected Aspect of the Progressive Movement: George W. Norris and Public Control of Hydro-electric
Power, 1913-1919," *Historian,* XXVII (May 1965), 350-65. And
while Lowitt has perhaps claimed a bit too much for the vague
stirrings in Norris's mind of a new attitude toward resource development, the area of conservation is quite obviously one in
which New Dealers continued progressive initiatives. Progressives
who were conservationists, wrote J. Leonard Bates, were early
committed to planning in the national interest, and "a few
wished to go farther than the New Deal ever went" (Bates, "Ful-
filling American Democracy: The Conservation Movement, 1907-

1921," *Mississippi Valley Historical Review,* XLIV (June 1957), 29-57). This view, advanced also by the veteran conservationist Judson King, in *The Conservation Fight, From Theodore Roosevelt to the Tennessee Valley Authority* (Washington, 1959), seems relatively invulnerable, despite qualifications introduced by books on conservation by Samuel P. Hays and Donald Swain. Hays, in his *Conservation and the Gospel of Efficiency: The Progressive Conservation Movement, 1890-1920* (Cambridge, 1959), depicts the early conservationists as more interested in efficient use than in preservation for public recreation or defending the rights of the general public against large lumber, mining, and grazing interests; the progressive conservationist thus appears to have been working in harmony with important business objectives, a circumstance which was certainly not present for the public power advocates of the 1930's. Swain, in *Federal Conservation Policy, 1921-33* (Berkeley, 1963), documents the intellectual and bureaucratic growth of the cause of conservation in the 1920's, and it makes it fairly obvious that progressive conservationists had a distance to go before they were ready for the efforts of the 1930's.

One of the most glaring differences between the two reform movements was the ethnic and class composition of both. So long as progressives were thought to be predominantly Yankee-Protestant and small town—and impressionistic as well as sample survey evidence has confirmed this for certain sectors of progressivism—it took no exhaustive knowledge of the New Deal coalition to conclude that these reform movements, resting upon different interests, could not share exactly the same goals. But J. Joseph Huthmacher, in his "Urban Liberalism in the Age of Reform," *Mississippi Valley Historical Review,* XLIX (September 1962), 231-41, has broadened the spectrum of progressivism to include urban elements later to become the backbone of the New Deal. Huthmacher performed a service in reminding us how much of urban-immigrant America was in political ferment in the progressive era, but he did not seem to sense either the true proportion of this element within progressivism or the possibility that the stirrings he noticed were not properly a part of progressivism at all. Arthur Mann's *Yankee Reformers in the Urban Age* (Cambridge, 1954) agrees with Huthmacher that the reform sentiment of the period was not confined to the small towns nor to

the sons of the Mugwumps, but encompassed—in Boston, at least
—the new ethnic and religious elements of urban, Eastern
America.

One could go on at considerable length citing surveys, biographies, and monographs which have added their weight to the interpretation of progressivism that maximizes its liberalism and
the importance of its successes, and minimizes the occasions when
it held back from the full extent of necessary reforms, leaving this
work to a generation that first had to suffer for the delay. Books
like Daniel Aaron's *Men of Good Hope* (New York, 1951) leave
the reader with a feeling that the reforms of the 1930's—and the
1960's, for that matter—represented the arrival of the American
public at positions taken by leading progressives many years ago.
A comprehensive statement of that view may be found in Dewey
Grantham's review article, "The Progressive Era and the Reform
Tradition," *Mid-America*, XLVI (October 1964), 227-51.

But from the earliest there were dissenting views, straws in the
wind hinting the possibility of other judgments. After the New
Deal, when both reform movements were in view, there continued to be dissent from the general interpretation which was so
friendly to both movements and sure of their essential identity.
Even as early writers like B. O. Flower (*Progressive Men, Women
and Movements of the Past Twenty-Five Years,* Boston, 1914) and
Benjamin DeWitt (*The Progressive Movement,* New York, 1915)
were writing the first congratulatory accounts and setting the
general tone for most historical writing through at least the early
1950's, men whose politics were further Left were making penetrating criticisms of progressive reform. Herbert Croly's *The
Promise of American Life* (New York, 1909), and Walter Lippmann's *Preface to Politics* (New York, 1913) and *Drift and Mastery* (New York, 1914) exposed the limited government and petit-
bourgeois thrust of much reform thought. John Chamberlain's
Farewell to Reform (New York, 1932) and Lincoln Steffens' *The
Autobiography of Lincoln Steffens* (2 vols., New York, 1931)
added to the indictment, and their corrosive comments on progressivism were all the more convincing, coming just at the collapse of a system which had supposedly been both cleansed and
conscience-stricken.

There were also those writing history who were satisfied with
progressivism but who did not like the New Deal, such as Edgar
E. Robinson (*The Roosevelt Leadership, 1933-45,* New York,

1955,) Arthur A. Ekirch, (*The Decline of American Liberalism* New York, 1955), or Raymond Moley, (*After Seven Years*, New York, 1939). In addition, there were those who did not like either, such as William A. Williams (*Contours of American History*, Cleveland, 1961) or Gabriel Kolko, (*The Triumph of Conservatism. A Reinterpretation of American History, 1900-1916*, Glencoe, 1963).

While these accounts did not always address themselves to the continuity question, the generally accepted continuity view could not survive a shift toward the Croly–Lippmann–Chamberlain attitude toward progressivism, nor toward the Robinson–Ekirch–Moley attitude toward the New Deal. And since the general version saw not only continuity, but was favorable to both reforms, it could not survive if the interpretation of men like Williams and Kolko gained strength.

But one of these shifts did begin to appear in much of the literature produced by professional historians after World War II. While the New Deal held the general approval of its historians, a critical attitude toward progressivism emerged, taking the form of a new attention to the shortcomings of the movement—its racial blindness, its ambivalence toward industrial concentration, its fundamental dislike of the labor movement, and so on. The effect, not lost on those who looked beyond progressivism to the larger reform tradition, was to open a gap between progressivism and the urban liberalism of the New Deal and after.

Edgar Kemler was a New Deal lawyer, not an historian, and his *The Deflation of American Ideals* (Washington, 1941), because of its brevity, and perhaps its timing, did not attract much attention. But Kemler's argument was a foretaste of much that would appear in professional circles later on: the progressive outlook was a hindrance, not a help, to the New Deal, and both the spirit and the surviving veterans of progressivism had to be either ignored or even fought as the New Dealers moved "from the moral approach to the engineering approach" (p. 45). Just after the War, Rexford Tugwell began a series of retrospective articles which touched, among other things, upon the New Deal's relationship to earlier progressivism. In a matchless style and with the special advantages of the insider, Tugwell virtually bracketed the "enraged progressives" with the "privileged conservatives" as groups who hindered, and finally defeated, the New Deal. For Tugwell the creative aspects of the New Deal arose from the "collectivist" school, including Croly, Van Hise, and Veblen, men who worked out the basis for a new ideology—he frequently called it the philosophy of "disciplined co-ordination"—during the progressive era. But he saw this ideology, despite the timing of its birth, as squarely opposed to that of the progressives. These articles, which appeared in *Western Political Quarterly* and *Ethics,* and which were to some extent summarized in Tugwell's *The Democratic Roosevelt* (Garden City, 1957), are cited in Bernard Sternsher, *Rexford G. Tugwell and the New Deal* (New Brunswick, 1964). The most important of them is Tugwell, "The New Deal: The Progressive Tradition," *Western Political Quarterly,* III (September 1950), 390-427.

Beginning in the early 1950's, more and more historical treatments of progressive ideas, leaders, or laws, concluded by noting that the mesh with the New Deal was far from perfect. John Blum, reflecting in his study of Wilson upon the New Freedom credo, saw in it "something of the spirit that was, years later, to lead many of its apostles to the Liberty League" (Blum, *Woodrow Wilson and the Politics of Morality,* Boston, 1956, p. 80). Robert Wiebe, at the end of a book on businessmen and progressive reform, estimated that the older progressives were alienated by the turn the New Deal took in 1935, rather than rejoicing in it as other historians have claimed. The anti-business tone of the second New Deal frightened the original progressive, whose connections with business, Wiebe sought to show, were often close and sympathetic (Wiebe, *Businessmen and Reform: A Study of the Progressive Movement,* Cambridge, 1962). Rush Welter argued that the older reformers broke with the New Deal in large numbers because it abandoned their cherished axiom of educating the whole people, and turned instead to serving as a cynical broker for various selfish interests: "Such objections to New Deal politics made an easy bridge by which former progressives might cross over to the conservative position, and . . . many made the journey" (Welter, *Popular Education and Democratic Thought,* New York, 1962, p. 316).

But the most influential statement of this sense of the shortcomings of progressivism and the gap between the two reforms was of course Richard Hofstadter's *The Age of Reform* (New York, 1955). Hofstader's subtle and well-known argument need not be summarized again—indeed, it is hard to summarize fairly at all. The excitement generated by the "status revolution" thesis has obscured the rest of Hofstadter's analysis of the progressive mind, but that analysis remains the most perceptive treatment of the many defensive aspects of the progressive enterprise, without, if one reads carefully, the loss of balance or even an essential sympathy.

Other historians who have made similar estimations of parts of the whole of progressivism, explicitly or implicitly strengthening the discontinuity argument, are David Noble, *The Paradox of Progressive Thought* (Minneapolis, 1958); William Leuchtenburg, in his introduction to a recent edition of Woodrow Wilson's *The New Freedom* (Englewood Cliffs, 1961) and, with admirable qualifications, in his *Franklin D. Roosevelt and the New Deal, 1932-40* (New York, 1963); Ray Ginger, *The Age of Excess* (New York, 1965); Arthur Mann, in his essay "The Progressive Tradition," in John Higham (ed.), *The Reconstruction of American History* (New York, 1962); Allan Nevins, in his Introduction to *The Journals and Letters of Brand Whitlock* (2 vols., New York, 1936); Richard Abrams, "The Failure of Progressivism," paper delivered at the Annual Convention of the Organization of American Historians, April 29, 1966.

The tendency to see shortcomings in progressive thought and practice, and the complementary and related tendency to become aware of important discontinuities between progressive reform and New Deal liberalism, has owed much to changing styles of research. The most important shift has been away from the "few articulate doubters," as Henry May calls the most penetrating progressive intellectuals, and away from such extraordinary documents as the Progressive Party Platform of 1912 or Lloyd's *Wealth and Commonwealth,* and toward a broader, more representative rank of reformer. May's *The End of Innocence* (New York, 1959) was based not only upon the usual "important" books by Croly, Ross, Beard and the others, but also upon best-sellers, political rhetoric of all sorts, popular magazines, second-rate history and sociology, and so forth. Not surprisingly, he found that the progressives offered "few answers to our most pressing questions" (p. 29). The chief concern of Hofstadter's *The Age of Reform,* already noted, was "not . . . with the best but with the most characteristic thinking." A desire to get a more representative level of progressive thought generated Daniel Levine's *Varieties of Reform Thought* (Madison, 1964).

While our interest in national politics and personalities is un-

likely to diminish, the past two decades have seen the completion of many studies, history and biography, of progressivism at
the state and local level. It would be wrong to contend that these
state and local studies have invariably unearthed a progressivism
less trenchant, less open-minded, less effective than we had
thought. Many of these studies are not interpretive, and some of
the best—Arthur S. Link's "The Progressive Movement in the
South, 1870-1917," *North Carolina Historical Review*, XXII
(April 1946), 172-95, Ransom E. Noble's *New Jersey Progressivism Before Wilson* (Princeton, 1946), or Hoyt L. Warner's recent
Progressivism in Ohio, 1897-1917 (Columbus, 1964)—have presented their corner of the progressive movement in a very favorable light. But a sizable, perhaps increasing, number of monographs on state and municipal reform have concluded on a note
that is substantially—although rarely entirely—critical. In varying degree, the following will serve to illustrate this interpretive
outcome: George Mowry, *The California Progressives* (Berkeley,
1950), Richard Abrams, *Conservatism in a Progressive Era: Massachusetts Politics, 1900-1912* (Cambridge, 1964), William D.
Miller, *Memphis During the Progressive Era, 1897-1916* (Ithaca,
1965).

Other sectors of progressive action, under close scrutiny for the
first time, have demonstrated less contact with the liberalism of
the 1930's than had been guessed. Jeremy Felt, in his *Hostages of
Fortune: Child Labor Reform in New York State* (Syracuse,
1965), found even this group of humanitarians, who sought public regulation of labor practices regarding children and who
have always been categorized as among the more "advanced"'
or "social justice" elements within progressivism, to be "an essentially conservative reform group" (p. 217) which achieved purely
"symbolic" victories. Although the New Deal outlawed child labor after they had failed to get their constitutional amendment,
the mere removal of children from the factories—which was the
sum total of their goals—did little "to reach the basic problem of
New York's youth," a conclusion which today's delinquency rates
seem to support. Another group on the cutting edge of progressivism, the housing reformers, emerges from Roy Lubove's sympathetic *The Progressives and the Slums: Tenement House Reform
in New York City, 1890-1917* (Pittsburgh, 1962) as courageous and
self-sacrificing men who nevertheless stubbornly refused to go beyond restrictive laws toward the public housing of the 1930's. Lu-

bove's story of a post-progressive group, told in *Community Planning in the 1920s: The Contribution of the Regional Planning Association of America* (Pittsburgh, 1963), suggests that the housing ventures of the New Deal and after had their intellectual and organizational origins after progressivism; Laurence Veiler, central figure in the progressive housing reform movement, disliked the New Deal.

Certain other progressive groups have been shown, in their aims or in their methods, to be unready for the pragmatic demands of the 1930's. Merle Curti's *Peace or War: The American Struggle, 1636-1936* (New York, 1936) leaves the peace progressives at the point of disaffection with Franklin Roosevelt, and demonstrates that up until 1936 their interests and those of the New Deals' had not intersected. Josephine Goldmark's article, "Fifty Years—The National Consumer's League," *Survey*, LXXXV (December 1949), 674-76, shows how the NCL had to move to a more radical style, dropping leaders like Newton Baker, before it could play the influential role during the 1930's that it eventually played. In another area, that of Negro rights, where the New Deal made some modest advances, the progressives seem to have had almost no interest: see Dewey Grantham, "The Progressive Movement and the Negro," *South Atlantic Quarterly*, LIV (October 1955), 461-77, and Gilbert Osofsky, "Progressivism and the Negro: New York, 1900-1915," *American Quarterly*, XVI (Summer 1964), 153-68. So few white Americans were interested in civil rights in the Roosevelt–Wilson years that progressivism, with its handful of pioneers such as Villard and Mary White Ovington and William English Walling, made a poor record where the Negro was concerned, but certainly not one without credits.

A feature of recent progressive historiography has been the growing number of career line analyses of samples recruited from many areas of progressive effort. These studies do not bear directly upon the problem of progressive–New Deal continuity, but rather have been stimulated by a desire to learn just who the progressives were. It has also been the purpose of many of them to validate or invalidate the "status revolution" thesis of Hofstadter's *Age of Reform*, an interesting problem which we need not go into here. But such studies have almost uniformly demonstrated the middle class, Yankee-Protestant composition of progressive groups (and of their conservative opponents as well, interestingly enough), and they serve to remind us how the New Deal coincided with the entrance into American political life of people of quite different class and ethnic backgrounds. The first two such recruitment studies were reported in George Mowry's *The California Progressives* (Berkeley, 1950) and in his "The California Progressive and His Rationale: A Study in Middle Class Politics," *Mississippi Valley Historical Review*, XXXVI (September 1949), 239-50, and in Alfred D. Chandler's "The Origins of Progressive Leadership," in Elting Morison (ed.), *The Letters of Theodore Roosevelt*, Vol. VIII (Cambridge, 1954), 1462-65. Others have followed, among them: George Mowry, *The Era of Theodore Roosevelt, 1900-1912* (New York, 1958), where Mowry reported an expanded sample of approximately 400; Jerome Clubb, "Congressional Opponents of Reform, 1901-13," unpublished Ph.D. dissertation, University of Washington, 1963; Henry J. Silverman, "American Social Reformers in the Late Nineteenth and Early Twentieth Century," unpublished Ph.D. dissertation, University of Pennsylvania, 1963; Richard B. Sherman, "The Status Revolution and Massachusetts Progressive Leadership," *Political Science Quarterly*, LXXVIII (March 1963), 59-65; William T. Kerr, "The Progressives of Washington, 1910-12," *Pacific Northwest Quarterly*, LV (January 1964), 16-27; Samuel P. Hays, "The Politics of Municipal Government in the Progressive Era," *Pacific Northwest Quarterly*, LV (October 1964), 157-69; Eli D. Potts, "The Progressive Profile in Iowa," *Mid-America*, XLVII (October 1965), 257-68; Norman Wilensky, *Conservatives in the Progressive Era: The Taft Republicans of 1912* (Gainesville, 1965); and Jack Tager, "Progressives, Conservatives, and the Theory of the Status Revolution," *Mid-America*, XLVIII (July 1966), 162-75.

Another focus of recent work has been on the relationship of progressivism to business, especially on the degree to which certain well-known progressive "regulatory laws" were desired by portions of the business community itself. To the extent that this is true—and the entire problem is far from settled—the progressive movement takes on the aspect of a counterattack by business interests against other business interests. An early and important book which revealed the force of sectional rivalry behind certain progressive laws was Samuel P. Hays, *The Response to Industrialism, 1885-1914* (Chicago, 1957). Gabriel Kolko, *The Triumph of Conservatism: A Reinterpretation of American History, 1900-1916* (Glencoe, 1963), attempts to overturn the old idea that industry was becoming monopolistic, and argues instead that progressivism was engineered by businessmen hurt by increasing competition. Robert Wiebe, *Businessmen and Reform: A Study of the Progressive Movement* (Cambridge, 1962), found that the line between business interests and reform objectives was often blurred. In James Weinstein's "Organized Business and the City Commission and Manager Movements," *Journal of Southern History*, XXVIII (May 1962), 166-82, and George B. Tindall, "Business Progressivism: Southern Politics in the 1920's," *South Atlantic Quarterly*, LXII (Winter 1963), 92-106, certain aspects of progressivism are seen to thrive in the business-oriented 1920's.

One of Edgar Kemmler's claims (in *The Deflation of American Ideals*) was that the New Dealers "withdrew human character from the range of our reforms." The moralistic side of progressivism was undeniably not congenial to the spirit of the new liberalism, and the question of continuity here becomes a close question as to the degree and types of moralism present in progressivism, and what became of such attitudes (or the organizations formed to defend them) during the 1930's. The standard works dealing with progressive temperance reformers—Andrew Sinclair's *Prohibition: Era of Excess* (Boston, 1962), James H. Timberlake's *Prohibition and the Progressive Movement* (Cambridge, 1963), and Joseph Gusfield's *Symbolic Crusade: Status Politics and the American Temperance Movement* (Urbana, 1963)—leave no doubt of the animosities between these reformers and the urban elements in the New Deal coalition. A less successful attempt to associate progressives (California progressives, in this case) with illiberal social ideals is Roger Daniels, *The Politics of Prejudice: The Anti-Japanese Movement in California and the Struggle for Japanese Exclusion* (Berkeley, 1962).

If the subsequent careers of certain progressives, such as Josephus Daniels or George Norris, appeared to connect the two reform periods, other careers persuaded the observer of the opposite view. Lawrence Levine's book, *Defender of the Faith: William Jennings Bryan: The Last Decade* (New York, 1965), demonstrated with sympathy and brilliance that Bryan in the 1920's, fighting science and cities and drink, was working toward the same ends as when he was a leading progressive. In Bryan's thought reform and reaction were two sides of the same thing, Levine shows, and Bryan was perfectly consistent throughout his public career. Stanley Coben's *A. Mitchell Palmer: Politician*

(New York, 1963) traced progressivism to a final position on the Right of the New Deal in the life of an important progressive. Allan Nevins recounted the same process in his Introduction to the *Journals and Letters of Brand Whitlock*. Because other biographies reported this sort of outcome, several scholars have been led to estimate that such careers might not be atypical. Richard Hofstadter wrote in *The Age of Reform* (p. 303): "Naturally there was also some continuity in personnel . . . . However, one could draw up an equally formidable list . . . [of those who] later became heated critics of the New Deal." Apparently one could, and in the behavior of progressives who lived into the 1930's there did not seem to be any clear answer for those who wished to know where the progressive impulse meshed with the New Deal and where it did not. In scattered places one could find complaints that the old progressives did not appear to take the unambiguous stand for the New Deal that might have been predicted. Robert M. Miller's study of social Christianity in the interwar period, *American Protestantism and Social Issues, 1919-39* (Chapel Hill, 1958), reported that the old social gospel progressives were dispersed all the way from reaction to continuing radicalism, with no discernible pattern. Kenneth Hechler, in his study of congressional Insurgency, made a similar report: "In view of the divergent opinions of the surviving Insurgents, it cannot be stated with any conclusiveness that the New Deal represents a realization and extension of their aims." (Hechler, *Insurgency: Personalities and Politics of the Taft Era* (New York, 1940), p. 276.) Russel B. Nye wrestled with contradictory evidence in his study of Midwestern progressives, and wearily concluded that "old" progressives in the 1930's were "uncertain." "Analyzing its [the New Deal's] relationship to the older strain of progressivism is not a simple task," he confessed, and he added that the Midwestern progressives had felt about the New Deal that "there was something about its spirit, and about its methods, that seemed to ring false." (Nye, *Midwestern Progressive Politics* (East Lansing, 1951), pp. 341, 347). Pages 327-49 of Nye's book contain the most acute discussion I have seen of the general problem of progressive response to the New Deal. Louis Filler, despite his many spirited and to my mind exaggerated defenses of the Muckrakers, shows a fine understanding of the political and moral confusions that came upon them as they aged; see Filler, *Crusaders for American Liberalism* (New York, 1939), pp. 25-29.

Further damage was done to the supposition of strong continuity in personnel by two studies which compared urban "machine" politicians with progressives who had fought them, and found that it was the former who were enthusiastic about the New Deal: see J. Joseph Huthmacher, "Charles Evans Hughes and Charles Francis Murphy: The Metamorphosis of Progressivism," *New York History*, XLVI (January 1965), 25-40, and George C. Rapport, *The Statesman and the Boss* (Washington, 1961), a study of Frank Murphy and Woodrow Wilson. Indeed, it has even been persuasively argued that Al Smith, whose New York governorship is widely credited with being the intermediate step between progressivism and New Deal liberalism, was being consistent when he complained that the New Deal was alien to his own political philosophy; see Samuel Hand, "Al Smith, Franklin D. Roosevelt, and the New Deal: Some Comments on Perspective," *Historian*, XXVII (May 1965), 366-81. An unpublished dissertation by Paul L. Silver, "Wilsonians and the New Deal," University of Pennsylvania, 1964, is the only study I have seen which addresses itself directly to the problem of continuity of personnel, and Silver finds all of his six Wilsonians at odds with the New Deal.

Certain studies of aspects of the New Deal strengthen the feeling that new men and new approaches shouldered aside progressive personalities and precedents. An incomplete but suggestive list might include the following: Donald R. McCoy's published work on political radicalism (*Angry Voices: Left of Center Politics in the New Deal Era*, Lawrence, 1958; "The Progressive National Committee of 1936," *Western Political Quarterly*, IX (June 1956), 454-69; "The National Progressives of America, 1938," *MVHR*, XLIV (June 1957), 75-93); Paul Conkins' fine study of daring and largely futile efforts at community planning and resettlement, *Tomorrow A New World: The New Deal Community Program* (Ithaca, 1959); two contemporary accounts of the new advisers surrounding Roosevelt, Joseph Alsop and Robert Kintner, *Men Around the President* (New York, 1939), and John Franklin Carter's *The New Dealers* (New York, 1934); John G. Hill's article, "Fifty Years of Social Action on the Housing Front," *Social Service Review*, XXII (June 1948), 160-79, which demonstrates that most progressive housing reformers hung back from public housing; and Harry Malisoff's three articles, "The Emergence of Unemployment Compensation: I," *Political Science Quarterly*, LIV (June 1939), 237-58, "II," (September

1939), 391-420, and "III," (December 1939), 577-99, describing
how little of the groundwork in this area had been done by 1934
when the administration began its study.

As our information has increased, so has our respect for the
need for qualification, for careful attention to subdivisions and
subgroups, for accounts that allow for complicated and overlap-
ping line of descent. Awareness of these complexities is present
in what I would choose as the three best treatments of the relationship between progressivism and the New Deal: Russel Nye,
Midwestern Progressive Politics, pp. 327-49; Arthur Schlesinger, Jr., *The Crisis of the Old Order* (Boston, 1957), pp. 17-45, 93-
152; and William E. Leuchtenburg's *Franklin D. Roosevelt and
the New Deal, 1932-40* (New York, 1963), chap. xiv. The approach of historiographical maturity in any area, it seems, is her-
alded by an end to incautious generalization. With the extension
of monographic studies for both periods of government bureaus,
voluntary associations, ideas both popular and philosophic, the
legislative process, perceived interests of major economic groups,
and especially more individual and collective biographies, we
may hope that historians will converge upon a rendering of the
progressive account which, rooted firmly in a large body of reliable data, will narrow those wide swings of interpretation which
have discouraged the American who comes to us for an understanding of his past.

I I

What follows is a bibliography listing the main sources I used in
reconstructing the political attitudes of progressives in the 1930's.
No full listing of these sources is possible, for clues and fragments
of evidence turned up in countless places, and to list them all
would overextend an already lengthy account. No attempt will
be made to cite the sources used in compiling basic biographical
data, although the search for such information was a major part
of my research task. The sources which follow bear on the center
of the inquiry, political attitude.

PRIMARY SOURCES

Manuscripts

Baker, Newton D. Library of Congress.
Baker, Ray Stannard. Library of Congress.
Bass, Robert Perkins. Dartmouth College Library.
Bennet, William Stiles. Syracuse University Library.
Borah, William E. Library of Congress.
Bristow, Joseph L. Kansas State Historical Society.
Brown, William Adams. Union Theological Seminary.
Brooks, John Graham. Possession of Lawrence Graham Brooks, Medford, Massachusetts.
Burke, John. University of North Dakota Library.
Burleson, Albert Sidney. Library of Congress.
Capper, Arthur. Kansas State Historical Society.
Churchill, Winston. Dartmouth College Library.
Colby, Bainbridge. Library of Congress.
Commons, John R. Wisconsin Historical Society.
Crane, Charles R. Institute of Current World Affairs.
Creel, George. Library of Congress.
Davenport, Frederick Morgan. Syracuse University Library.
Dickson, Edward A. University of California at Los Angeles.
Dunne, Finley Peter. Library of Congress.
Ely, Richard T. Wisconsin Historical Society.
Fisher, Irving. Yale University Library.
Folks, Homer. New York School of Social Work.
Garfield, James G. Library of Congress.
Ghent, William James. Library of Congress.
Glass, Carter. University of Virginia Library.
Good Neighbor League. Franklin D. Roosevelt Library, Hyde Park.
Hichborn, Franklin. University of California at Los Angeles.
Houston, David F. Houghton Library, Harvard University.
Hughes, Charles Evans. Library of Congress.
Irwin, Wallace. Bancroft Library, Berkeley.
Johnson, Hiram. Bancroft Library, Berkeley.
Kirkland, James H. Vanderbilt University Library.
Lenroot, Irvine. Library of Congress.
Lindsay, Samuel McCune. Columbia University Library.
McAdoo, William Gibbs. Library of Congress.
McReynolds, James C. University of Virginia Library.

National Child Labor Committee. Library of Congress.
Nelson, James Mandt. Wisconsin Historical Society.
Norris, George. Library of Congress.
Oral History Collection, Columbia University: Recollections of William Stiles Bennet, Frederick Morgan Davenport, Homer Folks, Burton J. Hendrick, George Rublee, Walter Sachs, and John Spargo.
Osborn, Chase S. University of Michigan Library.
Owen, Robert L. Library of Congress.
Parker, John M. University of North Carolina Library.
Peabody, George Foster. Library of Congress.
Pinchot, Amos. Library of Congress.
Pinchot, Gifford. Library of Congress.
Poindexter, Miles. University of Virginia Library.
Progressive National Committee of 1936. Library of Congress.
Robins, Raymond. Wisconsin Historical Society.
Roosevelt, Franklin D. Franklin D. Roosevelt Library, Hyde Park.
Ross, Edward A. Wisconsin Historical Society.
Russell, Charles Edward. Library of Congress.
Seligman, Edward R. A. Columbia University Library.
Shaw, Albert. New York Public Library.
Simkhovitch, Mary Kingsbury. Women's Archives, Radcliffe College.
Steffens, Lincoln. Columbia University Library.
Stelzle, Charles. Columbia University Library.
Stewart, Ethelbert. University of North Carolina Library.
Stimson, Henry L. Yale University Library.
Stimson, Marshall. Huntington Library.
Sullivan, Mark. Library of Congress, and Hoover Institution on War, Revolution and Peace.
Survey Associates. Social Welfare History Archive Center, Minneapolis.
Taussig, Frank W. Houghton Library, Harvard University.
Taylor, Graham. Newberry Library.
Tumulty, Joseph. Library of Congress, and Possession of Joseph Tumulty, Jr., Washington, D. C.
Villard, Oswald Garrison. Houghton Library, Harvard University.
Wald, Lillian. New York Public Library.
Walling, William English. Wisconsin Historical Society.
White, William Allen. Library of Congress.

Public Documents

U. S. *Congressional Record.* 1933-38.
U. S. Temporary National Economic Committee, *Investigation of Con-*

centration of Economic Power, December 1, 1938–January 19, 1940, various dates; Parts 1-35.

Newspapers and Periodicals (1933-38)

American Economic Review
American Association for Labor Legislation Review
Atlantic Monthly
Bangor (Maine) *Daily News*
Chicago Tribune
Cleveland Plain Dealer
Harper's Magazine
Harrisburg (Pennsylvania) *Patriot*
Harvard College *Anniversary Reports*
Milwaukee Journal
Nation
New Republic
New York *Daily News*
New York *Herald Tribune*
The New York Times
"News Releases" of the *Index Number Institute*
Proceedings of the National Conference of Social Work
Review of Reviews
San Francisco Examiner
Saturday Evening Post
Social Service Review
Survey
Survey Graphic
Topeka Capital
Topeka State Journal
Vital Speeches
Wichita Eagle
Yale Review

Articles and Books

Addams, Jane. *Twenty Years at Hull House.* New York: Macmillan, 1911.
———. *The Second Twenty Years at Hull House.* New York: Macmillan, 1930.
Allen, Henry J. *Landon: What He Stands For.* New York: Mail and Express, 1936.

Andrews, John B. *Administrative Labor Legislation*. New York: Harper and Brothers, 1936.

————. *Labor Laws in Action*. New York: Harper and Brothers, 1939.

Baker, Ray Stannard. *American Chronicle: The Autobiography of Ray Stannard Baker*. New York: Charles Scribner's Sons, 1945.

Bingham, Alfred M., and Selden Rodman, eds. *Challenge to the New Deal*. New York: Falcon Press, 1934.

Brown, William Adams. *A Teacher and His Times*. New York: Charles Scribner's Sons, 1940.

Churchill, Winston. *The Uncharted Way*. Philadelphia: Dorrance, 1940.

Cobb, Elisabeth. *My Wayward Parent: A Book About Irvin S. Cobb*. Indianapolis, Ind.: Bobbs-Merrill, 1945.

Cobb, Irvin S. *Exit Laughing*. Indianapolis, Ind.: Bobbs-Merrill, 1941.

Commons, John R. *Myself*. New York: Macmillan, 1934.

————. "The New Deal and the Teaching of Economics," *American Economic Review*, XXV (March 1935), 11.

————. "Communism and Collective Democracy," *American Economic Review*, XXV (June 1935), 212-23.

————. *The Economics of Collective Action*. New York: Macmillan, 1950.

Creel, George. *Rebel At Large: Recollections of Fifty Crowded Years*. New York: G. P. Putnam's Sons, 1947.

————. "Four-Flush Radicals: Reed of Missouri," *Harper's Weekly*, LIX (August 8, 1914), 124-6.

Daniels, Josephus. *Shirt-Sleeve Diplomat*. Chapel Hill, N. C.: University of North Carolina Press, 1947.

Devine, Edward T. *Progressive Social Action*. New York: Macmillan, 1933.

————. *When Social Work Was Young*. New York: Macmillan, 1939.

Dewey, John. *Individualism Old and New*. New York: Minton, Balch, 1931.

————. *Liberalism and Social Action*. New York: G. P. Putnam's Sons, 1935.

————. "The Future of Liberalism," *School and Society*, XLI (January 19, 1935), 73-7.

Dunne, Philip, ed. *Mister Dooley Remembers*. New York: Harper and Brothers, 1963.

Eastman, Max. *Enjoyment of Living*. New York: Harper and Brothers, 1948.

————. *Reflections on the Failure of Socialism*. New York: Devin-Adair, 1955.

———. "I Acknowledge My Mistakes," in *An Evening with the National Review*. New York: National Review Incorporated, 1960.

———. *Of Love and Revolution*. New York: Random House, 1964.

Ely, Richard T. *Ground Under Our Feet: An Autobiography*. New York: Macmillan, 1938.

Ely, Richard T. *Hard Times: The Way In and the Way Out*. New York: Macmillan, 1931.

Ely, Richard T., and Frank Bohn. *The Great Change*. New York: T. Nelson and Sons, 1935.

Fisher, Irving. *After Reflation, What?* New York: Adelphi, 1933.

———. *100% Money*. New York: Adelphi, 1935.

Fisher, Irving Norton. *My Father, Irving Fisher*. New York: Comet Press, 1956.

Fosdick, Raymond B. *Chronicle of a Generation*. New York: Harper and Brothers, 1958.

Gilman, Charlotte Perkins. *The Living of Charlotte Perkins Gilman: An Autobiography*. New York: Appleton-Century-Crofts, 1935.

Goldwater, Barry M., ed. *The Speeches of Henry Fountain Ashurst*. Phoenix, Ariz.: University of Arizona Press, 1956.

Hapgood, Hutchins. *A Victorian in the Modern World*. New York: Harcourt, Brace, 1939.

Hapgood, Norman. *The Changing Years*. New York: Farrar and Rinehart, 1930.

Hendrick, Burton J. *Bulwark of the Republic: A Biography of the Constitution*. Boston: Little, Brown, 1937.

Holmes, John Haynes. "Forty Years Of It!" Sermon delivered in Community Church, New York, February 9, 1947. Privately printed.

———. *I Speak for Myself: The Autobiography of John Haynes Holmes*. New York: Harper and Brothers, 1959.

Hooker, Helen M., ed. *A History of the Progressive Party, 1912-16*, by Amos Pinchot. New York: New York University Press, 1958.

Howe, Frederic C. *Confessions of a Reformer*. New York: Charles Scribner's Sons, 1925.

———. *Denmark: The Co-operative Way*. New York: Harcourt, Brace, 1936.

Hull, Cordell. *The Memoirs of Cordell Hull*. 2 vols. New York: Macmillan, 1948.

Hunter, Robert. *Revolution: Why, How, When?* New York: Harper and Brothers, 1940.

Ickes, Harold L. *The New Democracy*. New York: W. W. Norton, 1934.

————. *The Autobiography of a Curmudgeon.* New York: Reynal and Hitchcock, 1943.

————. *The Secret Diaries of Harold Ickes.* 2 vols. New York: Simon and Schuster, 1953.

Irwin, Wallace. "I Am a Product of Child Labor," *Harper's,* CLXXV (August 1937), 324-7.

Irwin, William Henry. *The Making of a Reporter.* New York: G. P. Putnam's Sons, 1942.

Johnson, Walter, ed. *Selected Letters of William Allen White, 1899-1943.* New York: Henry Holt, 1947.

Kellogg, Paul U. "A Century of Achievement in Democracy," *Proceedings* of the National Conference of Social Work, 1-29. New York: Columbia University Press, 1939.

Kellor, Frances. *American Arbitration: History, Functions, and Achievements.* New York: Harper and Brothers, 1948.

Kilpatrick, Carroll, ed. *Roosevelt and Daniels: A Friendship in Politics.* Chapel Hill, N. C.: University of North Carolina Press, 1952.

Lewis, William Draper. *Interpreting the Constitution.* Charlottesville, Va.: Michie Press, 1937.

Lief, Alfred, ed. *The Brandeis Guide to the Modern World.* Boston: Little, Brown, 1941.

Lindsey, Benjamin B., and Rube Borough. *The Dangerous Life.* New York: Horace Liveright, 1931.

Lippmann, Walter. *Drift and Mastery.* New York: Kennerly, 1914.

————. "Recovery by Trial and Error," *Yale Review,* XXIV (September 1934), 1-13.

————. "The Permanent New Deal," *Yale Review,* XXIV (June 1935), 649-67.

————. *Interpretations: 1933-35.* New York: Macmillan, 1936.

————. *The Good Society.* Boston: Little, Brown, 1937.

Luhan, Mabel Dodge. *Movers and Shakers.* New York: Harcourt, Brace, 1936.

McAdoo, William Gibbs. *Crowded Years.* Boston: Houghton Mifflin, 1931.

McClure, Samuel Sidney. *My Autobiography.* New York: F. Ungar, 1963.

McConnell, Francis J. *Christianity and Coercion.* New York: Cokesbury Press, 1933.

————. *By The Way: An Autobiography.* New York: Abingdon-Cokesbury, 1952.

Masters, Edgar Lee. "The Genesis of Spoon River," *American Mercury,* XXVIII (January 1933), 38-55.

———. *Across Spoon River*. New York: Farrar and Rinehart, 1936.

Mathews, Shailer. *New Faiths For Old: An Autobiography*. New York: Macmillan, 1936.

Moley, Raymond. *After Seven Years*. New York: Harper and Brothers, 1939.

Myers, Gustavus. *America Strikes Back*. New York: Ives Washburn, 1936.

———. *The Ending of Hereditary American Fortunes*. New York: Julian Messner, 1939.

Nearing, Scott. *Democracy Is Not Enough*. New York: Island Workshop Press, 1945.

———. *Economics For The Power Age*. New York: John Day, 1952.

———. *Man's Search For The Good Life*. Harborside, Maine: Social Science Institute, 1954.

———. *Freedom: Promise or Menace?* Harborside, Maine: Social Science Institute, 1961.

———. *The Conscience of a Radical*. Belmont, Mass.: Wellington Press, 1965.

Nevins, Allan, ed. *The Journals and Letters of Brand Whitlock*. 2 vols. New York: Appleton-Century, 1936.

Norris, George. *Fighting Liberal: The Autobiography of George W. Norris*. New York: Macmillan, 1945.

Ovington, Mary White. *The Walls Come Tumbling Down*. New York: Harcourt, Brace, 1947.

Owen, Robert L. *The National Economy and the Banking System of the United States*. Washington, D. C.: Government Printing Office, 1939.

Pease, Otis, ed. *The Progressive Years*. New York: George Braziller, 1962.

Philips, Harlan B., ed. *Felix Frankfurter Reminisces*. New York: Reynal, 1960.

Pinchot, Gifford. *Breaking New Ground*. New York: Harcourt, Brace, 1947.

Polier, Justine W., and James Waterman Wise, eds. *The Personal Letters of Stephen Wise*. Boston: Beacon, 1956.

Poole, Ernest. *One of Us*. New York: Macmillan, 1934.

———. *The Bridge: My Own Story*. New York: Macmillan, 1940.

Record, George L. *How to Abolish Poverty*. Jersey City, N. J.: George L. Record Memorial Association, 1936.

Robins, Elizabeth. *Raymond and I*. New York: Macmillan, 1956.

Ross, Edward A. *Seventy Years of It*. New York: Appleton-Century, 1936.

————. "Freedom in the Modern World," *American Journal of Sociology*, XLII (January 1937), 459-61.

Rowell, Chester H. "A Positive Program for the Republican Party," *Yale Review*, XXV (March 1936), 443-52.

Russell, Charles Edward. *Bare Hands and Stone Walls*. New York: Charles Scribner's Sons, 1933.

————. "An Old Reporter Looks at the Mad-House World," *Scribner's Magazine*, XCIV (October 1933), 225-30.

Schilpp, Paul A., ed. *The Philosophy of John Dewey*. New York: Tudor, 1939.

Schroeder, Theodore A. *Conservatisms, Liberalisms, and the New Psychology*. Cos Cob, Conn.: Next Century Press, 1942.

————. *A New Concept of Liberty: From an Evolutionary Psychologist*. Berkeley Heights, N. J.: Oriole Press, 1940.

Sedgwick, Ellery. *The Happy Profession*. Boston: Little, Brown, 1946.

Sheldon, Charles M. *Doctor Sheldon's Scrapbook*. Topeka, Kan.: Christian Herald Association, 1942.

Simkhovitch, Mary Kingsbury. *Neighborhood: My Story of Greenwich House*. New York: W. W. Norton, 1938.

————. *Here Is God's Plenty: Reflections on American Social Advance*. New York: Harper and Brothers, 1949.

Sinclair, Upton. *The Way Out*. New York: Farrar and Rinehart, 1933.

————. *The Autobiography of Upton Sinclair*. New York: Harcourt, Brace, 1962.

Spargo, John. "The Federal Administration Retards Economic Recovery," *Annals* of the American Academy of Political and Social Science, CXXVIII (March 1935), 16-24.

————. "Republicans Must Choose," *Review of Reviews*, XCII (December 1935), 22-6.

Sparks, George F. *A Many-Colored Toga: The Diary of Henry Fountain Ashurst*. Phoenix, Ariz.: University of Arizona Press, 1962.

Steffens, Lincoln. *Upbuilders*. New York: Doubleday, Page, 1909.

————. *The Autobiography of Lincoln Steffens*. 2 vols. New York: Harcourt, Brace, 1931.

————. *Lincoln Steffens Speaking*. New York: Harcourt, Brace, 1936.

Stelzle, Charles. *A Son of the Bowery: The Life Story of an East Side American*. New York: George Doran, 1926.

Stimson, Henry L., and McGeorge Bundy. *On Active Service in Peace and War*. New York: Harper and Brothers, 1947.

Strong, Sydney D., ed. *What I Owe to My Father*. New York: Henry Holt, 1931.

Sullivan, Mark. *The Education of an American.* New York: Doubleday, Doran, 1938.

Tarbell, Ida M. *New Ideals in Business.* New York: Macmillan, 1916.

————. "Is Our Generosity Wearing Thin?," *Scribner's Magazine,* XCVII (April 1935), 235-7.

————. *The Nationalizing of Business, 1878-1898.* New York: Macmillan, 1936.

————. *All In The Day's Work.* New York: Macmillan, 1939.

Taussig, Frank W. "Wanted: Consumers," *Yale Review,* XXIII (March 1934), 433-47.

Taylor, Graham. *Pioneering on Social Frontiers.* Chicago: University of Chicago Press, 1930.

————. *Chicago Commons Through Forty Years.* Chicago: Chicago Commons Association, 1936.

Villard, Oswald Garrison. "Pillars of Government: Costigan of Colorado," *Forum,* XCV (February 1936), 117-23.

————. *Fighting Years: Memoirs of a Liberal Editor.* New York: Harcourt, Brace, 1939.

Vincent, Merle D. "NRA: A Trial Balance," *Survey Graphic,* XXIV (July 1935), 333-7.

Voss, J. A., and William Hard. *Managerial Aspects of Labor.* New York: American Management Association, 1937.

Vrooman, Carl Schurz. *The Present Republican Opportunity: By A Democrat.* Chenoa, Ill.: Carl Vrooman, 1936.

Wald, Lillian D. *Windows on Henry Street.* Boston: Little, Brown, 1933.

Warburg, James Paul. *The Long Road Home: The Autobiography of a Maverick.* Garden City: Doubleday, 1964.

Wheeler, Burton K., and Paul F. Healy. *Yankee From the West.* New York: Doubleday, 1962.

"Where Are the Pre-War Radicals? A Symposium," *Survey,* LV (February 1, 1926), 556-9.

White, William Allen. *The Changing West: An Economic Theory About Our Golden Age.* New York: Macmillan, 1939.

————. *The Autobiography of William Allen White.* New York: Macmillan, 1946.

Winter, Ella, and Grenville Hicks, eds. *The Letters of Lincoln Steffens, 1920-1936.* 2 vols. New York: Harcourt, Brace, 1938.

Wise, Stephen S. *Challenging Years: The Autobiography of Stephen S. Wise.* New York: G. P. Putnam's Sons, 1949.

Witte, Edwin B. *The Development of the Social Security Act.* Madison, Wis.: University of Wisconsin Press, 1963.

Woll, Matthew, and William English Walling. *Our Next Step: A National Economic Policy.* New York: Harper and Brothers, 1934.

Zimand, Savel, ed. *Public Health and Welfare—the Citizen's Responsibility: Selected Papers of Homer Folks.* New York: Columbia University Press, 1958.

SECONDARY SOURCES

Adler, Cyrus. *Felix M. Warburg.* New York: The American Jewish Committee, 1938.

Aikman, Duncan. "California Progressivism Without a Progressive Movement," *Today,* I (January 13, 1934), 5-8.

Alexander, Jack. "The Man Behind the 'News,'" *Reader's Digest,* XXXIII (October 1938), 75-9.

Allen, Howard W. "Miles Poindexter: A Political Biography." Unpublished Ph.D. dissertation, University of Washington, 1959.

Allen, Howard W. "Miles Poindexter and the Progressive Movement," *Pacific Northwest Quarterly,* LIII (July 1962), 114-22.

Alsop, Joseph, and Turner, Catledge. *The 168 Days.* Garden City: Doubleday, Doran, 1938.

Armin, Calvin P. "Coe I. Crawford and the Progressive Movement in South Dakota," *Report and Historical Collections of the State Historical Society,* XXXII (1964), 23-221.

Balfe, Richard G. "Charles P. Neill and the U. S. Bureau of Labor: A Study in Progressive Economics, Social Work and Public Administration." Unpublished Ph.D. dissertation, University of Notre Dame, 1956.

Bannister, Robert C., Jr. "The Mind and Thought of Ray Stannard Baker." Unpublished Ph.D. dissertation, Yale University, 1961.

Beal, Vernon L. *Promise and Performance: The Political Record of a Michigan Governor.* Ann Arbor: University of Michigan Press, 1950.

Beaver, Daniel R. *A Buckeye Crusader.* Cincinnati: Privately printed, 1957.

Belcher, Wyatt. "Political Leadership of Robert L. Owen," *The Chronicles of Oklahoma,* XXXI (Winter 1953-54), 361-71.

Bocage, Leo J. "The Public Career of Charles R. Crane." Unpublished Ph.D. dissertation, Fordham University, 1962.

Brant, Irving. "How Liberal Is Justice Holmes?," *New Republic,* XCI (July 21, 1937), 294-9.

Bremner, Robert H. "Honest Man's Story: Frederic C. Howe," *American Journal of Economics and Sociology,* VIII (July 1949), 413-422.

Carter, Paul U. *The Decline and Revival of the Social Gospel: Social and Political Liberalism in American Protestant Churches, 1920-1940.* Ithaca: Cornell University Press, 1954.

Cassedy, James H. "Muckraking and Medicine: Samuel Hopkins Adams," *American Quarterly,* XVI (Spring 1964), 85-99.

Chalmers, David. "Ray Stannard Baker's Search for Reform," *Journal of the History of Ideas,* XIX (June 1958), 422-33.

———. *The Social and Political Ideas of the Muckrakers.* New York: The Citadel Press, 1964.

Cheslaw, Irving G. "An Intellectual Biography of Lincoln Steffens." Unpublished Ph.D. dissertation, Columbia University, 1952.

Childs, Herbert E. "Agrarianism and Sex: Edgar Lee Masters and the Modern Spirit," *Sewanee Review,* XLI (July 1933), 331-43.

Childs, Marquis, and James, Reston. *Walter Lippmann and His Times.* New York: Harcourt, Brace, 1959.

Clark, Glenn. *The Man Who Walked in His Steps.* St. Paul: Macalester Park Publishers, 1946.

Clough, Frank C. *William Allen White of Emporia.* New York: McGraw-Hill, 1941.

Coben, Stanley. *A. Mitchell Palmer: Politician.* New York: Columbia University Press, 1963.

Coleman, George W., ed. *John Graham Brooks and Helen Lawrence Brooks, 1846-1938: A Memorial.* Boston: Privately printed, 1940.

Cramer, Clarence H. *Newton D. Baker.* Cleveland: World, 1961.

Cronon, E. David. "A Southern Progressive Looks at the New Deal," *Journal of Southern History,* XXIV (May 1958), 151-76.

———. *Josephus Daniels in Mexico.* Madison: University of Wisconsin Press, 1960.

Crouch, W. W. "John Randolph Haynes and His Work for Direct Government," *National Municipal Review,* XXVII (September 1938), 434-40.

Current, Richard N. *Secretary Stimson: A Study in Statecraft.* New Brunswick: Rutgers University Press, 1954.

Curti, Merle. *Peace or War: The American Struggle, 1636-1936.* New York: W. W. Norton, 1936.

Davis, Allen F. "Raymond Robins: The Settlement Worker as Municipal Reformer," *Social Service Review,* XXXIII (June 1959), 131-141.

Dorfman, Joseph. *The Economic Mind in American Civilization*. 5 vols. New York: Viking Press, 1946-59.

———. *Institutional Economics: Veblen, Commons and Mitchell Reconsidered*. Berkeley: University of California Press, 1963.

Driscoll, Charles B. "A Disillusioned Reformer Faces Forty," *McNaught's Monthly*, V (January 1926).

Duffus, Robert L. *Lillian Wald: Neighbor and Crusader*. New York: Macmillan, 1938.

Dykhuizen, George. "John Dewey: The Vermont Years," *Journal of the History of Ideas*, XX (October 1959), 515-44.

Early, Stephen T., Jr. "James C. McReynolds and the Judicial Process." Unpublished Ph.D. dissertation, University of Virginia, 1954.

Ellis, Elmer. *Mr. Dooley's America: A Life of Finley Peter Dunne*. New York: Knopf, 1941.

Everett, John R. *Religion in Economics: A Study of John Bates Clark, Richard T. Ely and Simon N. Patten*. New York: Kings Crown Press, 1946.

Fausold, Martin L. *Gifford Pinchot: Bull Moose Progressive*. Syracuse: Syracuse University Press, 1961.

Feuer, Lewis S. "John Dewey and the Back to the People Movement in American Thought," *Journal of the History of Ideas*, XX (October 1959), 545-68.

Fine, Sidney. "Richard T. Ely: Forerunner of Progressivism, 1880-1901," *Mississippi Valley Historical Review*, XXXVII (March 1951), 599-624.

Fisher, Irving Norton. *A Bibliography of the Writings of Irving Fisher*. New Haven: Yale University Press, 1961.

Freund, Paul A. "The Liberalism of Mr. Justice Brandeis," *American Jewish Archives*, X (April 1958), 1-11.

Friedberg, Gerald. "Marxism in the United States: John Spargo and the Socialist Party of America." Unpublished Ph.D. dissertation, Harvard University, 1964.

Geiger, George R. *John Dewey in Perspective*. New York: Oxford University Press, 1958.

Goldmark, Josephine. *Impatient Crusader: Florence Kelley's Life Story*. Urbana: University of Illinois Press, 1953.

Graybar, Lloyd. "Albert Shaw's Ohio Youth," *Ohio History* LXXIV (Winter 1965), 29-34.

Greenbaum, Fred. "Edward P. Costigan: Study of a Progressive." Unpublished Ph.D. dissertation, Columbia University, 1962.

Hamilton, Marty. "Bull Moose Plays an Encore: Hiram Johnson and the

Presidential Campaign of 1932," *California Historical Society Quarterly*, X (September 1962), 211-21.

Harmon, M. Judd. "Some Contributions of Harold L. Ickes," *Western Political Quarterly*, VII (June 1954), 238-52.

Harter, Lafayette G. *John R. Commons: His Assault on Laissez-Faire.* Corvallis: Oregon State University Press, 1962.

Hartley, Lois Teal. "Edgar Lee Masters: A Critical Study." Unpublished Ph.D. dissertation, University of Illinois, 1949.

——. "Edgar Lee Masters—Biographer and Historician," *Journal of the Illinois State Historical Society*, LIV (Winter 1961), 56-83.

Hendel, Samuel. *Charles Evans Hughes and the Supreme Court.* New York: Columbia University Press, 1951.

Hertzler, J. P. "E. A. Ross: Sociological Pioneer and Interpreter," *American Sociological Review*, VI (October 1951), 597-613.

Hicks, Granville. "Lincoln Steffens: He Covered the Future," *Commentary*, XIII (February 1952), 147-56.

Hinshaw, David. *A Man From Kansas: The Story of William Allen White.* New York: G. P. Putnam's Sons, 1945.

Hinton, Harold B. *Cordell Hull.* London: Hurst and Blackett, 1942.

Hofstadter, Beatrice and Richard. "Winston Churchill: A Study in the Popular Novel," *American Quarterly*, II (Spring 1950), 12-28.

Hook, Sidney. *John Dewey: An Intellectual Portrait.* New York: John Day, 1939.

——, ed. *John Dewey: Philosopher of Science and Freedom.* New York: Dial, 1950.

Hull, Denison B. *The Legislative Life of Morton D. Hull.* Chicago: Privately printed, 1948.

Humes, D. Joy. *Oswald Garrison Villard: A Liberal of the 1920's.* Syracuse: Syracuse University Press, 1960.

Johnson, Claudius O. *Borah of Idaho.* New York: Longmans, Green, 1936.

Johnson, Walter. *William Allen White's America.* New York: Henry Holt, 1947.

Kehl, James A., and Samuel J. Astorino. "A Bull Moose Responds to the New Deal: Pennsylvania's Gifford Pinchot," *Pennsylvania Magazine of History and Biography*, LXXXVIII (January 1964), 37-50.

Keso, Edward E. *The Senatorial Career of Robert Latham Owen.* Nashville: George Peabody College, 1937.

Koerner, J. D. "The Last of the Muckrake Men," *South Atlantic Quarterly*, LV (April 1956), 221-33.

Lief, Alfred. *Democracy's Norris.* New York: Stackpole, 1939.

Losch, Christopher. *The New Radicalism in America.* New York: Knopf, 1965.

Lundberg, Ferdinand. *Imperial Hearst: A Social Biography.* New York: Equinox Press, 1936.

Lyon, Peter. *Success Story: The Life and Times of S. S. McClure.* New York: Scribner's, 1963.

McGeary, M. Nelson. *Gifford Pinchot: Forester and Politician.* Princeton: Princeton University Press, 1960.

McHenry, Dean E. *The Hichborn Story.* Los Angeles: John R. and Dora Haynes Foundation, 1950.

McKee, Irving. "Background and Early Career of Hiram W. Johnson, 1866-1910," *Pacific Historical Review,* XIX (February 1950), 17-30.

McKenna, Marian C. *Borah.* Ann Arbor: University of Michigan Press, 1961.

Marks, Jeannette A. *Life and Letters of Mary Emma Woolley.* Washington: Public Affairs Press, 1955.

Mason, Alpheus T. *Brandeis and the Modern State.* New York: Viking, 1936.

———. *Brandeis: A Free Man's Life.* New York: Viking, 1946.

———. "Charles Evans Hughes: An Appeal to the Bar of History," *Vanderbilt Law Review,* VI (December 1952).

Meiburger, Sister Anne V. "Efforts of Raymond Robins Toward Recognition of Soviet Russia and the Outlawry of War, 1917-33." Unpublished Ph.D. dissertation, Catholic University, 1958.

Meriwether, Lee. *Jim Reed: Senatorial Immortal.* Webster Groves, Missouri: International Mark Twain Society, 1948.

Miller, Robert M. *American Protestantism and Social Issues, 1919-39.* Chapel Hill: University of North Carolina Press, 1958.

Mims, Edward. *Chancellor Kirkland of Vanderbilt.* Nashville: Vanderbilt University Press, 1940.

"Mr. Justice Brandeis," *Harvard Law Review,* LV (December 1941).

Morison, Elting E. *Turmoil and Tradition: A Study of the Life and Times of Henry L. Stimson.* Boston: Houghton Mifflin, 1960.

Morrison, Joseph L. *Josephus Daniels Says . . . : An Editor's Political Odyssey from Bryan to Wilson to F.D.R., 1894-1913.* Chapel Hill: University of North Carolina Press, 1962.

Mowry, George. *The California Progressives.* Berkeley: University of California Press, 1950.

Neal, Nevin E. "A Biography of Joseph T. Robinson." Unpublished Ph.D. dissertation, University of Oklahoma, 1958.

Neuberger, Richard L., and Stephen B. Kahn. *Integrity: The Life of George W. Norris*. New York: Vanguard, 1937.

Neuman, Fred G. *Irvin S. Cobb: His Life and Letters*. New York: Rodale Press, 1938.

Nye, Russel B. *Midwestern Progressive Politics*. East Lansing: Michigan State University Press, 1951.

Osborn, Stella, ed. *An Accolade for Chase Osborn*. Sault St. Marie: Privately printed, 1940.

Paulson, Ross E. "The Vrooman Brothers and the American Reform Tradition." Unpublished Ph.D. dissertation, Harvard University, 1962.

Perkins, Dexter. *Charles Evans Hughes and American Democratic Statesmanship*. Boston: Little, Brown, 1956.

Pike, Albert H. "Jonathan Bourne, Jr.: Progressive." Unpublished Ph.D. dissertation, University of Oregon, 1957.

Pool, David de Sola. *H. Pereira Mendes: A Biography*. New York: Privately printed, 1938.

Pusey, Merlo J. *Charles Evans Hughes*. 2 vols. New York: Macmillan, 1951.

Rascoe, Burton, *Before I Forget*. Garden City: Doubleday, Doran, 1937.

Sageser, A. Bower. "Joseph L. Bristow: The Editor's Road to Politics," *Kansas Historical Quarterly*, XXX (Summer 1964), 153-62.

Seldes, George. *Lords of the Press*. New York: Julian Messner, 1938.

Shriver, Philip R. "The Making of a Moderate Progressive: Atlee Pomerene." Unpublished Ph.D. dissertation, Columbia University, 1954.

Silver, Paul L. "Wilsonians and the New Deal." Unpublished Ph.D. dissertation, University of Pennsylvania, 1964.

Smith, Harold S. "William J. Ghent: Reformer and Historian." Unpublished Ph.D. dissertation, University of Wisconsin, 1957.

Smith, Rixey, and Norman Beasley. *Carter Glass: A Biography*. New York: Longmans, Green, 1939.

Snow, Edgar. "Life and Letters of Charles R. Crane." Unpublished Ph.D. dissertation, Fordham University, 1955.

Socolofsky, Homer E. *Arthur Capper: Publisher, Politician, and Philanthropist*. Lawrence: University of Kansas Press, 1962.

Swanberg, William A. *Citizen Hearst*. New York: Scribner's, 1961.

Tebell, John. *An American Dynasty: The Story of the McCormicks, Medills, and Pattersons*. Garden City: Doubleday, 1947.

Thomas, Milton H. *John Dewey: A Centennial Bibliography*. Chicago: University of Chicago Press, 1962.

Titus, Warren I. "Winston Churchill, American: A Critical Biography." Unpublished Ph.D. dissertation, New York University, 1957.

Trattner, Walter. "Social Statesman: Homer Folks, 1867-1947." Unpublished Ph.D. dissertation, University of Wisconsin, 1964.

Voss, Carl Hermann. *Rabbi and Minister: The Friendship of Stephen S. Wise and John Haynes Holmes.* Cleveland: World, 1964.

Wade, Louise C. *Graham Taylor: Pioneer for Social Justice, 1851-1938.* Chicago: University of Chicago Press, 1964.

Ware, Louise. *George Foster Peabody.* Athens: University of Georgia Press, 1951.

Warner, Landon. "Henry T. Hunt and Civic Reform in Cincinnati, 1903-13," *Ohio History,* LXII (April 1953), 146-61.

Warner, Robert M. "Chase Osborn and the Progressive Movement." Unpublished Ph.D. dissertation, University of Michigan, 1957.

————. *Chase Salmon Osborn: 1860-1949.* Ann Arbor: University of Michigan, 1960.

Weaver, Earl J. "John Dewey: A Spokesman for Progressive Liberalism." Unpublished Ph.D. dissertation, Brown University, 1963.

Weingast, David E. *Walter Lippmann: A Study in Personal Journalism.* New Brunswick: Rutgers University Press, 1949.

Winkler, John K. *William Randolph Hearst: A New Appraisal.* New York: Hastings House, 1955.

Winter, Ella, and Herbert Shapiro. *The World of Lincoln Steffens.* New York: Hill and Wang, 1962.

Wittke, Carl. "Peter Witt, Tribune of the People," *Ohio Archaeological and Historical Quarterly,* LVIII (October 1949), 361-77.

Wreszin, Michael. *Oswald Garrison Villard: Pacifist at War.* Indianapolis: Indiana University Press, 1965.

Index

DATE DUE

MAY 3 '69			
JUN 3 '69			
MAR 27 1970			
MAR 10 '72			
72			
DEC 1 1972			
8:00 p.m.			
10:30 pm			
4:50			
NOV 03 '75			
FEB 6 '78			
GAYLORD			PRINTED IN U.S.A.